GREAT
GAMBLES
of the Civil War

GREAT GAMBLES
of the Civil War

Philip Katcher

ARMS AND
ARMOUR

*This book is dedicated
to the memory of Don Patterson,
a gentleman*

Arms and Armour Press
An Imprint of the Cassell Group
Wellington House, 125 Strand, London WC2R 0BB

Distributed in the USA by Sterling Publishing Co. Inc.,
387 Park Avenue South, New York, NY 10016-8810.

Distributed in Australia by Capricorn Link (Australia) Pty. Ltd,
2/13 Carrington Road, Castle Hill, NSW 2154.

British Library Cataloguing-in-Publication Data:
a catalogue record for this book is available from
the British Library

ISBN 1-85409-308-8

Designed and edited by DAG Publications Ltd.
Designed by David Gibbons; edited by Philip Jarrett;
printed and bound in Great Britain.

Jacket illustration:
The Defence of Little Round Top, by Keith Rocco;
reproduced by permission of the artist.

CONTENTS

CONTENTS

INTRODUCTION

Almost every action in life is a gamble of one sort or another. Does one get married? It may or may not work out. Does one choose to work for one company or another? One job may lead to a successful career, while the other to a dead end or dismissal. Does one choose to walk home after work, or take a bus? The bus may be involved in a traffic accident and passengers hurt, while a walker might become the victim of violence.

Most decisions in life, however, have no major consequences. The bus rider and pedestrian are equally likely to rach their destinations unharmed. But gambling adds so much to life that many people seek opportunities to indulge in it. They buy into pools or lotteries, or even visit casinos to gamble their money on the chance of accumulating even more. At least, that is what they say. In fact, the odds are so stacked against them that it is obviously the gamble rather than the result that provides the motivation.

War is in many ways the ultimate gamble. In the first place it requires a great deal of money, national treasure, to equip and arm men for war. But beyond that it involves lives, not just money. Both must be spent for one side to win.

It does not follow automatically that highly successful generals are also gamblers of both treasure and lives. Lieutenant General Thomas Jonathan 'Stonewall' Jackson was a prime gambler, splitting his corps away from a Confederate army that was already smaller than the attacker's army to make a swinging flanking attack in his greatest success at Chancellorsville. On the other hand, Major General George Thomas, whose solid stand at Chickamauga earned him the nickname 'Rock of Chickamauga', was so methodical in his preparations to attack Lieutenant General John B. Hood's army at Nashville in late 1864 that Lieutenant General U. S. Grant almost removed him, despairing of getting him to move at all. When Thomas did strike, however, his troops virtually wiped out Hood's army; the only example of a Civil War army being destroyed in the field. Both generals were successful, but only one had the soul of a gambler.

From its very beginning, the American Civil War of 1861-65 was a gamble. At first the gamble was political. Northern voters gambled that the southern states would not attempt to dissolve the nation if the majority of votes went to an anti-slavery president, Abraham Lincoln, a Republican from Illinois on record as being against the expansion of slavery to the western states. They gambled that majority rule was still the basic premise of the United States of America and that, despite their talk, the citizens of the southern states would respect that. Southern politicians gambled that northern voters would take the threats to break up the country seriously and not elect Lincoln. At the same time they gambled that they had the powers of persuasion to bring all southern citizens firmly on their side and make a southern nation a reality.

Northern voters lost their gamble. After Lincoln's election, South Carolina held a convention that voted to leave the Union. The state's politicians gambled correctly that they would find popular support for such a move. Then they gambled that they would be supported by fellow southern states, and that the northern states would allow them to leave in peace. Many far-sighted southerners, including Alexander Stephens, who would become the south's vice-president, disagreed. But they were in an overall minority. John Gill Shorter, a leading judge in Alabama, wrote to his daughter in December 1860 saying: 'the Union will be dissolved', and adding 'and there will be no war'.[1] Indeed, Alabamian Leroy P. Walker, soon to be the first Secretary of War of the new Confederate States of America, claimed that he would be able to mop up all the blood shed as a result of secession with a handkerchief.

Their gamble that southern states would support them was indeed correct. Very quickly after South Carolina's move, half a dozen nearby slave states also declared that they had left the Union. The group formed a new nation, the Confederate States.

Initially the second gamble, that the northern states would allow this to happen without resort to arms, also appeared to be successful. Indeed, Confederate buyers of equipment from arms to paper money were able to order what they needed from northern manufacturers without difficulty. The outgoing administration of President Franklin Buchanan, which had regarded southern interests favourably, was unable to drum up support for restoring the country by force because it seemed unable to decide what to do at all. The government vacillated, not calling for troops to occupy the southern states, but at the same time not willing to relinquish Federal property such as the forts that defended the coast.

Finally, Lincoln's administration took office. Initially, however, it did not seem to southern leaders to be any more decisive than Buchanan's. Indeed, low-level talks in the office of the US Secretary of State with southern leaders about the issue of southern independence were carried on even as the new Republican leadership decided what to do.

In any gamble there comes a time when the gamblers lose control of their bets. The dice are tossed, the cards are dealt, the wheel begins to spin. The gambler can only sit back and watch, hoping for the best. Such was the case with the southern gamble that they could leave the United States and form the Confederate States without any loss of property or life.

The move was up to the Lincoln administration, which decided to up the ante by authorising the resupply of a Federal fort, Fort Sumter, in the harbour of Charleston, South Carolina. It gambled that the city's administrators would allow this resupply, but the Confederates did not. They fired on *The Star Of The West*, the northern ship bringing fresh supplies. Although the Lincoln administration said it would not try another such mission, and the fort's commander admitted that his garrison would soon be starved out, the raising of the ante in this manner, unexpected as it was, scared the southern gamblers. They upped the ante themselves, stating that unless Fort Sumter was surrendered by a certain time it would be brought to submission by firepower. The northerners sat pat. His bluff called, Confederate President Jefferson Davis authorised the fort's besiegers to open fire.

That final political gamble cost the south the war. It would take years, and the cost would be astonishing. The reaction in the north was nothing like that anticipated by southern leaders. There was a burst of anger and a rush to get troops organised and down south to suppress what had become in northern minds a rebellion designed to destroy the best hope for free peoples everywhere. Lincoln had won the last hand of the political poker game played between the two sides.

Now, however, the game had largely been taken out of the hands of the political leaders. True, they would still organise the game, designate the leading players as commanders of their armies, and set the stakes by forming and equipping armies and declaring what the final victory would be. They could play side games against each other with European governments in an attempt to win them (and the supplies they could offer) to their sides, but it would be the commanders in the field who would actually play the great game of war. It would be up to them to pick their politician's gambles.

Yet, to a great extent, even the military gambles were often taken from the hands of the leading players. For example, Lee's gamble to turn the Union left at Gettysburg on the second day was foiled by a very minor player, a regimental commander from Maine, who gambled that Lee's men were as tired as his and that a bayonet charge by his out-of-ammunition men could disrupt Lee's movement. Indeed, Lee was aware of this, and considered it his task to get his men, who were ready, where he wanted them, give them a plan for success, and then sit back and watch them do the job. He knew that there were gambles at every level in war, from the highest headquarters to the lowest trench.

Some of the gambles in the accounts that follow were successful, some partly successful, and some simply failed. Some involved entire armies and others small forces. Some took place on land and some on the water. Some were taken by units on the defence, and some by attacking formations. The one thing common to them all is that they originated in the brain of a single individual – a commander – who chose an option that went against conventional wisdom, which almost always advises caution. It is always easiest to do the conventional thing, and one can hardly be faulted for doing it if one is unsuccessful. However, if one takes an unconventional approach and gambles on a big effort and loses, one has to suffer the consequences. Most generals do not like to take political heat; it does not help military careers. Yet the leaders who gambled, at whatever level, were different. They decided to take the unconventional approach and ignore cautious advice.

Sometimes the gamble was well thought out. It was presented to the originator's commanding officer and approved at the highest levels. Equipment could be ordered to the right places and men could be trained to the plan's specifications. At other times the gamble was impetuous, a decision reached in the heat of action, when the alternatives of victory and defeat stared the gambler in the face and there was no time for careful consideration of the options.

However, once the decision had been made and the game started, the outcome was largely out of the original planner's hands. Indeed, it would not even rest entirely in the hands of the men who had been launched on the gamble. No matter how dedicated, how brave, how well trained these men were, they could be beaten by a more dedicated, braver, better trained force. The men on the gambler's side might decide not to do what he wants to do. Front-line troops at Missionary Ridge, having cleared the rifle pits at the bottom of the hill, thought they were in an unsafe position, and many of them decided on their own to keep advancing up the hillside, regardless of orders.

Moreover, the forces of nature had to be contended with. Would rains so swell a creek that a force could not cross it? If so, an attack might fail or an escaping body might be caught. Had the weather been so dry that creeks were narrow? Then an attacking body might not have enough water and be so thirsty and weary that it could not stand a ferocious counterattack. Rainy weather could hide a unit on the march, but the resulting mud could bring that same unit to a virtual standstill.

Some things just cannot be predicted. The clank of a tin cup on the side of a tin canteen might betray an otherwise undetected movement. A fort that the best intelligence has placed in a particular area may not actually exist there, and a sudden attack might be launched against a phantom. An unlucky shot might hit an enemy ship's bulkhead, bounce back at cross range and blow up, killing the ship's captain. A fuse might be faulty, so a shell might not explode and a ship might not sink. A mounted courier could be captured and a vital message disclosed to the enemy. Ammunition crates might be cracked open to reveal ammunition of the wrong calibre.

After all, a gamble is still a gamble. Were it not, were any attack certain, then war would be vastly different. Indeed, so would be all of life.

Notes
1   Davis, William C., *A Government of Our Own*, New York, 1994, p.9.

A GAMBLE AT THE REGIMENTAL LEVEL
The 33rd Virginia at Manassas

THE GAMBLE: *that a newly recruited, untried regiment, in the heat of battle and without orders, can storm and take a Federal battery and thereby turn potential defeat into victory.*

'On to Richmond' was the cry of almost every newspaper in the north after Fort Sumter fell to southern cannon, and Richmond became the capital city of the new Confederate States of America. But Richmond was more than a political capital; it was a economic centre as well. It was in Richmond that most of the munitions of war, ranging from small-arms to cannon, were manufactured. It was there that much of the clothing of the Confederate army in the east was made. Were Richmond to fall, it would be certain death to the fledgling Confederacy. But capturing the city was an idea easier put on paper than accomplished.

The new regiments flocking to the Federal colours lacked military training and were not even fully equipped. It would take a great deal of practice in drill from the Bible of the infantry, Hardee's *Tactics*, for the raw officers and men to master such manoeuvres as 'Deploy column. Battalion outwards, face. March'. When the colonel ordered this, according to the manual:

> The column will deploy itself on the two companies at its head, according to the principles prescribed for the deployment of columns in mass. The captains of these companies will each, at the command *march*, place himself on the right of his own company, and align it by the right: the captain of the fourth will place himself in the rear rank, and the covering sergeant in the rank of file closers, at the moment the captain of the third shall come to its left to align it.[1]

Quite a bit of choreography for a regiment of as many as a thousand men, the vast majority of whom had been farmers, clerks and mechanics only days before. Indeed, even those who fancied themselves of a military bent and had been active in volunteer militia companies had rarely, if ever, participated in full battalion drills or even seen units larger than a company. It would take many months to get both sides ready for full nineteenth-century warfare.

This was one thing on which all the professional soldiers agreed. The only problem was that they did not have the time. Men from all over the north had been incensed to see the flag of their country fired on. They wanted revenge, they wanted an end to this breakaway republic, and they wanted it now.

By 29 June 1861 some 30,000 men from states as far away as Minnesota had gathered in the capital of the United States, Washington DC. They had turned it into one vast military camp, even sleeping in the capital building itself. The General in Chief of the United States Army, Winfield Scott, a veteran of the War of 1812 and the Mexican War, put together a plan that would slowly crush the new Confederacy to death. He would close southern ports, so that no munitions of war could reach their soldiers, capture the Mississippi River to cut the south in half, and advance south along all fronts slowly.

Politicians were not to allow him the luxury of time, however. Instead, the government turned to the commander of the troops around Washington, Major General Irwin McDowell, a professional soldier. At the president's request McDowell drew up a plan to advance directly south towards Richmond with his 30,000 men, to face a Confederate force of some 21,900 men under General P. G. T. Beauregard at Manassas Junction. Manassas was a sleepy little Virginia town, but an important crossroads, some 29 miles south-west of Washington. Potentially, Beauregard's troops could be reinforced by Confederate troops in the Valley of Virginia under General Joseph Johnston. According to McDowell's plan, however, nearby Federals under Major General Robert Patterson would pin this force down.

Lincoln approved McDowell's plan at a cabinet meeting on 29 June and ordered him forward. McDowell asked for still more time, pleading his troops' lack of training. 'You are green, it is true,' Lincoln replied, 'but they are green also.'[2]

McDowell issued his marching orders. His units would march in parallel columns, each unit carrying the National Colour prominently at all times, with small National Colours also carried by the artillery, to reinforce the notion that the US government was the final national authority. Finally, knowing that many of his men were clad in non-regulation uniforms, ranging from the grey of Wisconsin, New York, and Pennsylvania, to the red shirts of Minnesota and the sky blue of Indiana, and that many of the Confederate volunteers were equally differently attired, he stressed that in combat each commander had best be doubly sure that the troops on which he ordered fire were actually enemy soldiers. As it transpired, this would play an important part in the battle to come.

On 16 July McDowell and his green 'blue bellies' set off on what was essentially their first campaign march of any distance. It would be both a breaking-in and an actual campaign, a fact that concerned McDowell's professional soldier subordinates. In the minds of most of the rank and file, however, it was to be a short march and a glorious and short conflict. They would march to fight, drive the ill-mannered southern rabble off, take Richmond and end the war. In the meantime, many of them straggled behind as they stopped to pick blackberries in the bushes along the sides of the road to Manassas. They were not far removed from the mindset of the Maryland militia private who, only 50 years earlier, had carried a pair of dancing pumps in his knapsack when marching to meet the British who would burn Washington, thinking that after their quick victory they would be sure to be invited to the President's house for a victory ball.

One soldier of the 79th New York, a 'highland regiment', who wore the twin gold bars of a captain, insisted on wearing his dress kilt on the march. Seeing a pig loose, he drew his sword and chased it, despite his rank. The sight of a man in a 'skirt' waving a sword and running after a squealing pig was too much for his soldiers, who called out remarks such as 'Put on your drawers!' and 'Take off that petticoat!' Finally the pig dashed under a fence and the captain, not prepared to lose his supper, leapt over it 'and in the act made such an exhibition of his attenuated anatomy as to call forth a roar of laughter'.[3] If this was the way in which company commanders were to behave, who could expect much from the privates?

The advancing Federals met little resistance. A few Confederate cavalrymen fired long-range pistol or carbine shots, but rarely hit a target. As the Union troops tramped down the dusty roads they heard axes banging away in woods ahead of them and found, when they arrived, felled trees across the roads. Federal pioneers, in advance of the infantry, quickly tossed them aside.

In the meantime, on 8 July, Beauregard, aware that his green army was significantly smaller than that of the Federals, ordered his troops entrenched at Fairfax Court House to fall back via Centreville to Bull Run if McDowell's troops appeared at their front. There the Confederates would find a natural line of defence along the creek, where steep banks and deep waters made it impossible for artillery to cross and slow, at best, for infantry, save at a few well-known fords and bridges.

When Federal skirmishers finally clashed with Confederate outposts, the Confederate commander gave the orders to retreat. Their retreat was hasty: 'The road was strewn with provisions & clothes thrown away by the Secesh [a northern nickname for supporters of southern secession] & our advance', wrote a member of the 2nd Michigan. 'I saw more than 2 wagon loads of blankets & jackets in one heap.' The Federals moved on to the nearby town, Germantown, where they:

> ... found several houses in flames & the men of our brigade burned nearly all the rest before they left. It was but a small village & like most of the farm houses was recently deserted by the inhabitants. Some other buildings were burned during the day. A very neat breastwork intended to rake the road to Germantown was abandoned about two hours before we arrived. The enemies [sic] campfires were still burning brightly. The men here stole everything movable.[4]

These scenes, which novice soldiers certainly saw as evidence of the unwillingness of the Confederates to fight, made them even more confident of a short battle – if, indeed, there was to be a battle. On the other hand, Beauregard was counting on his retreat making the Federals overconfident and thereby easier to defeat.

McDowell realised that any chance of his movement passing unnoticed was now lost. The Confederates would be prepared. He wanted his men to push on quickly, and ordered one column to take Centreville at the first light of 18 July. The others were to press on to turn the enemy's right. Personal reconnaissance, however, showed this to be an unlikely option. The roads, McDowell saw for himself, were too narrow and crooked to bring large numbers of infantry, cavalry and artillery down. He faced the options of a frontal assault at Mitchell's or Blackburn's Fords, or a movement around the enemy left. This area appeared to be more open and capable of being crossed by troops. McDowell picked the flanking movement.

McDowell's basic battle plan was good enough. On 18 July his troops reached Centreville. The next morning they would move against their first enemy determined to make a stand.

A frantic Beauregard, who had learned of McDowell's approach from a woman spy in Washington, wired Richmond for reinforcements. A brigade not far south at Fredericksburg, consisting of two infantry regiments and a battery, was put on the road north immediately. Other regiments in Richmond boarded railroad cars for a ride to what appeared to be a future battleground, and he called for Johnston's troops in the Valley to slip away from Patterson's Federals and join him at Bull Run. This latter move was problematic at best. Johnston's troops would not only have to lose their opponents, but they would have to take a long railroad trip, while McDowell's Federals were only a short march away. Indeed, by the time Beauregard found out that Johnston had been ordered to join his force, he felt it was too late to make the trip in time. 'McDowell will be on us early tomorrow when we must fight him and sell our lives as dearly as possible,' he told his staff.[5]

Regardless of his feelings of success or failure, Beauregard, whose main joy in life seems to have been making elaborate battle plans, went to work on his own map. He did not intend simply to draw up his regiments along the creek and fight a static, defensive battle. Instead, he planned almost a mirror operation of that planned by McDowell, although he was unaware of this at the time. As McDowell moved to turn Beauregard's left, Beauregard would move to turn McDowell's left.

The Federals started early on the morning of the 18th, the lead division entering Centreville at about 9 a.m. Once again, what they found there – abandoned earthworks, trenches and even a signal tower – indicated a Confederate rout to them. The leading Union brigade passed through the town and halted at a spring to gather water for the hot, thirsty troops. While the bulk of the men filled their canteens, the brigade commander sent a force of several companies on towards Blackburn's Ford across the Bull Run. Accompanied by the division commander, the reconnoitring troops reached the ford only to discover that it was unguarded.

Quickly the orders went out for the rest of the brigade to march to the ford. A two-gun section of Battery G, 1st US Artillery, went with them and deployed when it reached a point about half a mile from the ford. Its commander had several rounds fired across the creek to determine what enemy strength, if any, was present there. A section of Louisiana's Washington Light Artillery returned fire, and the first major battle of the Civil War had begun.

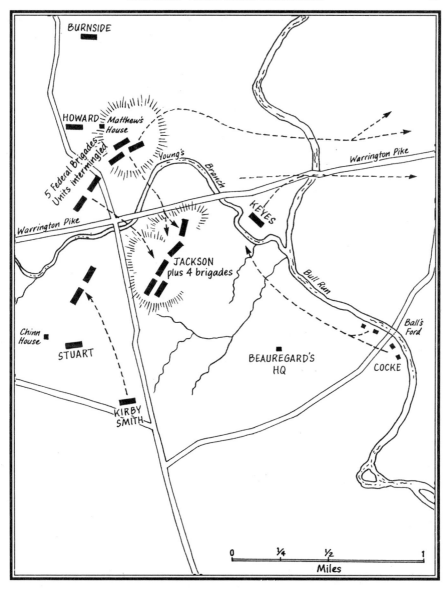

Other Federal artillery arrived and joined the fray, while infantry deployed into line of battle and pressed forward. Men of both sides went into action here in grey uniforms, while both sides had flags with dark blue cantons with white stars on them and red and white bars filling the rest of the flag. Virginians and United States forces both carried dark blue colours with seals painted in their centres. Federals marched almost next to Confederates before discovering their mistake and receiving unexpected volleys.

As more Federals entered the fight, the Union army's chief engineer arrived. He saw that the infantry was holding the Confederates well enough, as suited McDowell's plan of holding them in the centre while turning their left. However, the Federal commander on the spot was too aggressive for the engineer's taste. He, and a captain from McDowell's staff who had also recently arrived at the source of the gunfire, asked the division commander to hold back his attack. Their pleas fell on deaf ears; the attack was pressed on.

The Confederates near Blackburn's Ford had the advantage of being hidden in thick woods, while the Federals came at them across relatively open fields. Not only did the woods hide the southern strength, but they also protected the southern shooters. The Federal attack stalled, despite being reinforced by yet another brigade and more artillery. Finally, the Federals halted in line and let their artillery duel it out with the Confederate guns.

At about 4 p.m. McDowell, perhaps alerted by his staff captain as to the overly aggressive fight at Blackburn's Ford, arrived on the scene. He was most distressed by what he found there. The division commander asked to be allowed to continue his assault, saying that he could beat Beauregard by sunset. McDowell, upset that his plans were being so ignored, told him that this fight was not to be the main fight at all. None the less, to salvage what could be salvaged, and so as not to lower morale, McDowell told the general to take the high ground before halting where he was for the night. McDowell himself then turned back to Centreville to set up a new headquarters.

Instead of following McDowell's orders to make a limited assault, however, the Federal division commander faced his brigades about and headed back to Centreville. 'The men retired sullen & many of them sad from the field,' a Michigan private recalled. 'I know I felt mad and anxious to try it again.'[6] So far everything was going the Confederates' way.

The morning of the skirmish at Blackburn's Ford, the War Department in Richmond telegraphed Johnston in the Valley to move as quickly as possible to Beauregard's position. Johnston, having received confirmation from Beauregard that the Federals were indeed ready to attack, ordered his troops to strike their tents, douse their fires, shoulder their muskets and move out. The first troops to take to the road were the First Brigade, Virginia Volunteers, led by a strange Virginian named Thomas Jonathan Jackson. Jackson, an 1848 West Point graduate and lately a professor of artillery tactics at the

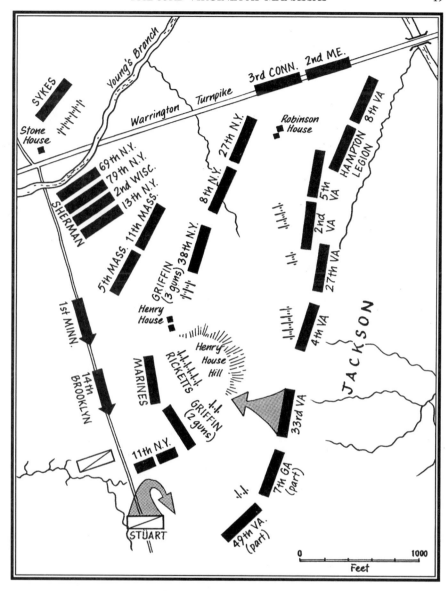

Virginia Military Institute, finished the Mexican War in 1848 as a brevet major owing to his bravery in action.

His First Brigade consisted of units raised in the Valley of Virginia. Their designations were the 2nd, 4th, 5th, 27th and 33rd Volunteer Virginia Infantry Regiments. In addition, in keeping with the Confederate army's practice of attaching an artillery battery to each infantry brigade, the Rockbridge Artillery of Lexington, Virginia, accompanied the infantry. 'The

Lousy Thirty-third' was the nickname of the last regiment to join the 1st Virginia Brigade, earned because it was the first in the new brigade in 1861 to become infested with those friends of every Civil War soldier, the body louse.

The 33rd was not one of those socially prominent Virginia regiments which had roots in volunteer companies of the eighteenth century. Its men, mostly farmers owning small plots of land, came largely from the west, from the Valley of Virginia. Most of them had gathered after Virginia had left the Union and their state was threatened by northern invaders. The regiment was not uniformly dressed or equipped. At least one company of the regiment carried smooth-bore flintlock muskets into this battle. They were a variety of men from all walks of life and social levels. The one thing they had in common was that very few of them were professional soldiers.

Indeed, the man they elected colonel, Arthur Campbell Cummings, a 49-year-old native Virginian, had graduated from the Virginia Military Academy in 1844. He had served as a captain in the Mexican War, being awarded the brevet rank of major for his service, but in the decades after the war he had returned to civilian life, working as a lawyer and farmer in Abingdon. He could hardly have been described as a professional soldier.

Jackson, as yet a commander of unknown quality, marched his brigade until about 2 a.m., when he finally halted the men for a couple of hours' rest. While they slept as though dead, lying wrapped in their blankets where they fell, he personally kept watch. Before dawn, Jackson roused his weary troops and got them under way once again. By 6 a.m. the First Brigade had reached the Piedmont Station, where Jackson allowed them to break ranks and eat breakfast. He had hurried them so much that the brigade reached the station before the railroad cars that would take them east to Manassas Junction had arrived.

The train arrived and the troops boarded. The trip east was painfully slow, but many of the men were seeing a part of the country they had never seen before on a method of transportation they had not previously used, so it was all novel to them. After an eight-hour ride, during which only 30 miles had been covered, the train arrived. The men, ready for action, jumped off the cars only to discover from local civilians who watched them arrive that the Federals had attacked on the previous day and had been driven off near Blackburn's Ford. Excitement gave way to disappointment, and the exhausted men once again rolled up in their blankets and fell asleep.

Before they slept, however, many of the men, concerned that both sides were wearing the same types of uniforms, did what they could to prepare. 'We tore all the feathers out of our hats,' wrote 33rd Virginia Private John O. Casler, 'because we heard that the Yanks had feathers in theirs, and we might be fired on by mistake, as our company was the only one that had black plumes in their hats.'[7]

The rest of Johnston's command followed them, not all arriving until late on the 20th. Now, however, the Confederates under Beauregard, to whom Johnston deferred as knowing the ground best, had 35,000 men to meet a Federal force of 37,000. McDowell's worst fear, of facing this combined force, had come true. Beauregard arranged his force with most of it defending his right on Mitchell's Ford, where he expected the Federals to come again.

Unfortunately for Beauregard's grand plans, this was not where McDowell planned to attack. He intended to swing the bulk of his forces to Sudley Ford, on the far Confederate left, which his chief engineer had found to be relatively unguarded. At 8 p.m. in the evening of Saturday the 20th he gathered his generals and issued orders to put his forces under way. However, these soldiers were not alone. Behind them came the cream of Washington society, their wicker picnic baskets packed full of champagne and cold chicken. They planned to find some convenient hill when the battle began to watch the victory they knew was to follow. Among them were six US senators, including radical Republican Benjamin Wade of Ohio, and a score of members of the House of Representatives. Ladies in wide-hooped crinoline dresses, carrying parasols as protection against the burning sun, accompanied them.

They missed the beginning of the battle, for reveille in the lead Federal formations was sounded at 2 a.m. on 21 July. The volunteers, not yet used to striking camp in the dark, took an hour to be formed up and ready to march. It then took another hour in the darkness to reach Cub Run, and it was not until 6 a.m. that Colonel J. B. E. Sloan of the 4th South Carolina saw a Federal officer plant a flag near a fording place. At about that time the first cannon fired, signalling that McDowell's troops opposite the Warrenton Turnpike stone bridge were in place and ready to demonstrate against the Confederates across the creek.

The demonstration failed. The Confederate brigade commander at the spot was not fooled, and only committed his skirmishers against the deployed but stationary Federal troops. At about 7.30, when the Federals at the stone bridge had found a ford nearby, a Confederate signal officer, E. Porter Alexander, saw dust rising above the trees, glints from shiny musket barrels and the tips of flags. 'Look to your left,' he signalled Beauregard's headquarters, using a new semaphore system of flags to convey his message. 'You are turned.'[8]

Luckily for Beauregard the turning movement was anything but easy or quick. The road that led to Sudley Ford was too narrow for an infantry regiment, let alone artillery. Pioneers slowly cleared the way as the infantry started and stopped behind them. Moreover, a guide picked a wrong road, one that took a very roundabout way to the Ford and would cost the attackers dearly. It was not until 8.45 that McDowell's first troops reached and crossed Bull Run at Sudley Ford.

Beauregard, however, did not realise his good fortune. Instead, he seemed to become confused, sending contradictory orders to some officers, not changing the orders for his planned attack to others, and hurrying reinforcements to the left. Expecting an attack on his right rather than his left, at 7 a.m. he had sent orders to Jackson to bring the First Brigade up to Mitchell's Ford. He now changed those orders, having Jackson, along with brigades commanded by Brigadier General Bernard Bee and Colonel Francis Bartow, go to the aid of the troops on the left.

The troops there were having a hard time, being pressed back by overwhelming Union numbers. Only a desperate charge by a Louisiana Zouave battalion, Wheat's Tigers, stalled the Federals. Bee's troops from Alabama and Mississippi were the first to arrive and go into line to the right of the South Carolina brigade, whose left lay on the Sudley Ford road, along Matthews Hill. They were followed shortly by Barstow's two Georgia regiments. All had come up at the double in the hot weather, and were thirsty and weary from their run. As they went forward into line they came under well directed Federal cannon fire.

Once in line the three brigades advanced, only to be met by heavy and well aimed Union fire. 'It was a whirlwind of bullets,' a survivor recalled. 'Our men fell constantly. The deadly missives rained like hail among the boughs and trees.'[9] They held the ground they had won for as long as an hour, taking casualties all the time as they repelled Federal attacks. Finally, at about 11.30, surrounded on three sides by advancing Federals, the badly battered Confederates retreated from Matthew's Hill to a new line along Henry Hill. Additional reinforcements in the form of South Carolina's Hampton's Legion joined the Confederate line on Matthew's Hill, but also fell back slowly to the line on Henry Hill. Beauregard's left had been turned.

Henry Hill, however, had already been occupied by Confederate troops. They were men of the First Brigade. Jackson, who had been up since 4 a.m., had his men up early, making strips of white cotton to be tied around their caps for identification in the field. He had received his orders to march towards Mitchell's Ford, and was on the way when he heard the heavy volleys of infantry and the booms of artillery to the Confederate left. Rather than wait for new orders, he turned his brigade in the direction of the firing, sending a courier ahead of him to notify Bee that he and his men were coming.

At about 11.30, as the Confederates were fleeing from Matthew's Hill, Jackson's men started up the slope of Henry Hill. Seeing the disaster in his front, Jackson halted his men just below the crest of the hill and ordered them to lie down. The men wanted to get into the battle, rather than stop and wait. 'The balance of the brigade was in line of battle behind the brow of a small ridge,' wrote Private Casler. 'We were halted at the foot of this ridge and Colonel Cummings told us that it was General Jackson's command that our regiment should depend principally on the bayonet that day, as it was a [smooth-bore] musket regiment.'[10]

'The firing in our front was terrific,' a Virginian later wrote, 'and why we did not render immediate and timely assistance to Bee I could never learn.'[11] Instead, artillery drawn up along the hill line provided covering fire for the fleeing Confederates.

Bee himself, drawn along with the retreating men like a piece of wood on a wave, asked some men in the Brigade what command it was. The nearby soldiers told him, pointing to where Jackson sat motionless on his horse, watching the enemy approach. Bee rode over to him. 'General, they are beating us back,' he cried to the Virginian.

'Sir, we'll give them the bayonet,' was the curt reply.[12] Jackson then formed his brigade from behind the hill where it had been hidden in full line. Casler recalled:

Our regiment marched up the hill and formed "left in front", on the left of the brigade, and on the entire left of our army. As we passed by the other regiments the shells were bursting and cutting down the pines all around us, and we were shaking hands and bidding farewell to those we were acquainted with, knowing that in a few moments many of us would be stretched lifeless on the field.[13]

His spirits apparently renewed, Bee rode back to where his men had gathered in the relative safety of the back slope of Henry Hill. The mass of different uniform styles showed that the men there were from virtually every unit in his command. Of them all, only the grey frock coats trimmed with black tape of the 4th Alabama were worn by men who seemed to retain some unit cohesion. However, all of the field officers of that regiment were missing. 'What regiment is this?' he asked one of the men.

'Why, general,' came the reply, 'don't you know your own troops? This is all that is left of the 4th Alabama.'

A moment of shock overcame Bee, then he regained his composure and asked the troops: 'Will you follow me back to where the firing is going on?'

'To the death,' was the reply. Then Bee made another statement, one that has caused puzzlement as to its meaning ever since. A newspaper correspondent said it went something like this: 'There is Jackson standing like a stone wall. Let us determine to die here, and we will conquer. Follow me.'[14] Today it is unclear whether he meant that Jackson's lack of movement should be inspirational and he complimented the Virginian, or, as Major Thomas Rhett of Jackson's staff later claimed, he was furious that Jackson allowed the non-Virginia brigade to be mauled while the First Brigade stood several hundred yards away without making an effort to come up and reinforce Bee's troops. Whatever the case, it came to be considered a compliment; one which would forever link the word 'stonewall' with both Jackson and the First Brigade, as Bee was to die in this battle.

In fact, Bee had only moments left to live, as he charged the survivors of his brigade straight into the guns of two regular US Army batteries, Battery D, 5th US Artillery, led by Captain Charles Griffin, and Battery I, 1st US Artillery, led by Captain J. B. Ricketts. Both were strong batteries of well trained troops. Battery D comprised two 10lb Parrott guns, two old 6lb smooth-bore guns and two 12lb howitzers, especially useful in close fighting against infantry. Battery I had six 10lb Parrotts.

The fire of these twelve guns tore great gaps in the ranks of Bee's men. After moving only 100 yards towards the guns, most of the men turned and dashed for the safety of the rear. Only the company around Bee himself continued, and even these turned shortly after and made for the rear. Bee himself tried to rally his men, then turned and seemed to ride alone straight for the Federal guns. He fell, mortally wounded. Taken to the rear by one of his aides, he died within a few hours.

As Bee was drawing his last breaths, Beauregard and Johnston arrived on Henry House Hill. There they found Bee's troops milling in the rear, and Johnston directed the 4th Alabama colour sergeant to place his flag on the right of the First Brigade. Slowly, individual soldiers began to form up on this colour and other regiments began to re-form on the line. By 1 p.m. a new defence line of nine full regiments had been drawn up based on the First Brigade.

Anxious to take advantage of their success so far, McDowell ordered Ricketts' and Griffin's two batteries forward, almost to the crest of Henry Hill, to within a few hundred feet of the Confederate line. He promised that they would have sufficient infantry, including the 11th New York, a regiment made up of New York City firemen dressed in Zouave uniform which was not noted for its discipline but was believed to consist of fierce fighters.

The two batteries limbered up, although both commanders thought the move a mistake, mistrusting the quality of the 11th New York. They quickly reached their assigned position, whereupon sniper fire immediately began taking its toll on their horses. Ricketts, believing the fire came from the Henry family house nearby, had it fired on to drive out the supposed sharpshooters. One of his rounds mortally wounded the old bedridden widow who lived there, one of the first civilians to die in the war.

Meanwhile the 11th New York, along with the 14th New York State Militia Regiment, the '14th Brooklyn' who also wore red trousers and dark blue jackets, moved up to the gun line. 'Boys,' said one 33rd sergeant who had been ahead of his men and watched as the New Yorkers advanced, 'there is the prettiest sight from the top of the hill you ever saw; they are coming up the other side in four ranks, and all dressed in red.'[15]

As the New Yorkers reached the gun line, Jackson's men rose to their feet and gave a full brigade volley in which, one brigade member recalled, 'we literally mowed them down'.[16] The 14th, however, on the right, approached where the left flank regiment of the Brigade, the 33rd Virginia, lay mostly hidden in scrub pines and woods. Colonel Cummings, unsure of the lie of the land as he had only just reached this position, was not positive of the identity of the approaching troops. Before the battle he had passed out an identification sign for his men, in addition to the white stripes worn around their hats. This consisted of raising the palm to the forehead, like a salute, and saying 'Sumter'.

Cummings stepped out ahead of his regiment and gave the field sign. It seemed to him that one of the approaching officers returned the sign, and

Cummings ordered the 33rd to hold its fire. A few shots still rang out from his ranks. 'Cease firing,' he called out. 'You are firing on friends.'

'Friends, hell,' Private Casler muttered to his mate. 'That looks like it.'[17] Hardly had Cummings spoken those words, however, when a volley from the 14th convinced him that he was wrong.

A firefight then broke out on both sides, but it was shortlived. Hardly had the First fired its volley when the 1st Virginia Cavalry, led by Colonel J. E. B. Stuart, arrived and decided from the stars and stripes carried by the 11th New York that they had a target of opportunity in front of them. Stuart quickly gave the order to draw sabres and charge. Although the Federals had time for one volley, which emptied a number of saddles, the Confederates were rapidly among them, sabres flashing, before they could reload and fire again. Some Confederates used their carbines and pistols at this close range instead of sabres, which were not available to them all. In a moment they passed through the infantry, swung around, and rode through them again, causing more casualties on both sides. The New Yorkers were badly shaken, and their officers struggled to re-form their shattered companies.

But as the cavalry rode off, the Federal artillery continued to pound Jackson's line and the guns drawn up along it. One shell disembowelled Beauregard's horse as he rode along the line to cheer the men. Splinters from another round slightly wounded Jackson, who also had a finger broken by a musket ball.

Cummings now decided to make the biggest gamble of his career. He had received no orders to do anything but hold his position unless Federal infantry drew within 30 yards of his position, and they had not done so. Indeed, his position was apparently secure enough, without any immediate nearby threat. There was no particularly strong reason for him to do anything but remain drawn up in line, partly protected by the woods, with the rest of the brigade.

On the other hand, he felt that his regiment had been unsettled both by the approach of the 14th Brooklyn and the advance of the two batteries. He was worried that another Federal push would break them. As Cummings later wrote:

There had been some confusion in the regiment, produced by a solid shot being fired towards the regiment and tearing up the ground, together with the appearance of some red-coats on our left. Previous to this time the enemy's artillery fire had been directed towards the regiments of the brigade and at Pendleton's Battery. This little confusion in the regiment, and the fact of the men being raw and undisciplined, made me uncertain as to what would be the result, if I waited, as directed by General Jackson, until the enemy was within thirty paces. And, therefore, as soon as I returned to the regiment I ordered the charge, without waiting...'[18]

So, to beat the enemy to the punch, he decided to charge. It was the kind of gamble that would always be appreciated by Jackson, although at this early stage of the war nobody knew that.

Without waiting for additional orders, or even notifying Jackson or others in the Brigade, Cummings ordered the men to fix bayonets. Then came the rest of his quick orders: 'Attention! Forward March! Charge bayonets! Double quick!'[19] The regiment suddenly darted out of the woods by itself, yelling as the men came on. The timing could not have been better. The two New York regiments were in the process of re-forming and were actually behind the gun line, the guns masking their musketry. The batteries, whose commanders were so intently watching their fronts and were therefore unsure of the position of the New Yorkers behind them, essentially were on their own.

'Captain, don't fire there,' Major William F. Barry, McDowell's chief of artillery, told Griffin as the 33rd moved forward. 'Those are your battery support.'

'They are Confederates,' Griffin replied. 'As certain as the world, they are Confederates.'

'I know they are your battery support,' Barry concluded.[20] Griffin, not believing but obedient, told his battery not to fire on the 33rd, turning his guns again towards the crest of Henry Hill.

In much the same way, Sergeant Major Edward Davis pleaded with Colonel Willis Gorman to have his 1st Minnesota fire on the advancing 33rd. However, Gorman, like Barry, apparently believed the Virginians to be Federal reinforcements and refused to fire on them.

Cummings had the 33rd march towards the right of Griffin's battery, some 50 yards away. On the way the regiment had to halt to scale a snake-rail fence. As they were re-forming, an officer stepped to the front and made what apparently was a brief speech to them.[21] Then they moved off and wheeled towards the battery. When they were some 40 yards away, Griffin, still not trusting Barry's word, gave word to prepare to limber up the guns. Barry, however, reassured him that the 33rd was actually the 11th New York. Union Brigadier General Samuel Heintzelman, however, sitting on his horse near the true 11th, was not mistaken. On seeing the 33rd move out he ordered the 11th to move forward and charge the 33rd. At that moment, however, Cummings halted the 33rd and commanded: 'Ready, aim, fire!'

One of those firing was a company commander, Captain Randolph Barton, who carried an old US Army non-commissioned officer's sword as his badge of rank but had added a flintlock musket to his personal arsenal. 'This gun, after two futile efforts, I fired at a man on horseback in the battery, one of the drivers, I think,' he later wrote.[22]

'That was the last of us,' moaned Griffin. 'We were all cut down.'[23] Almost every cannoneer was either wounded or dead. So many of the battery horses fell that it became impossible to save the guns. Ricketts was wounded, fell from his saddle and was captured. One veteran later wrote that, on the volley of the 33rd:

> ... all was confusion. Wounded men with dripping wounds were clinging to caissons, to which were attached frightened and wounded horses. Horses attached to caissons rushed through the infantry ranks. I saw three horses galloping off, dragging a fourth, which was dead.
>
> The dead cannoneers lay with the rammers of the guns and sponges and lanyards still in their hands. The battery was annihilated by those volleys in a moment. Those who could get away didn't wait. We had no supports near enough to protect us properly, and the enemy were within seventy yards of us when that volley was fired.[24]

The effects of the close-range volley were also felt by the 1st Minnesota, a red-shirted regiment that had been sent to reinforce the 11th. The regimental colour bearer 'was hit by three balls before he fell and after that he loaded and fired some three or four times,' before dying. Thirty men in the regiment's colour company were wounded or killed, while the flag itself was 'riddled with bullets'.[25]

Griffin ran back to the 11th and pleaded with them to charge and save his guns. They were not moved. Instead, they fired one sloppy volley and retired, a would-be-heroic regiment that would not remain on the muster rolls long. The 1st Minnesota, too, would not move forward, but at least it stayed where it was and began returning fire on the 33rd.

Griffin ran back and, helped by a couple of men and two horses, managed to save one gun. Others saved a couple of caissons, posted far to the rear of the gun line. An irate Griffin reported:

In this charge of the enemy, every cannoneer was cut down and a large number of horses killed, leaving the battery (which was without support in name) perfectly helpless. Owing to the loss of men and horses, it was impossible to take more than three pieces from the field. Two of these were afterwards lost in the retreat, by the blocking up of the road by our own forces and the complete exhaustion of the few horses dragging them.[26]

The Virginians swarmed around the rest of the guns. One of the 33rd's members who had been an artilleryman in the Mexican War called out to some nearby Virginia soldiers: 'Boys, let's turn the guns on them'.[27] The words had hardly left his mouth when he fell, shot dead.

Jackson, seeing the success of the 33rd, ordered an advance by the rest of the brigade. Before that could happen, however, Federal gunfire concentrated on the 33rd forced the regiment back. The men retreated, unable to bring Griffin's guns back with them, but the rest of the Brigade pressed on until stiffened Federal resistance halted them and drove them back. The battle for Henry Hill settled down into a fierce firefight, with small advances and retreats on both sides for two hours. Federals, thrown into action a regiment at a time, would charge, and Jackson's fire would push them back. Ricketts' and Griffin's guns however, remained silent, mute monuments in no-man's land. Both sides reinforced their lines, but both were beginning to lose men from the firing lines by straggling. Many of the untrained volunteers were tired, hot and thirsty, and had simply had enough of fighting. Streams of unharmed men, dragging their muskets, straggled towards the rear.

A fresh Virginia brigade arrived at about 4 p.m. and dashed forward just as another Confederate brigade was trying its luck at a charge. The combination this late in the day was just too much for the average Union soldier, and units began to break up. Some fell back slowly, in good order; others simply ceased to exist as the men made their way back towards Centreville and even on to Washington. Beauregard, seeing what was happening, ordered a general advance. Confederate artillery, firing through the fleeing ranks, hit a wagon crossing the stone bridge on the Warrenton Pike, blocking it. Now panic set in in many Union units. Soldiers joined civilian spectators in fleeing back to Washington.

The victory had so disorganised the Confederate army, however, that the generals could not properly move it forward as units to capture as much equipment and personnel as they might have done. Nor could they go on the offensive and take Washington, as Jackson wanted. But it was a stirring first battle for the Confederates, and the victory was largely due to the gamble taken by Colonel Arthur Cummings. It was his capture, without orders, of the two regular batteries that set in motion the eventual victory. It was the war's first 'great gamble'. The cost, however, had been high. Of the 450 men Cummings took into the battle, 43 were dead and 140 wounded. The cost was also directly human. Afterwards, men of the 33rd found three of their number killed by a single shell, brothers Holmes Conrad Jr. and Tucker Conrad, and their cousin Peyton Harrison.

Notes
1 Hardee, W. J., *Rifle and Infantry Tactics*, Raleigh, NC, 1862, p.130.
2 Sandburg, Carl, *Abraham Lincoln, the Prairie Years and the War Years*, New York, 1954, p.252.
3 Davis, William C., *Battle at Bull Run*, Baton Rouge, Louisiana, 1977, pp.916-97.
4 Sears, Stephen W., *For Country Cause & Leader, The Civil War Journal of Charles B. Haydon*, New York, 1993, pp.51-52.
5 Davis, William C., *op. cit.*, p.111.
6 Davis, William C., *op. cit.*, p.124.
7 Casler, John O., *Four Years in the Stonewall Brigade*, Dayton, Ohio, 1994, p.22.
8 Davis, William C., *op. cit.*, p.166.
9 Davis, William C., *ibid.*, p.179.
10 Casler, John O., *op. cit.*, p.25.
11 Davis, William C., *op. cit.*, p.196.
12 Davis, William C., *op. cit.*, p.196.
13 Casler, John O., *op. cit.*, p.25.
14 Davis, William C., *op. cit.*, p.197.
15 Casler, John O., *op. cit.*, p.26.
16 Davis, William C., *op. cit.*, p.206.
17 Casler, John O., *op. cit.*, p.27.
18 Casler, John O., *op. cit.*, p.36.
19 Casler, John O., *op. cit.*, p.27.
20 Davis, William C., *op. cit.*, p.211.
21 Robertson, James I., Jr., *The Stonewall Brigade*, Baton Rouge, Louisiana, 1963, p.41.
22 Casler, John O., *op. cit.*, p.42.
23 Davis, William C., *op. cit.*, p.212.

24 Gross, Warren Lee, *Recollections of a Private*, New York, 1890, p.14.

25 Moe, Richard, *The Last Full Measure*, New York, 1993, p.50.

26 Scott, Robert N., ed, *The War of the Rebellion: A Compilation of the Official Records of the Union and Confederate Armies* (hereinafter *ORs*), Washington, 1884, Series I, Vol. II, p. 394.

27 Casler, John O., *op. cit.*, pp.28-29.

The 20th Maine Charges at Gettysburg

THE GAMBLE: *that a regiment, out of ammunition, having been under attack for several hours, can drive a vastly superior force back by the use of the bayonet and thereby save the far left flank of the army.*

In late June and early July 1863 the seemingly ever-victorious Confederate Army of Northern Virginia and its famed commander, Robert E. Lee, were on the way north again. They had come this way nearly a year before, only to be stopped on the Antietam Creek in Maryland. This time, however, they had stolen a march on the commander of the Army of the Potomac, Major General Joseph Hooker. The Federal army finally discovered where they had gone and headed after them, being careful to place themselves between the enemy and the United States capital city of Washington. Hooker, who had dropped the ball at Chancellorsville, was replaced on the line of march by a native Pennsylvanian, George Gordon Meade.

Lee's men swarmed through Pennsylvania, heading almost to Harrisburg, the state capital, while others drove east through York to the Susquehanna River. One group headed to the small town of Gettysburg, hearing there were shoes to be had there. The only problem was that Federal cavalrymen led by hard-fighting Brigadier General John Buford had beaten them to and through the town and taken the high ground on the other side. Figuring that the blue troops ahead of them were only militia and dismounted cavalry, the Confederate infantry drove forward. Fighting was heavy as the breech-loading carbines of the Union troopers took their toll. Infantry and artillery from the Union I Corps arrived on the field, joined shortly thereafter by more from the XI Corps.

The chance meeting engagement had now turned into a fully fledged battle, much to the dismay of Robert E. Lee. Lee normally depended on his cavalry, led by jaunty Major General J. E. B. Stuart, for information on the enemy in his front. Stuart, however, had taken his cavalry corps on a long raid around the Federal army and captured a long supply train – which also slowed his movements – but had not brought Lee vitally needed intelligence. Lee preferred not to bring on a full-scale battle without Stuart. Moreover, his infantry was spread all over the Pennsylvania countryside, and getting them concentrated would take time. He did not know how much time he would have before Meade could concentrate his new command against him.

Still, by 1 July the Confederates had largely found success. By the end of the day the Confederate infantry had almost smashed the XI Corps and had done a great deal of damage to the I Corps. They had taken the high ground outside Gettysburg itself, and then pushed on and through the small town. The Federals had fallen back to a tall hill just south of the town, Culp's Hill, and the low ridge line, known as Cemetery Ridge from the town cemetery on its ground. Although the Confederate general on the ground, Richard Ewell, had failed to press on and take Culp's Hill as the night fell on the evening of the first evening, the Confederates were still well situated. Their southern line wrapped around with its left facing Culp's Hill and its right down a low ridge across the valley from Cemetery Ridge. Called Seminary Ridge from the Lutheran seminary located on it, the position lay in a wooded belt that offered protection from prying northern eyes as well as shot and shell.

Lee sent orders to all of his far-flung units to march through the night to Gettysburg, as did Meade to his units. Then both sides prepared for the next morning.

Before sunrise one of Lee's corps commanders, Lieutenant General James Longstreet, rode over to Lee's headquarters tent to ask for orders. Lee had none for him yet, although he generally planned to attack on a flank or two. This tactic had served him best at his recent victory at Chancellorsville. But a successful flank attack called for detailed knowledge of the ground over which the attack was to pass, and the enemy in its way. As yet the Confederate cavalry had not arrived, and neither had much of the infantry. Lee's knowledge of the Federal positions, hidden by the dark, was at best imperfect. He told Longstreet to wait as Confederate engineer officers scouted the flanks. Longstreet waited through daybreak as Lee rode over to the right himself to examine the ground there.

While Lee and his engineers were scouting, the Federals were reinforcing. During the night the II Corps arrived and was placed on Cemetery Ridge next to Culp's Hill, which was manned by the small XII Corps. The

III Corps was placed towards the left of the II Corps. On the left of the III Corps stood two steep hills, Little Round Top, closer to the Federal position, and, beyond that, Big Round Top. The V Corps had arrived behind them and was drawn up as reserves. The VI Corps was still on the way up.

Lee returned to his headquarters a little after 10 a.m., and the scouting reports he sought came shortly after that. Looking at his maps, he decided on his plan. He would attack on either flank. Culp's Hill, which Ewell had left the night before, would be the target for one assault, which would mainly serve as a demonstration to keep the Federals busy. The other attack would fall on the Union left, guarded by the two Round Tops. It would be an attack *en echelon*, designed to roll up the Federal line and destroy its army. At about 3 p.m. marching orders went out to Longstreet's troops, who had been allowed to stack arms, unsling their accoutrements and rest in whatever shade they could find. Not only was it hot, but the humidity was high, as was usual in that part of Pennsylvania in July. Breathing was hard enough; it was really unpleasant to have to move around. None the less, once the units were ready they faced south and marched off to the attack.

'General Lee ordered his reconnoitring officer to lead the troops of the First Corps and conduct them by a route concealed from the view of the enemy,' recalled Longstreet, whose I Corps troops were to make the attack on the Federal left. 'Under the conduct of the reconnoitring officer, our march seemed slow, – there were some halts and countermarches.'[1] The blistering July sun rose and began to fall without the Confederate attack. Even those in the ranks could see that time was being lost. Colonel William C. Oates of the 15th Alabama, one of Hood's units, thought that: 'There was a good deal of delay on the march, which was quite circuitous, for the purpose of covering the movement from the enemy.'[2]

The general direction of the attack was described to Major General John B. Hood as south of Gettysburg, along the Emmitsburg Road. Hood wrote:

Before reaching this road, however, I had sent forward some of my picket Texas scouts to ascertain the position of the enemy's extreme left flank. They soon reported to me that it rested upon Round Top Mountain; that the country was open, and that I could march through an open woodland pasture around Round Top, and assault the enemy in flank and rear; that their wagon trains were parked in the rear of their line, and were badly exposed to our attack in that direction.[3]

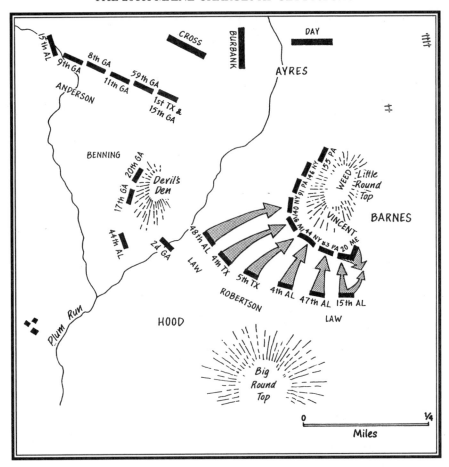

Hood, always vigorous in the attack, hesitated to attack the enemy's position in his front, instead asking permission to attack the enemy's exposed position. Permission was refused, Longstreet ordering a direct assault on the Union left in accordance with Lee's original orders.

At about 3.30, Hood's artillery opened fire and his infantry deployed into line. The Army of the Potomac's chief signal officer, Captain L. B. Norton, reported:

Now it would be impossible to hide the attack. A station was established upon Round Top Mountain, on the left of our line, and from this point the greater part of the enemy's forces could be seen and their movements reported. From this position, at 3.30 p.m., the signal officer discovered the enemy massing upon General Sickles' left, and reported that fact to General Sickles [commander of the III Corps] and to the general commanding [Meade].[4]

Watches were not co-ordinated in the two armies. One student of the battle, after studying when events happened and the times participants said they occurred, decided that watches in Lee's army were set some 20 minutes ahead of those in Meade's.[5] Therefore it would have been about ten to four, Confederate time, when the US Signal Corps station on Big Round Top reported the massing of Hood's troops.

As it turned out, probably neither Sickles nor Meade received the Signal Corps message. They had been in a conference of all corps commanders at Meade's headquarters, behind the centre of the line at Cemetery Ridge. When the conference broke up, shortly after 3 p.m., Meade rode over to examine Sickles' defences at his part of the line. Meade was accompanied by Richard Warren, his chief engineer, and Henry Hunt, chief of the Union artillery. Sickles, a politician appointed to general rank because of the support he could bring to the Lincoln administration, had placed his defences badly, but after looking the line over and deciding to leave it where it was, Meade returned to his headquarters. Warren rode on up to the top of Little Round Top to see what he could of the enemy.

When he got there he saw something suspicious across the valley of Plum Run in a fringe of trees on Snyder Ridge. He sent an orderly to a III Corps battery with a request to toss a couple of rounds at the trees. The battery commander, not having any other targets in his front, quickly complied. The rounds drove some Confederates and their tell-tale scarlet, blue crossed, square battle flags out into the open.

In horror, Warren realised that Confederate infantry could easily take the commanding position of Little Round Top, which was manned only by some Signal Corps troops and Warren with his staff. From that position they could roll up the entire Union army. It would be a Chancellorsville all over again, but this time deep in the north itself. Could the country stand such a defeat?

Warren hurried a staff officer to Sickles, asking that a brigade be sent to the position as quickly as possible. There was not a single brigade in reserve in Sickles' corps. In the meantime, and in desperation, Warren, who saw fresh V Corps troops arriving behind Little Round Top, tore down the hillside to the white rectangular flag bearing the red Maltese Cross that represented the headquarters of the First Division, V corps. Its commander, Brigadier General James Barnes, reported:

> General Warren, of the staff of General Meade, came up, riding rapidly from the left, and pointing out the position of the elevation known as the Round Top, not far off and toward the left, urged the importance of assistance in that direction. [Major] General [George] Sykes [V Corps commander] yielded to his urgent request, and I immediately directed Colonel Vincent, commanding the Third Brigade, to proceed to that point with his brigade. Colonel Vincent moved with great promptness to the post assigned to him. The brigade consisted of the Sixteenth Michigan, the Forty-fourth New York, the Eighty-third Pennsylvania, and the Twentieth Maine Regiments.[6]

All told, the brigade counted about 1,000 muskets on its battle line.

As the brigade pulled into position, Vincent posted them. The 16th Michigan was placed on the right of the brigade, its flank touching the left flank of the Third Division. The 44th New York was next in line, with the 83rd Pennsylvania on its left. At the extreme left of the line, on the very end of the Union line, went the 20th Maine.

Up to that point the 20th Maine had not achieved an exceptionally brilliant military record. It had been organised in Portland, Maine, in the late summer of 1862, and was mustered into Federal service on 29 August 1862 under Colonel Adelbert Ames and assigned to the First Division, V Corps of the Army of the Potomac. That corps had been maintained in reserve at the Battle of Antietam, so the regiment saw no action there. It was only minimally involved in the Battle of Fredericksburg, and it missed Chancellorsville altogether because its men were quarantined with smallpox. While the army fought its hard fight, the 20th had been guarding a telegraph wire.

On this hot day the 20th had 358 men and 28 officers present for duty, including company cooks and servants, who did not have to handle a musket but who did not want to miss what they knew would be an important fight. In addition, the regiment had been assigned 120 men from the 2nd Maine who had volunteered for that regiment when it was mustered in for a two-year term but had signed papers for three years' service. Although they had demanded that they be discharged with the rest of the regiment, the army had held that they owed their country another year of duty. This they refused to do, so they had been sent to the 20th as mutineers awaiting courts martial. According to orders, if they accepted duty in the 20th they would avoid this fate. Otherwise they could serve prison terms if the colonel of the 20th did not just shoot them out of hand, as he had apparently been authorised to do. The colonel did not shoot the prisoners; he simply had them follow along on the 26 miles the regiment marched on 1 July to reach the battlefield.

Ames, however, had caught the eye of army top brass and had been promoted. Command of the regiment then fell to its lieutenant colonel, 35-year-old Joshua Lawrence Chamberlain. Chamberlain was not a professional soldier, having been a professor of rhetoric and revealed religion at Maine's Bowdoin College. He had taken a sabbatical in 1862, explaining that he was going to travel in Europe. Instead he secured an appointment as lieutenant colonel of the new 20th Maine. Chamberlain had been joined in the regiment by his younger brother, Thomas, who had been named a lieutenant in Company G. In July 1863 he was serving as the regimental adjutant. A third brother, John, had joined the Christian Commission. Since the regiment had no surgeon in the summer of 1863, Chamberlain had asked for John's service as medical director of the regiment, and his request had been granted.

The three brothers led the regiment, ahead of the regiment, riding abreast. Suddenly a Confederate solid shot flew by them. Chamberlain halted his horse. 'Boys,' he said to his brothers, 'I don't like this. Another such shot might make it hard for mother. Tom, go to the rear of the regiment, and see that it is well closed up! John, pass ahead and look out a place for our wounded.'[7]

The area to which the brigade had been assigned was well suited for defence, and would be hard to attack successfully. Colonel James Rice of the 44th New York later reported:

The ground occupied by the brigade in line of battle was nearly that of a quarter circle, composed mostly of high rocks and cliffs on the centre, and becoming more wooded and less rugged as you approached the left. The right was thrown forward somewhat to the front of the ledge of rocks, and was much more exposed than other parts of the line. A comparatively smooth ravine extended along the entire front, perhaps 50 yards from our line, while on the left and beyond a high and jagged mountain rises, called Round Top hill.[8]

As Vincent's brigade filed into position, the Confederates swept into the field below the Federals. Confederate Major General E. M. Law wrote:

Advancing rapidly across the valley which separated the opposing lines, all the time under a heavy fire from the [Union] batteries, our front line struck the enemy's skirmishers posted along the farther edge of the valley. Brushing these quickly away, we soon came upon their first line of battle, running along the lower slopes of the hills known as Devil's Den, to our left of Round Top, and separated by Plum Run valley. The fighting soon became close and severe. Exposed to the artillery fire from the heights in front and our left, as well as to the musketry of the infantry, it required all the courage and steadiness of the veterans who composed the Army of Northern Virginia – whose spirit was never higher than then – to face the storm. Not one moment was lost. With rapidly thinning ranks the grey line swept on, until the blue line in front wavered, broke, and seemed to dissolve in the woods and rocks of the mountain-side. The advance continued steadily, the centre of the division moving directly upon the guns on the hill adjoining Devil's Den on the north, from which we had been suffering so severely. In order to secure my right flank, I extended it well up on the side of Round Top ...[9]

Hood himself fell, an arm mangled by enemy artillery fire.

Private Jonathan Stevens of Company K, 5th Texas, was one of the attackers:

As we start up the mountain we got a plunging volley from the enemy, who are posted behind the rocks on the crest. They are not more than 25 or 30 steps away and well protected behind the rocks, while we are exposed to their fire. Their first volley was most destructive to our line. Every line officer of my regiment is shot down except one man – the major. Now, for the first time in the history of the war, our men begin to waver. We are suffering terribly. Finally they begin to go back. Their idea is to fall back, re-form and come back again. Just at this juncture Captain Hubert calls out for Company K to stand fast. Only eleven men stand their ground – 3 officers and 8 men – but we stand and make a fight. The balls are whizzing so thick around us that it looks like a man could hold out a hat and catch it full.[10]

But the Confederate line pressed on.

Stray rounds flew over their heads as the men of Vincent's Brigade prepared for battle. Vincent himself rode to the front, to where the 20th Maine would be posted. He was a well-built young man, with a magnificent pair of sideburns. Chamberlain saw him as he arrived at the head of his regiment and rode over to him. 'I place you here,' Vincent said as he saw Chamberlain ride up. 'This is the left of the Union line. You understand? You are to hold this ground at all costs!'[11]

Chamberlain did not like the look of Big Round Top, which overlooked his line, hidden as it was in the trees and rocks. He ordered Captain Walter G. Morrill's Company B to be detached as skirmishers, extending from the left flank across a hollow between the two hills. He told the company commander to act as circumstances required, but the purpose of Company B's position was to prevent the 20th being taken by surprise from the left or rear.

What Chamberlain did not know was that, while the 20th was the whole regiment on the far Union left, there actually were other Union combat troops on his left. There were other Federals around from the 2nd US Sharpshooters, a specially raised unit of marksmen trained to fight as skirmishers. They wore all-green uniforms, as opposed to the dark blue coats and sky blue trousers of the other Federal infantry, as marks of their unique status, and were armed with breechloading Sharps rifles. Earlier, the 2nd had all been in the area Chamberlain was to defend, but, save for the one company, had been withdrawn to another part of the field. They had been posted to the right of Little Round Top, on the other side of Plum Run, when the Confederates attacked along there on the left of the III Corps.

Major Homer Stoughton, 2nd Sharpshooters commander, reported:

I held my position until their line of battle was within 100 yards of me and their skirmishers were pushing my right flank, when I ordered my men to fall back, firing as they retired. My left wing retreated up the hill and allowed the enemy to pass up the ravine, when they poured a destructive fire into his flank and rear. The right wing fell back gradually until they mingled with the regiments composing the Second Brigade, and remained till night, when the brigade was relieved.[12]

In fact, some of the 2nd, fighting in loose skirmish order, drifted across the front of Little Round Top until they came in touch with Company B of the

20th Maine, who had drawn up their line behind a stone wall along the left of the rest of the regiment.

Colonel Rice came over to the left of his line, where his regiment and Chamberlain's touched, to take a look at the position with Chamberlain and discuss the fighting to come. Below them they could see Confederates pouring around the left of the III Corps and moving up towards the base of the Round Tops.

It was a stirring, not to say appalling sight: here a whole battery of shot and shell cutting a ragged chasm through a serried mass, flinging men and horses like drift aside; there a rifle volley at close range, with reeling shock, hands tossed in air, muskets dropped with death's quick relax, or clutched with last, convulsive energy, men falling like grass before the scythe – others with manhood's proud calm and rally; there a little group kneeling above some favourite officer slain, his intense spirit still animating the fiery steed pressing headlong with empty saddle to the van; here, a defiant regiment of ours, broken, slaughtered, captured; or survivors, of both sides crouching among the rocks for shelter from the terrible crossfire where there is no rear![13]

But the Confederates came on relentlessly.

While the men of Company B were filing into position the artillery firing ceased, and musket shots to the right indicated an enemy attack had finally reached the brigade's position. Confederates rushed at the front of the brigade again and again, only to fall back, badly blooded. Finally they shifted a little to the Union right, hitting the line in front of the 16th Michigan. Here they were a bit more successful, driving back the Michigan boys. Colonel Vincent fell, mortally wounded. Troops from the 140th New York, originally ordered to reinforce the III Corps, arrived on the scene and drove back the Confederates, who were exhausted from fighting and climbing over rocks and trees. The line was restored and there was a momentary lull.

On the Confederate side, General Law told Colonel William C. Oates, commander of the 15th Alabama Infantry, that Oates was Chamberlain's opposite in this battle, as his regiment represented the extreme right of the Confederate line. His orders to Oates were 'to hug the base of Great Round Top and go up the valley between the two mountains, until I found the left of the Union line, to turn it and do all the damage I could'. His regiments would be supported by the 47th Alabama. The 15th, with 44 officers and 644 musketmen, was the strongest regiment in the attacking force.

While the general and colonel talked, the men of the two regiments waited in line of battle, their arms stacked. They had already marched 28 miles in the previous 24 hours, much of the time in the hot sun, and many of the men had drained their canteens. Oates had authorised two men from each company, 22 men in all, to gather the canteens from their companies and fill them with water from a well Oates had seen some 100 yards in the rear of their battle line. They were dipping the canteens in the cool water as Law ordered Oates to move off. Oates later wrote:

> It would have been infinitely better to have waited five minutes for those twenty-two men and the canteens of water, but generals never ask a colonel if his regiment is ready to move. The order was given and away we went. The water detail followed with the canteens of water, but when they got into the woods they missed us, walked right into the Yankee lines, and were captured, canteens and all. My men in the ranks, in the intense heat, suffered greatly for water.[14]

On such small details do the fates of nations often hang.

The Alabamians had not got far when they received a surprising fire on their left flank from Federal skirmishers, many apparently from the 2nd Sharpshooters, who had drifted far to their right. The rolling fire of the skirmishers, trained in independent and accurate fire, continued. Oates looked back for new orders from an expected courier. None arrived, and he let the troops march on. Lieutenant Colonel Isaac B. Feogin of the 15th fell with a leg wound; he would loose the limb on an operating table.

Concerned about the damaging fire, Oates changed the direction of his line of march on the right and, accompanied by the 47th Alabama, attacked in the direction of the Sharpshooters. The skirmishers fell back towards Big Round Top as the Confederates came on, chasing the Federals instead of moving ahead between the two mountains as originally ordered. Oates deployed three companies of the 47th as skirmishers and formed the remaining men into a single battle line. Then he advanced up the mountain. He said:

> The sharpshooters retreated up the south front of the mountain, pursued by my command. In places the men had to climb up, catching to

the rocks and brushes and crawling over the boulders in the face of the fire of the enemy, who kept retreating, taking shelter and firing down on us from behind the rocks and crags which covered the side of the mountain thicker than grave-stones in a city cemetery. Fortunately they usually over-shot us.[15]

Finally the two regiments reached the top of the mountain, as their foes scampered down the other side, back towards the stone wall where Company B, 20th Maine, was hidden.

The climb had taken its toll on the already tired Alabama troops. They lacked their canteens and there were no springs on the side of Big Round Top. Oates let his men drop their muskets on the ground and take a break. As they were all catching their breaths, one of those mounted staff officers so derided by infantrymen found the colonel. He asked why the Confederates were not moving on, and Oates explained their situation. The captain then said that Hood had been wounded and replaced by Law, who ordered Oates to 'press on, turn the Union left, and capture Little Round Top, if possible, and to lose no time.'[16] Oates argued that he should wait there for artillery to come up, but was overruled. So he called his weary men to their feet and the two regiments started down the hill to cross the ravine, right towards where the 20th Maine waited. It was now 6 p.m., and there was about an hour and 40 minutes of daylight left.

At that moment, however, the 20th Maine was not waiting for Oates' men. Instead, their attention was taken by Confederates coming up past the rocks and low shrubs on their front. These were soldiers of the 4th Alabama, with some overlapping troops from the 47th Alabama. The command to fire was given, and rolls of smoke poured down the hillside as Confederates fell wounded and dead. The Federal line was holding. Suddenly, Lieutenant James H. Nichols, commander of Company K, posted in the centre of the regiment's line, saw something to his left. He felt sure he had seen more Confederates behind the attackers, coming down the slope from Big Round Top.

Corporal Elisha Coan, a member of the regimental colour guard, recalled:

... some of the bullets came from our front and soon some officers [others] came from our left lengthwise of the regiment line, I said to my comrade on my right they are getting on our flank. Just then an officer from the left of our line came up to Colonel Chamberlain and reported that the enemy was flanking us and getting in our rear.[17]

Chamberlain climbed on top of a large rock, bullets clipping twigs near him, and tried to see through the smoke and brush. He recalled:

Thick groups in grey were pushing up along the smooth dale between the Round Tops in a direction to gain our left flank. There was no mistaking this. If they could hold our attention by a hot fight in front while they got in force on that flank, it would be bad for us and our whole defence.[18]

The force coming down was Oates' regiment, stronger than Chamberlain's, and his reinforcing regiment. Chamberlain had to decide what to do. The conventional tactic would have been to face about the entire regiment, strung out in a single line of companies facing the front, and wheel it, hinged on the 83rd Pennsylvania, in a single line to the left to form another single line. But there were problems with this. First, keeping dress on an entire regiment wheeling in line is very difficult, even on a flat, open field. Doing it in broken ground would be virtually impossible. Moreover, his regiment was already heavily engaged, fighting off attacking Confederates. He would have to detach several companies as skirmishers to cover the wheeling movement, and thereby shorten his line. At the same time, the Confederates already attacking could easily brush by his skirmishers and attack the main body, who would have their backs to the enemy. Finally, the ground he had to give up was high ground, and would cede an advantage to the enemy.

Chamberlain called the company commanders to his side and quickly gave them his orders. Companies E, I, K, D and F, the centre and right wing, or half, of the regiment would extend their line to the left. Where the battle line had been set up two men deep, it would now be a single line of men. Chamberlain himself would take the regimental colours to what would now be the end of the line on Company F. The companies to the left of F – A, H, C and G, which made up the left wing of the regiment – would wheel about to the left and fall back to 'refuse the left flank'. Chamberlain would lead the way and post the colours first, then the four left companies would march down to him and turn, as the other companies extended their lines to fill in.

This manoeuvre was even more complicated to perform, especially under heated fire on broken terrain, but Chamberlain's men managed it. They arrived just in time, ducking behind trees and boulders, as Oates led his men forward. Oates had not seen the Maine men, hidden by the brush, move in his front. He wrote:

Advancing rapidly, without any skirmishers in front, the woods being open without undergrowth, I saw no enemy until within forty or fifty steps of an irregular ledge of rocks – a splendid line of natural breast-works running about parallel with the front of the Forty-seventh regiment and my four left companies, and then sloping back in front of my centre and right at an angle of about thirty-five or forty degrees. From behind this ledge, unexpectedly to us, because concealed, they poured into us the most destructive fire I ever saw. Our line halted, but did not break.

Oates' men began to fall, while others halted and began to return the fire. 'I could see through the smoke men of the Twentieth Maine in front of my right wing running from tree to tree back westward toward the main body, and I advanced my right, swinging it around, overlapping and turning their left.'[19]

The Alabamians had fixed bayonets, but the Maine men had not yet done so. Despite the sudden shock of the Federal volley, the southern troops came on, closing with the Federals. In desperation, the Maine troops turned their muskets around, using the butts like clubs and fighting off the Confederates. Chamberlain wrote:

The edge of conflict swayed to and fro, with wild whirlpools and eddies. At times I saw around me more of the enemy than of my own men; gaps opening, swallowing, closing again with sharp convulsive energy; squads of stalwart men who had cut their way through us, disappearing as if translated. All around, strange, mingled roar–shouts of defiance, rally, and desperation; and underneath, murmured entreaty and stifled moans; gasping prayers, snatches of Sabbath song, whispers of loved names; everywhere men torn and broken, staggering, creeping, quivering on the earth, and dead faces with strangely fixed eyes staring stark into the sky.[20]

Only two of the colour guard were standing. Colour Sergeant Andrew Tozier, his regimental flag dug into the earth and leaning against his shoulder, picked up a musket and fired as rapidly as possible. Chamberlain saw this, and called for his adjutant to get a couple of men to help defend the colours. Several mutineers of the 2nd Maine picked up muskets and joined in the fight, smashing into the Confederates. Chamberlain made a mental note to have their courts martial dismissed if they survived. He also saw a boy with a bad gash in his head and sent him to the rear to safety, but moments later he saw the young soldier back in line, a bloody bandage wrapped around his head.

One Maine soldier made a grab for the colour of the 15th Alabama, only to fall with a bayonet in his head at the hand of Sergeant Pat O'Connor of the Confederate unit's colour guard.

Lieutenant Colonel Michael Bulger, commander of the 47th, fell, shot through a lung. With this his regiment fell back in some confusion. As those men fell back, however, Oates ordered the 15th to change direction to the right and swing around, with the intention of enfilading the Federal line and, relieving the 47th, so as to gain the enemy's rear and drive him from the hill:

> My men obeyed and advanced about half way to the enemy's position, but the fire was do destructive that the line wavered like a man trying to walk against a strong wind, and then slowly, doggedly, gave back a little; then with no one upon the left or right of me, my regiment exposed, while the enemy was still under cover, to stand there and die was sheer folly; either to retreat or advance became a necessity.[21]

The Confederates fell back only a short way. Captain DeBernie Waddell, adjutant of the 15th, asked Oates for permission to take 40 or 50 men further down the right of the line to some rocks where they could rake Chamberlain's line. Oates gave permission and the group set off. The others halted where they were, badly winded. Many of their officers, including Colonel Oates' brother, had been killed or seriously wounded. Still, Oates rallied his men and, passing through the ranks with his sword drawn, yelled: 'Forward, men, to the ledge!'[22] The Confederates came on, driving right into the Federal line. Some of the Federals fell back to another rocky ledge near the first one, and Oates believed he had taken the position, but the men from Maine dashed back at them. Oates recalled that he held that position as the 20th Maine companies attacked him five times, and the two lines, in little groups, fell back and went forward time and again.

Exhaustion eventually overcame the fighters on both sides, and the front became quiet but for the odd shot. The Confederates rested behind one ledge, wishing for their missing canteens, while the Federals, with their canteens to hand, took refuge behind the next ledge up the hill. The Maine men went out and gathered the many dead and wounded and brought them to safety. The men on the firing line pulled out the tin containers in their cartridge boxes and put ammunition from the bottom of the tins on the top so that it was easily reached. Most, however, were totally out of ammunition, and searched the cartridge boxes of nearby downed comrades to find what they could. Most of them had fired the 60 rounds they had brought into battle. Chamberlain sent his adjutant to the commander of the 83rd to ask for a company as reinforcements, as a third of the 20th Maine was out of action. The commander's answer was that the 83rd did not have a company to spare, but he could extend his line a bit if the 20th wanted to shift down. This Chamberlain did, but his regiment was still too thinly spread to defend its ground adequately.

The situation was desperate. Chamberlain had to decide what to do. 'It did not seem possible to withstand another shock like this now coming on,' he reported, adding 'Only a desperate chance was left for us.'[23] He would take a huge gamble that the enemy was unbalanced by its defeats, and order a bayonet charge, his left wheeling down towards the centre. He went to the left to tell the senior captain there of his plan, limping because his left leg had been badly bruised when a bullet struck his iron sword scabbard and his right instep had been hit by flying debris. Then he returned to the colour company and yelled 'Bayonets!'

Before he could give any further orders, however, Captain Holman S. Melcher, commander of the colour company, came up and asked if he could take his company forward during the lull to gather his wounded. 'Yes, sir, in a moment,' Chamberlain replied. 'I am about to order a charge.'

Melcher ran back to his company, his sword drawn and waving in the air, and dashed forward through the battle line to where his company wounded lay, yelling 'Come on! Come on! Come on, boys!' for his company to follow him.[24] The men of his company, carrying the regimental colours and having heard the first command to fix bayonets, leaped up and ran down with him. Others, in all about 170 of the regiment, assumed they had not heard the command to charge and dashed down with them, straight at the 15th

Alabama. Others, too, from the 83rd, dashed forward as they saw Confederates fleeing across their front.

Chamberlain would later speak of the charge as if it were a well schemed thing, resulting from a plan that all understood. Although he did have it in mind to make a bayonet charge, charging *en echelon* or as a wheel on the right, in truth it was more impromptu than that. In his official report he described the action thus: 'Holding fast by our right, and swinging forward our left, we made an extended "right wheel", before which the enemy's second line broke and fell back, fighting from tree to tree, many being captured until we swept the valley and cleared the front of nearly our entire brigade.'[25] In fact, the 'right wheel' largely happened by accident when men saw and joined the charge.

Oates had his problems, too, although Chamberlain was unaware of them. Not only were his men exhausted and his casualties heavy, but he had just received word that two entire regiments were coming on his right. In reality they were the men of the 2nd Sharpshooters and Company B, 20th Maine, who were now advancing towards the sounds of the guns. Oates watched as they drew within range and began to open fire on his men. He asked for help from the 4th Alabama, only to have his courier return with the word that no other Confederates were in sight, and the woods between the 15th and 4th Alabama Regiments were swarming with Federals. His company commanders, concerned that they were taking fire from several areas, asked him to order a retreat. 'Return to your companies,' Oates told them. 'We shall sell out as dearly as possible.'[26] Then, after a few moments' thought, Oates realised that they were correct and ordered a general retreat.

Oates' men were pulling out just as Chamberlain's hit. Confederates ran everywhere they could. Many ran back to the Big Round Top, but most ran back towards the main Confederate line on Plum Run. About 80 retreated to the north-east, where they were captured in the Weikert Farm Lane. Chamberlain himself, sword in hand, was suddenly confronted by a Confederate officer who aimed his pistol straight at Chamberlain and pulled the trigger. Something must have happened to the pistol; perhaps the percussion cap had fallen off the cone, as often happened. In any case, the pistol did not go off and just as quickly the Confederate handed the sword he carried in his other hand to the Maine colonel.

Colonel Bulger of the 47th was found by a captain as he lay wounded. 'I am a lieutenant colonel,' Bulger told the officer, 'and I will not surrender my sword to an officer of equal rank.'

'Surrender your sword, or I will kill you,' replied the captain, flushed in the heat of battle.

'You may kill and be damned,' Bulger said. 'I shall never surrender my sword to an officer of lower rank.'

By now a bit cooler, the amused captain sent for a colonel to accept the Alabama colonel's surrender.[27]

A member of the colour guard involved in the charge recalled that they met little opposition:

Some threw down their arms and ran, but many rose up, begging to be spared. We did not stop but told them to go to the rear, and we went after the whipped and frightened rebels, taking them by scores and giving those too far away to be captured deadly shots in the back. After chasing them as far as prudent, we "rallied around the colours" and gave three hearty cheers, and then went back to our old position, with our prisoners. Two of our boys guarded 81 in one squad to the rear.[28]

Fearful of a Confederate counterattack, when the Federals reached the bottom of Little Round Top Chamberlain ordered them halted. Then they slowly returned to their original position, stopping to pick up wounded and capture prisoners on the way. Oates described the ground over which they had come: 'The blood stood in puddles in some places on the rocks; the ground was soaked with the blood of as brave men as ever fell on the red field of battle.'[29]

The attacking Federals had taken some 300 Confederates, besides Bulger, as prisoners. About 100 of them had been wounded. Another 60 dead Confederates were found on the ground over which they had fought.[30] Oates reported:

After all had got up, I ordered the rolls of the companies to be called. When the battle commenced, four hours previously, I had the strongest and finest regiment in Hood's Division. Its effectives numbered nearly 700 officers and men. Now 225 answered at roll-call, and more than one-half of my officers had been left on the field.[31]

The loss to the 20th Maine, which had saved the Union left and quite possibly the battle, was some 130, of whom 40 had been killed or mortally wounded.[32] Since Company B, which had 50 men, had been out of the main fight, the 20th actually had 308 officers and men on its main battle line during the battle. Chamberlain's wild gamble, combined with some of the toughest fighting by any regiment during a war marked by tough fighting, had won the day.

Notes

1 Longstreet, James, *From Manassas to Appomattox*, New York, 1991, pp.365-366.
2 LaFantasie, Glenn, *Gettysburg*, New York, 1992, p.78.
3 Hood, John B., *Advance and Retreat*, New York, 1993, p.57
4 *ORs*, Series I, Vol. XXVII, Part I, p.202.
5 Stewart, George R., *Pickett's Charge*, Greenwich, Connecticut, 1963, p.5.
6 *ORs*, op. cit., pp.600-601.
7 Chamberlain, Joshua L., *Through Blood and Fire at Gettysburg*, Gettysburg, Pennsylvania, 1994, p.9.
8 *ORs, op. cit.*, pp.616-617.
9 Johnson, Robert O., and Buel, Clarence E., *Battles and Leaders of the Civil War*, New York, 1956 (hereinafter *B&L*); E. M. Law, 'The Struggle for "Round Top"' Vol. III, pp.323-324.
10 Stevens, Jno. W., *Reminiscences of the Civil War*, Hillsboro, Texas, 1902, p.114.
11 Chamberlain, Joshua, L., *op. cit.*, p.10.
12 *ORs, op. cit.*, pp.518-519.
13 Chamberlain, Joshua L., *op. cit.*, p.13.
14 LaFantasie, Glenn, *op. cit.*, p.87.
15 LaFantasie, Glenn, *ibid*, pp.85-86.
16 LaFantasie, Glenn, *ibid.*, p.87.
17 Styple, William B., ed., *With a Flash of His Sword*, Kearny, New Jersey, 1993, p.82.
18 Chamberlain, Joshua L., *op. cit.*, p.14.
19 LaFantasie, Glenn, *ibid.*, pp.90-91.
20 Chamberlain, Joshua L., *op. cit.*, pp.16-17.
21 LaFantasie, Glenn, *op. cit.*, p.96
22 LaFantasie, Glenn, *ibid.*, p.97.
23 *ORs, op. cit.*, p.624.
24 Cross, David F., 'Mantled in Fire and Smoke', *America's Civil War*, January 1992, p.41.
25 *ORs, op. cit.*, p.624.
26 Pfanz, Harry W., *Gettysburg, the Second Day*, Chapel Hill, North Carolina, 1987, p.234.
27 LaFantasie, Glenn, *op. cit.*, p.95.
28 Styple, William B., *op. cit.*, p.78.
29 LaFantasie, Glenn, *op. cit.*, p.99.
30 Styple, William B., *op. cit.*, p.143.
31 Styple, William B., *ibid.*, p.134.
32 Pullen, John J., *The 20th Maine*, Greenwich, Connecticut, 1962, p.136.

Brown takes the CSS *Arkansas* to Vicksburg

THE GAMBLE: *that an ironclad built of inferior material and with poor engines can pass by a much larger enemy fleet and escape to deep waters, where it can do maximum damage.*

In terms of defending its many harbours and waterways, the south at the outbreak of the Civil War had severe disadvantages. Although it had an army that could draw on its volunteer companies and militia, it had no navy. It had very few shipyards, few experienced naval contractors, and even fewer ships' carpenters. It had virtually no machinery to produce ships' engines.

Moreover, the lack of manufacturing facilities meant that much of what the south needed, not only to fight a war, but to maintain basic civilian existence, had to be imported through its ports. And, with its lack of available hard currency or rich natural resources, the south depended on shipping its cotton abroad to maintain its war effort. Yet the official policy of the new government of the Confederate States was to defend every inch of its territory, including coastal cities. A navy had to be created. It would be up to the Confederacy's new Secretary of the Navy to get that job done.

The job was given to Stephen R. Mallory, a Floridian who had served on the US Senate's navy committee before the war. Fortunately for the cause he was a bright individual, receptive to new ideas, something not terribly common among the usually very conservative naval types. Mallory was aware that both the British and French navies had developed ships with iron-plated sides during the Crimean War. These vessels could deflect shots fired by enemy ships or forts without receiving much damage, while their heavy guns could do great harm to any enemy. 'I regard the possession of an iron-armoured ship as a matter of the first necessity,' Mallory wrote the chairman of the House Committee on Naval Affairs on 7 May 1861, adding, 'Inequality of numbers may be compensated by invulnerability; and thus not only does economy but naval success dictate the wisdom and expediency of fighting with iron against wood, without regard to first cost.'[1]

At first Mallory sent agents to Europe to find the ironclads he wanted. However, no navies there wanted to sell any such ships, which had just entered their fleets. His agents did manage to secure contracts for several armoured ships with British builders, but these ships would take many months to build and man, and even then there was always the danger that the British government would seize them as being in violation of the neutrality of Her Majesty's government. For the short term, the southern navy would have to be created in the south.

This brought some of its own problems. There was only one rolling mill in all of the south capable of rolling two-inch-thick iron plate, the Tredegar Iron Works, on the bank of the James River in the Confederacy's capital city of Richmond. The lack of experienced shipbuilders who could produce those beautifully curvaceous ships' hulls meant that, whatever kind of ship Mallory finally authorised, it would largely have to be built by house carpenters. These men, skilled woodworkers in their own ways, still produced items having angles rather than curves.

In early June, Confederate Navy Lieutenant John M. Brooke, a former professional US Navy officer, produced a plan for an ironclad that could be produced by southern builders. Using only the plate available, it would be essentially a floating battery. Its deck was actually submerged in the water, and the superstructure was little more than an ironclad fort with sloping walls to deflect enemy shot and protect its own guns, which were inside. The top would be open, with a grate laid over it. The idea of submerging the decks at the bow and stern was to gain buoyancy and speed.

In July 1861 Mallory ordered his subordinates to build an ironclad vessel on the hull of an old US Navy wooden frigate, the USS *Merrimac*, that had been burned at the war's outbreak to prevent its falling into southern hands. When it was raised, naval engineers found that its machinery was largely usable after minor repairs. Moreover, the hull itself had been untouched by fire.

Before the new ironclad, to be rechristened the CSS *Virginia*, could be finished and her sea trials begun, Mallory had to respond to the cries for help from other port cities. By the end of August he had authorised three similar vessels in the west. More followed quickly, including two ironclads laid down at Fort Pickering, below Memphis, Tennessee, in October 1861, one named *Tennessee* and the other *Arkansas*. Both of these were designed to be 165 feet long by 11 1/2 feet wide, with 35-foot-tall superstructures.

They were to have 18-inch-thick sides of mixed iron plate and railroad iron and wood bolted together. The low-pressure engines had two screws and were to be able to propel the vessels at about eight knots. Each would have a complement of 200, of all ranks. The *Arkansas* was armed with two 9-inch smooth-bore guns, two 8-inch smooth-bores, two 6-inch rifled guns, and two 32lb smooth-bores.

John Shirley, the builder, had contracted to finish both ships by Christmas Eve, 1861, but the problems of hiring skilled workmen, finding the necessary material and getting it to the job site delayed both vessels considerably. 'Our work goes on very slowly, and it seems impossible to get it done faster,' wrote the soon-to-be executive officer Lieutenant Henry K. Stevens of the *Arkansas* in March. This was fine with him, as he believed that the ship was 'a humbug, and badly constructed'.[2]

News of the fall of New Orleans brought fear to the heart of the senior naval officer in Memphis. On 5 June 1862 he ordered the *Tennessee*, which was not as close to completion as the *Arkansas*, burned. The *Arkansas*, still unable to travel under its own steam, he ordered towed to 'some swamp until she can be completed.'[3] All the woodwork on the ship had been finished except the captain's cabin, which, in typical Victorian style, was elaborately furnished with decorative touches in wood. But armour had yet to be laid on the casemate, although the hull had been armoured from the main deck to about a foot below water level. The main problem, however, was that the engines and boilers had yet to be finished, even though all of the basic equipment had been installed.

Lieutenant Charles H. McBlair assumed command of *Arkansas* while it was being towed to the Yazoo River, then up to Greenwood, Mississippi. There was no dry dock there; in fact there was no shipyard at all, and the work crew moored the ship to a pier while work proceeded. It went slowly, too slowly to please the army and local civilians, who wanted to see the ship protecting them from a river-borne enemy. After some persuasion, Secretary Mallory replaced McBlair with another captain.

The new man was Lieutenant Commanding Isaac N. Brown, a native Kentuckian and the son of a Presbyterian minister. He had been a career US Navy officer before the war, with almost 28 years of service under his sword belt. He was not a shrinking violet. McBlair, who was quite insulted at being ousted from one of the few Confederate commands available, protested, and Brown noted later that he 'came near shooting him, and must have done so had he not consented and got out of my way'. Brown then went after the rest of the crew, one of them writing home that 'Brown is a pushing man'. Another wrote that he 'was not afraid of responsibility and there is nothing of the Red Tape about him ...'[4]

Brown was dismayed at the first sight of his new command:

> The vessel was a mere hull, without armour; the engines were apart; guns without carriages were lying about the deck; a portion of the railroad iron intended as armor was at the bottom of the river, and the other and far greater part was to be sought for in the interior of the country.[5]

One thing that Brown discovered almost immediately was that Greenwood, safely hidden away as it might have been, was not a good place to finish an ironclad. There were poor railroad and road connections by which to have material shipped. Housing for crew and workers was limited at best, men having to sleep aboard the unfinished craft. Additional workmen could not be hired in the area. He therefore looked down river to Yazoo City, a river port town which, as its citizens went off to serve in the army and its commerce dried up, had become a shell of its pre-war self. None the less, there were still facilities there with equipment for steamboat repair, and some trained personnel were available to man them. Moreover, the largest sawmill for miles around was in Yazoo City. It was, Brown decided, a much better place to finish off his ship, and he had her towed there.

Brown set his men to work with a vengeance. He even managed to get a small powder manufactory set up in Yazoo City to make precious gunpowder for his guns. He stripped two stranded gunboats of their four guns, and obtained the rest of his battery from Memphis by barge. He had solid shot cast in Jackson, Mississippi, and six gun carriages were manufactured in that state capital. He had orders issued impressing all local blacksmiths and mechanics into work on his ship, and had slave labour donated by local planters. Local planters also provided much of the food eaten by his sailors and labourers while they were getting the ship seaworthy.

Days on the river were exceptionally hot and humid, miserable enough to sicken hard workers quickly. Much of the work was therefore done at night, by the sparking light of pine flares or the flickering light of candles. Malaria, brought by mosquitoes that bred in the swampy river waters, felled other workers. Lieutenant Stevens wrote home: 'I have not much time for writing now, as my whole day from five in the morning until seven in the evening is taken up, and I am then pretty tired'.[6]

But the ship was taking shape. Brown described her as looking:

> ... as if a small seagoing vessel had been cut down to the water's edge at both ends, leaving a box for guns amidships. The straight sides of the box, a foot in thickness, had over them one layer of railway iron; the ends closed by timber one foot square, planked across by six-inch strips of oak, were then covered by one course of railway iron laid up and down at an angle of thirty-five degrees. These ends deflected over-head all missiles striking at short range, but would have been of little security under a plunging fire. This shield, flat on top, covered with plank and half-inch iron, was pierced for 10 guns – 3 in each broadside and 2 forward and aft. The large smoke-stack came through the top of the shield, and the pilot-house was raised about one foot above the shield level.[7]

A senior Confederate Navy officer examined the vessel and reported back to the Secretary of the Navy that she was a poor excuse for a man-of-war, indeed. His report said: 'The *Arkansas* is very inferior to the *Merrimac* in every particular. The iron with which she is covered is worn and indifferent, taken from a railroad track, and is poorly secured to the vessel; boiler iron on stern and counter; her smoke-stack is sheet iron.'[8]

All the time, US Navy vessels drew closer from the south. Apart from forts along the river, such as at Baton Rouge and Vicksburg above New Orleans and some above Yazoo City, the way was fairly well open for the US Navy to travel up and down the whole river. Farragut's ability to take his fleet past Forts St Philip and Jackson below New Orleans made this quite clear. Vicksburg, like those earlier fallen forts, was regarded as rather impassable, but Farragut began probing that citadel with his ships as early as 24 May. Major General Earl Van Dorn, commander of Vicksburg, was worried that he could not fend the Yankees off with shore batteries alone, and asked President Davis to release *Arkansas* to him for the city's defence. 'It is better to die game and do some execution,' he wrote the chief army officer at Yazoo City, 'than to lie and be burned up in the Yazoo.'[9]

Brown received orders from the army's Van Dorn to get under way as quickly as possible, and to attack the Union flotilla gathered north of the city before Farragut could pass under the guns of Vicksburg and unite his vessels into one squadron. He could simply have disregarded these orders, because he did not report to the army's commander but to the senior Naval officer, Captain George Hollins, commander of the Upper Mississippi. Moreover, Van Dorn also advised Brown that there were 37 enemy men-of-war in sight of Confederate pickets, and more were known to be up-river. An inferior craft such as the *Arkansas*, with its poor engines producing a top speed of six knots in still water and its lack of trained crew, would have very little chance of passing such a naval force. Any move against such a force would probably lead to the loss of one of the rare Confederate ironclads; and it would certainly be Brown's last sea command. Going south as Van Dorn had asked would be a major gamble, with most of the cards stacked against the Confederates.

Brown decided to take that gamble. In fact he decided on an even greater gamble than simply getting to Vicksburg. He gambled that he could dash past the Union gunboats, inflicting a fair bit of damage to them, and then anchor at Vicksburg. There he would recoal. Once *Arkansas* had recoaled and had any damage repaired, using the excellent facilities to be found at Vicksburg, he would dash past the southern Union flotilla, down the river, past New Orleans and out into the Gulf of Mexico. From there he would sail on to the safe harbour of Mobile, Alabama, which was still in Confederate hands. With his vessel added to the strength of that city's naval flotilla, the Confederates could then destroy the Federal blockading force outside that harbour. With the blockade lifted, international law decreed that the city would remain open for a minimum of 30 days. Moreover, the Confederate flotilla there would be strong enough to resist any attempt of the Federal navy to re-establish its blockade.

It was quite a large gamble. Brown's one ship, with its rickety engines and landsmen crew, would have to challenge a vastly superior Union fleet, not to mention guns all along the shore, especially in and around New Orleans. But the prize if the gamble paid off would be the end of the blockade and the opening of a major southern port to all the manufacturers of Europe, as well as to the cotton-planters of the south. Large gambles merit large prizes.

He had to move quickly, even before the ship was fully ready, because the river's water began to fall rapidly. Soon it would be too shallow for *Arkansas*, which drew $11\frac{1}{2}$ feet of water where she was tied up. On 20 June the *Arkansas* set sail for Liverpool Landing, a point some 25 miles down the river where the Confederates had built a set of obstructions to prevent Union warships from moving up-river. Once there, work began again on the ship, while Brown searched for sufficient men to fill her complement of some 232 officers and men. He did not manage to get enough men until mid-July.

Finally, on 14 July, Brown had the engines fired up, the lines cast loose, and began the voyage. It would be both the ship's shakedown cruise and its initial combat cruise. There were problems to shakedown. Steam leaked from the engines into the magazine and dampened the powder. Brown anchored his ship and had tarpaulins spread along the bank near an old sawmill. The powder was then spread over the tarpaulins to dry in the sun. He decided to keep the ship there, rather than move on into a group of Union boats which he knew was not far down-river from his position. The men were allowed to lower their hammocks and bed down for the night. They were awakened early next morning to a breakfast of a coffee substitute, real coffee being almost non-existent in the Confederacy.

At daybreak Brown had the ship cast off and resumed his voyage. Knowing that Union men-of-war awaited his arrival, he had battle preparations made. Sand was strewn on the decks to prevent slipping on blood, tourniquets were issued to division officers, division tubs were filled with drinking water, fire buckets were put in place, small-arms were issued and the magazines were opened. His pilot brought him into the 'Old River', a Mississippi River channel that the Yazoo River followed before entering the main river. Then, as they were steaming along, a lookout suddenly called out that he had spotted ships ahead of them. Brown and his officers easily identified them as Union warships, an ironclad and two wooden gunboats. The ironclad, the *Carondelet*, was in the centre of the ships, which were on line. They were on a reconnaissance mission, looking for the *Arkansas*.

Brown had expected to encounter these ships, and his plan was to ram the ironclad and then, in the confusion caused by its sinking and while survivors were being taken aboard the wooden ships, escape down-river. He had the beat to quarters sounded, and then addressed his gun crews on the main deck:

Gentlemen, in seeking the combat as we now do, we must win or perish. Should I fall, whoever succeeds to the command will do so with the resolution to go through the enemy's fleet, or go to the bottom. Should they carry us by boarding, the *Arkansas* must be blown up; on no account must she fall into the hands of the enemy. Go to your guns.[10]

The rays of a burning sun beating on the iron sides of the ship, which had been painted a dull brown colour for camouflage (described by Farragut as 'chocolate colour'[11]), caused most of the men to strip off their shirts before going to the guns. Many tied handkerchiefs around their foreheads to keep the sweat out of their eyes. Officers left their woollen coats in their cabins, appearing on the deck in shirtsleeves. To buy some time so that he could get closer before gunfire began, Brown did not have the Confederate naval jack raised on his ship.

Even without the flag, those aboard the Union ships quickly realised that the *Arkansas* would soon be among them. It was the last thing they had expected. 'I do not think she will ever come forth,' no less a person than David Farragut had written to the Secretary of the Navy as recently as 10 July.[12]

Lieutenant Joseph Ford, captain of the army ram *Queen of the West*, one of the wooden ships, realised he had no chance at all against a heavily armoured ram, especially going up-stream, where his greater speed would be nullified. He quickly gave orders to put about, and within minutes his ship had disappeared from the scene, much to the disgust of the officers on the remaining two vessels.

On board the other wooden ship, the *Tyler*, Lieutenant Commander William Gwin decided to fire his bow guns at the southern ironclad and then swing round to give the stern guns a chance, fighting as both Union and Confederate vessels continued downstream. He reasoned that the noise would rouse the rest of the Union fleet down-river, which would then be prepared and could join the fight. Without consulting Gwin, Commander Henry Walke, captain of the *Carondelet*, decided to do the same.

As it transpired, the three should have planned a strategy for fighting the ironclad, as their separate decisions virtually gave Brown the victory. The *Tyler* was a faster vessel than the heavier *Carondelet*, and soon left the Federal ironclad behind, a target for all of the *Arkansas's* forward guns. Brown chased the Union ship, planning to ram her if possible. 'I had determined,' he wrote, 'despite our want of speed, to try the ram or iron prow upon the foe, who were gallantly approaching.'[13] Initially, Brown ordered his bow guns to remain silent, trying to build up sufficient speed to smash into the Union ship's bow. Most of the cannonballs from the *Carondelet's* stern guns bounced harmlessly off the sides of the *Arkansas*.

One Irish crewman stuck his head out of a gunport to see how the fight was going, and unfortunately his head and a Union cannonball occupied the same space at the same time. Two officers were standing near the headless corpse, 'and fearing that the sight of the mangled corpse and blood might demoralise the gun's crew, sprang forward to throw the body out of the port and [one of them] called upon the man nearest him to assist. "Oh! I can't do it, sir!" the poor fellow replied, "It's my brother." The body was thrown overboard.'[14]

Finally, Brown, realising that his faulty engines would not propel the southern ironclad fast enough, ordered the two bow guns to open fire. By chance, and owing to poor Union planning, Brown found the Achilles' heel of the armoured Federal craft, her weakly defended stern, and his fire began doing damage to the *Carondelet*. For two hours the two boats headed downstream, towards where the Yazoo flows into the main body of the Mississippi. Brown's craft came nearer and nearer, until the two vessels were so close that Brown ordered his bow guns silenced because they were too close to fire safely. But at this point the river was so narrow that Brown was afraid of running aground in ramming the enemy ironclad. He therefore ordered the *Arkansas* to drive past the *Carondelet*, firing a full broadside into her as the Confederate ship floated past.

The blast put an end to the *Carondelet*. The ship had been pierced through and through by rounds from the *Arkansas*; in all, thirteen rounds had penetrated her hull. Her deck pumps and boats were shot away. Her steam gauge, three escape pipes, and two water pipes were cut by cannon fire. One round split the wheel ropes, and the Union ironclad floated helplessly into a tangle of low-lying willow trees on the bank. Steam poured out of her gun ports. Four of her crew were killed, another fifteen wounded, and sixteen were missing. Unharmed survivors leapt from her decks and swam for the shore. The Confederates cheered as white flags appeared at various portholes of the Union ship.

The *Tyler* was now running ahead of the *Arkansas*, and Brown ordered his craft to make for the Union boat. Gwin realised that he had no chance if the southern boat got too close, and he was too lightly armed, with only one 32lb cannon at his stern, to keep her away. He had all the coal possible poured into her furnaces and aimed ahead as fast as the huge paddles could take her. Confederate fire raked her decks, killing eight Federals and wounding another sixteen, including a number of soldiers of the 4th Wisconsin Infantry who had been detailed to serve as sharpshooters on the *Tyler*. At the same time, Gwin's well-trained gun crew fired carefully at the *Arkansas*.

Their shots took their toll. One struck the pilot house, which rose above the gundeck armour. The concussion knocked Brown off his feet, dashing him to the deck. He later wrote that he ran his hand over his pounding head, worrying about being fatally wounded, 'but this gave me no concern after I had failed to find any brains mixed with the handful of clotted blood I drew from the wound and examined'.[15]

While he was recovering, another shot penetrated the armour of the prominent pilot house, tearing away a piece of the ship's wheel, mortally wounding the chief pilot, John Hodges, and wounding the Yazoo River pilot, putting him out of commission. The last greatly concerned Brown, since Mississippi River pilots did not know the channel through which his ship was now passing. The *Arkansas'* smokestack was located behind the pilot house, and rounds that did not hit the house tore through the smokestack. The ship was holed several times, and several breechings, which connected the stack and the ship's steam pipes, were cut. Pressure began to fall, dropping more than 100lb/in² in a matter of minutes. Brown no longer had enough boiler pressure to ram an enemy vessel. The *Tyler* was safe from Gwin's worst fear.

Moreover, steam now poured like a hot liquid from pipes running through the enclosed gun deck, adding to the heat already radiating from the bulkheads. A record 120°F was recorded on the gun deck, while the engineering staff had to brave temperatures that reached 130° in the engine room. Members of the engine crew staggered on to the relatively cooler gun deck for a breath of air, and those manning the silent broadside guns were detailed to take their place. The ship's executive officer found that no man could work below for more than 15 minutes, and soon had teams organised to relieve the engine room staff. No breeze, save for that created by the speed of the ship, flowed over the top of the gun decks on this windless day.

Brown himself was passing by a hatchway when a bullet from a Union sharpshooter, obviously spent and travelling beyond its killing range, smashed into his left temple. He was thrown, unconscious, down through the hatch to the gundeck below, landing between two guns. 'I awoke as if from sleep,' he recalled, 'to find kind hands helping me to a place among the killed and wounded.'[16] Brown staggered to his feet and made his way back to his battle station to resume command.

Suddenly, at 7.15 a.m., the *Tyler* burst on to the main Mississippi River a dozen miles above Vicksburg, not far from where a squadron of over 30 Union ships lay quietly, not expecting any trouble. Lookouts on the Union ships saw the *Tyler* and *Arkansas* arrive almost neck-and-neck, while the *Queen of the West* sped before them. Their first thought was that the *Tyler* had taken a prize and was bringing it to their anchorage. While the firing had been heard down-river, it was generally assumed that the three Union vessels had been exchanging shots with Confederate river-front batteries and ambushing guerrilla bands. Shortly, however, observers noted that the Union vessel and the other ship were firing at each other. The squadron officers ordered beat to station; the decks were cleared and the guns rolled out, ready for action.

Not all of the 30 Union ships were warships; a large number were transports. These were generally anchored on the Vicksburg side of the river, while four lightly armoured, wooden-hulled rams, manned by soldiers under Army Lieutenant Colonel Alfred Ellet, were on line near the Yazoo side, directly in the way of the approaching *Arkansas*. Eight deep-draught Naval ships commanded by David Farragut, part of the fleet that took New Orleans, were anchored in line behind the army rams. Three centre-wheeled boats, each carrying thirteen cannon, were in line between that line and Vicksburg. A number of small mortar boats were even closer to Vicksburg.

'Brady, shave that line of men-of-war as close as you can, so that the rams will not have room to gather headway in coming out to strike us,' Brown yelled at his pilot.[17] In what must have seemed a lifetime on the Confederate craft, the *Arkansas* closed and then passed the line of army rams before they could spring into life.

However, the lead boat, the *Lancaster*, got under way and aimed her ram directly at the approaching ironclad. 'Go through him, Brady,' Brown shouted to the pilot.[18] Before she hit, however, a round from a bow gun tore through the Union boat and opened up a steam drum. Boiling steam filled the boat, scalding most of the crew. Men hurled themselves into the cooling waters of the river. 'We passed by and through the brave fellows struggling in the water under a shower of missiles intended for us,' Brown recalled.[19] Many were never seen again. Behind them, Farragut's New Orleans veterans opened fire. His flagship, the *Hartford*, exchanged shots with the southern ironclad, as did the *Kineo*, the first to fire.

The *Arkansas* closed with the two, exchanging round after round. According to Brown, his ironclad 'ran by them at pistol-shot distance.'[20] The dense, foul-smelling smoke, reeking of sulphur, lay heavy on the river and gun decks. All of the ships involved were taking a pounding, iron and wood being torn apart and the blood of sailors splashing across the decks.

'The heat on the gun deck from rapid firing, and the concussion from shot and shell striking the ship on all sides, was terrific,' wrote Master's Mate John A. Wilson of her crew. 'Men and officers alike fought their guns clad only in pantaloons and undershirts.'[21]

A round from the *Hartford* actually broke through the Confederate iron, bursting in the enclosed gun deck. Four men of a 32lb gun crew fell, dead, while 'The Captain of the gun standing at my right was knocked down by the concussion and so great was the shock that he lost his mind and never recovered'.[22] In addition, the gun captain, Lieutenant George Gift, was wounded in his right shoulder. Master's Mate Wilson wrote:

> An XI-inch solid shot entered the ship's side above my gun, smashing in the bulkhead, killing two men and the powder boy, wounding three others, and knocking me senseless, cutting my head and nose. I was taken below, wounds were dressed, and returned to my gun shortly afterwards. The same shot continued on across the deck, passing through the lower part of the smokestack, killing eight of Midshipman Scale's men and wounding three others (as they were running out their gun). It finally struck the opposite bulkhead, broke in half, and fell on deck.[23]

Another shot burst near a gunport, killing a sponger and knocking down other gun crew members. Other rounds tore more holes in the smokestack, further reducing the draw, while a lucky hit knocked the ship's colour from its staff. Midshipman Dabney Scales grabbed a new colour and, under fire, scrambled up a ship's ladder to replace the piece of red, white and blue bunting. The replacement was also torn away by enemy fire, and only Brown's direct order stopped Scales from making another dash to replace it, despite the enemy fire. By now the *Arkansas* was able to move only a knot faster than the current carrying her downstream.

Lieutenant Gift recalled:

> We were passing one of the large sloops-of-war when a heavy shot struck the side abreast of my bow-gun, the concussion knocking over a man who was engaged in taking a shot from the rack. "He rubbed his hip, which had been hurt, and said that would hardly strike twice in a place". He was mistaken, poor fellow, for immediately a shell entered the breach made by the shot and, bedding itself in the cotton-

bale lining on the inside of the bulwark proper, exploded with terrible effect. I found myself standing in a dense, suffocating smoke, with my cap gone and hair and beard singed. The smoke soon cleared away, and I found but one man (Quartermaster Curtis) left. Sixteen were killed and wounded by that shell, and the ship set on fire. Stevens, ever cool and thoughtful, ran to the engine-room hatch, seized the hose and dragged it to the aperture. In a few moments the fire was extinguished, without an alarm having been created.[24]

Everywhere the crew looked they saw an enemy vessel, and Federal soldiers on either river bank added to the confusion with their musket fire. 'I had the most lively realisation of having steamed into a real volcano,' Brown wrote, 'the *Arkansas* from its centre firing rapidly to every point of the circumference without the feat of hitting a friend or missing an enemy.'[25]

For half an hour the *Arkansas* took, and inflicted, damage. Finally, however, she passed the last Union ship in the line, the *Benton*, before it could get under way to stop her. The *Benton* followed, accompanied by another Union ship, as the *Arkansas* rounded the bluff and came under protective fire from batteries in the Vicksburg fortifications. Brown, standing with his officers on the top of the gun deck to see the confusion they had left behind them, had brought his ship to Vicksburg. Some 20,000 of the city's residents and soldiers from the garrison lined the riverbanks to cheer as she pulled up to her anchorage. Master's Mate Wilson, bleeding from a smashed nose, looked around at the sight on the gundeck: 'Blood and brains bespattered everything, whilst arms, legs, and several headless trunks were strewn about'. Civilians who gathered to greet the victorious ship turned away in horror.[26] One officer who brought his men to help remove her wounded recalled:

The embrasures, or portholes, were splintered, and some were nearly twice the original size; her broadside walls were shivered, and great slabs and splinters were strewn over the deck of her entire gunroom; her stairways were so bloody and slippery that we had to sift cinders from the ash pans to keep from slipping.[27]

Twelve of the crew were dead and another three seriously wounded, as well as some additional minor wounds among another fifteen of her officers and men.

Almost as soon as the ironclad had moored, Brown, promoted to the rank of commander for his action, tried to replace her crew with trained personnel and worked at repairing the damage. Even he had to admit that the *Arkansas* was too battered to continue on to challenge the Federal fleet at New Orleans. None the less, she would make it significantly harder for the Union navy to rule the Mississippi. 'It was a bold thing,' said Farragut, reporting the *Arkansas*' passage to his superior flag officer. He excused her escape by saying: 'She was only saved by our feeling of security'.[28] The Federal Navy made several passes by her in an attempt to sink the ironclad, all of which were unsuccessful. All the time, the officers and men continued to repair her as they trained army artillerymen in the art of naval gunnery. Finally, Lieutenant Stevens, the ship's acting captain while Brown was lying in a sick bed, ordered steam raised and the *Arkansas* was on its way to support an army attack on the state's capital city, Baton Rouge.

Unfortunately the machinery was not up to the trip, the southern-made engines continuing to fail at inopportune moments. While the army's attack failed, the *Arkansas* came into view of a Federal flotilla which was searching for the ironclad. The Union boats, although out of range, opened fire as the *Arkansas* moved into the stream to ram the leading Federal ship, the *Essex*. At that moment the engines quit for good, leaving the heavy vessel floating helplessly shorewards. Stevens ordered his men to scuttle the ship, destroy everything possible and abandon her. Stevens himself, tears pouring down his cheeks, set fire to his cabin and the wardroom. A grenade he was putting into one of the engines blew up in his hands, badly burning him, and he had to be helped off the ship, one of the last of the crew to leave. At noon on 6 August, less than three months after *Arkansas* had been towed from Memphis, flames reached her powder magazine and she blew up. She had been in active service only 23 days, yet Brown's gamble in taking her downstream, instead of destroying her before she could even be launched, which would have been the prudent move, upset the Union schedule on the Mississippi and put its vastly superior Navy unexpectedly on the defensive.

Notes
1 Still, William N., Jr., *Iron Afloat*, Columbia, South Carolina, 1985, p.10.
2 Still, William N., Jr., *ibid.*, p.62.
3 Still, William N., Jr., *ibid.*, p.62.
4 Still, William N., Jr., *ibid.*, p.64.
5 *B&L*, Vol. 3, p.572.
6 Still, William N., Jr., *op. cit.*, pp.65-66.

7   *B&L*, Vol. 3, p.572.
8   Sharf, J. Thomas, *History of the Confederate States Navy*, New York, 1976, p.307.
9   Still, William N., Jr., *op. cit.*, p.66.
10 Sharf, J. Thomas, *op. cit.*, pp.310-311.
11 *Official Records of the Union and Confederate Navies in the War of the Rebellion*, Washington, 1905, (hereinafter *ORN*), Series I, Vol. 19, p.3.
12 Still, William N., Jr., *op. cit.*, p.6.
13 *B&L*, Vol. 3, p.574.
14 Sharf, J. Thomas, *op. cit.*, p.314.
15 *B&L*, Vol. 3, p.574.
16 *B&L*, Vol. 3, p.575.
17 *B&L*, Vol. 3, p.576.
18 *B&L*, Vol. 3, p.576.
19 *B&L*, Vol. 3, p.576.
20 *ORN*, Series I, Vol. 19, p.68.
21 *ORN*, Series I, Vol. 19, p.133
22 Still, William N., Jr., *op. cit.*, p.70.
23 *ORN*, Series I, Vol. 19, p.133.
24 Sharf, J. Thomas, *op. cit.*, pp.319-320.
25 *B&L*, Vol. 3, p.576.
26 *ORN*, Series I, Vol. 19, p.133.
27 Still, William N., Jr., *op. cit.*, p.71.
28 *ORN*, Series I, Vol. 19, p.4.

The USS *Monitor* Creates a Naval Revolution

THE GAMBLE: *that a wholly unproven steel ship, the USS* Monitor, *can first of all stay afloat and, beyond that, can fight and hold off a more conventionally designed ironclad battery.*

When the United States government learned in July 1861 of Confederate plans to build an ironclad warship within striking distance of its ships at Fortress Monroe, Virginia, there was great concern, to put it mildly. The US Navy, led by a civilian with little naval experience, Secretary of War Gideon Welles, learned of the Confederates at Norfolk raising the old US frigate USS *Merrimac* from where it lay underwater. The young Confederate Navy was now converting her hull into an ironclad. Welles recalled:

> We, of course, felt great solicitude in regard to this proceeding of the rebels, not lessened by the fact that extraordinary pains were taken by them to keep secret from us their labours and purposes. Their efforts to withhold information, though rigid, were not wholly successful, for we contrived to get occasional vague intelligence of the work as it progressed.[1]

Welles himself had thrown cold water on previous attempts to interest the US Navy in ironclads. That summer, an offer came from British shipbuilder John Laird Sons & Company of Liverpool to build armoured gunboats, but it was refused out of hand. According to the Assistant Secretary of the Navy, the navy's Engineer in Chief, Benjamin Isherwood, 'thought ironclads a humbug and [naval warship designer John] Lenthal[l] shrank from touching the subject first at that period when fatal days and months were passing.'[2]

The month the Confederates began work on their *Virginia*, the name given to the ironclad being built on the hull of the *Merrimac*, Senator James

W. Grimes introduced legislation in the Senate calling for the construction
of armoured ships, based on European experiences. The bill, which allo-
cated $1.5 million for the construction of three ironclads, called for a com-
mittee to study the situation and approve several designs to be used. The
three-man board was made up of Commodores Joseph Smith and Hiram
Paulding and Captain Charles H. Davis, none of who had any knowledge
of or experience with ironclads. In the meantime, the Navy advertised on 7
August for proposals for such vessels from:

> ... parties who are able to execute work of this kind, and who are
> engaged in it, of which they will furnish evidence with their offer, for
> the construction of one or more ironclad steam vessels of war, either of
> iron or wood and iron combined, for sea or river service, to be not less
> than ten nor over sixteen feet draught of water; to carry an armament
> of from eighty to one hundred and twenty tons weight, with provisions
> and stores for from one hundred and sixty five to three hundred per-
> sons, according to armament, for sixty days, with coal for eight days.
> The smaller draughts of water, compatible with other requisites, will
> be preferred. The vessels to be rigged with two masts, with wire rope
> standing rigging, to navigate at sea.[3]

They were handed a batch of seventeen detailed proposals for such warships. Two appealed to the board almost immediately.

The first was essentially a standard warship with rail and plate armour
fastened to her sides rather like aluminium siding on a house. To be called
the *Galena*, her design was submitted by C. S. Bushnell & Company of
New Haven, Connecticut, and would cost $235,000. The second was a
steam frigate proposed by Merrick & Sons of Philadelphia, Pennsylvania. It
was bigger than the Bushnell vessel and would cost $780,000. It was this
one that the board felt was 'the most practicable one for heavy armour'.[4]
The other ship, the board felt, would be too top-heavy with all the armour
and the guns above the waterline.

Bushnell, learning of the board's reservations, talked about his plans and
the board's objections to a leading iron founder in New York, who suggested
he take the calculations to a well-known Swedish engineer who had lived in
the United States since 1839 and had designed ships for the Navy before.
That engineer, John Ericsson, agreed to see Bushnell's design. After some
study he said that the ship would float and withstand shot fired from some

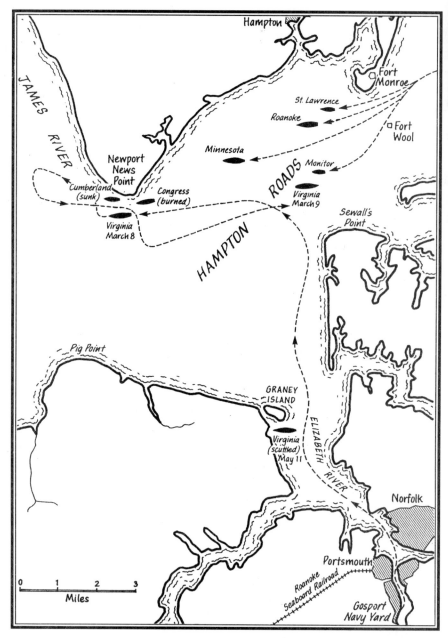

distance away. And, while Bushnell was there, Ericsson dug out some old designs for an ironclad he had produced in 1854 with an idea of selling the design to the French Navy for use in the Crimean War. Nothing had come of his proposal for his 'iron-clad steam-battery' with its novel low sloped deck and single hemispherical revolving turret in its centre mounting but two guns.

Bushnell must have been taken quite aback by the revolutionary designs for every feature of the boat that were revealed as Ericsson unrolled the long sheets of blueprints. The boat was 172 feet long above the water, with an iron-plated deck and low sides. Below the water the hull was of wood, 122 feet long and 34 feet wide. The different structures above and below the water would effectively protect her from ramming.

A cylindrical turret sat directly amidships. In it were mounted two large-calibre naval guns. It was turned by power generated by the ship's engine, upon commands delivered via a speaking tube connected to the pilot house. The pilot house itself was rectangular structure some three feet ten inches tall that sat well forward towards the bow. It was made like a log cabin, the 'logs' being wrought-iron blocks with a slit almost an inch wide to allow the captain and helmsman to see out while still being protected from enemy shot. An iron plate sat on top of the house; this could be pushed up and away as an emergency hatch. The anchor well was just before the pilot house.

The pilot house opened into a passageway that led to the captain's quarters. The wardroom, with entrances to the officer's cabins, was just past that. Beyond that lay the crew's quarters, with room for only half of the crew to sleep at a time, the rest being presumed to be on duty. Various doors off the crew's quarters led to areas where the ship's stores were kept. Beyond that, directly under the turret, lay the galley. The two engines lay towards the stern. Single-cylindered steam engines, they were also of a novel design, including cranks and connecting rods that enabled them to work together smoothly. For that reason, each engine required only one cylinder instead of the normal two, saving much space. Power was transmitted to a four-bladed propeller hung in a cavity under the stern overhang for protection. Since virtually all activity took place below water level, ventilation was a major consideration, and Ericsson had designed blowers with separate steam engines that would draw 7,000ft of air from pipes on deck to the very lowest part of the hull below decks. The system would force out the hot air, since hot air rises, and leave the living quarters relatively cool and fresh.

The overall result was something unlike any previous warship ever built. Bushnell realised this, of course, but he also realised that this was something worth gambling on; that this novel design just might revolutionise naval warfare. Ericsson had suffered a bad experience with US Navy officials when a gun on the *Princeton*, which he had designed some years earlier, exploded during a demonstration, killing a number of important government officials. Despite this misadventure, Bushnell pleaded to be allowed to take the plans to the Navy's Board. Ericsson finally agreed.

Instead of returning to Washington, Bushnell took the plans for the novel boat to Hartford, Connecticut, where Welles was overseeing his family's packing for the move to Washington. Welles was greatly impressed by the plans, and told Bushnell to take them to the Board in Washington right away. Beyond that, Welles wrote, 'Deeming the subject of great importance, and fearing the Board would be restrained by the limit of twenty-five days [in which to submit designs], I immediately followed, and arrived in Washington almost as soon as Mr Bushnell with the model'.[5] Welles reached Washington about the same time as Bushnell because Bushnell had stopped off in Troy, New York, to obtain a letter of introduction to Lincoln himself from some friends of the Secretary of State. Fearing that the novelty of the plan would deter the Board, naval officers being well known for their lack of gambling instinct when it came to ship designs, Bushnell went directly to the President.

Lincoln, he later said, was 'greatly pleased' by the plan and agreed to accompany Bushnell to the Board meeting on 13 September. Indeed, the meeting that day went largely as Bushnell feared, some of the Board being vehemently opposed to the plan, while others did find some merit in it. Finally Lincoln said: 'All I have to say is what the girl said when she stuck her foot into the stocking. It strikes me there's something in it.'[6]

The Board agreed to meet again the following day, to hear Bushnell's entire presentation of the ship's plans yet again. This meeting, which Welles attended, also ended in deadlock, the general feeling being against building the vessel. Bushnell, a remarkably persistent individual who was not, after all, presenting plans in which he had a vested interest, spoke to each Board member individually. He finally persuaded Paulding and Smith to agree to have one of the ships built if Davis agreed. Davis, however, was another matter. 'Take the little thing home and worship it,' he finally told Bushnell, 'as it would not be idolatry, because it was in the image of nothing in the heaven above or on the earth beneath or in the waters under the earth.' Davis clearly was not a gambler.

A lesser man would have given up by that point. Bushnell, however, was not a lesser man. He knew that the only way to get the Board to agree to build the unusual craft was to have Ericsson himself present the plans. Yet Ericsson's previous dealings with the US Navy had so soured him that there was no way he could be persuaded to go to Washington. Bushnell therefore tricked Ericsson when he visited him a short time later. He told the Swede that the Board had accepted the plans totally, and would authorise the boat's construction, adding that at least one Board member called the inventor a genius and the boat worthy of him. There was just one thing, he added as Ericsson glowed in the warmth of the praise. Davis did not understand a couple of points, and they were so technical that it would take Ericsson to clear them up. Would it be possible for the inventor to explain these points to the Board himself? Ericsson swallowed the bait. He would go to Washington immediately.

Once there, he was told that the boat had already been discussed and rejected. In a huff, he turned to go, and then Smith said that the problem had been that the board felt the boat lacked sufficient stability. Ericsson immediately launched into a painstaking explanation of how the boat would be stable in rough weather, then described the vessel in detail and gave a vivid account of her attributes.

The Board was enthralled; following Ericsson's presentation they discussed it among themselves and then asked the inventor to return after lunch. He did, making the presentation again with Welles present. Welles then asked the boat's cost, and was told it would be about $275,000. Welles then polled the board. This time only Pauling demurred, still fearing that the boat lacked stability. Ericsson wearily went over his plan again, and finally convinced Pauling that it would work.

At 3 p.m. Ericsson was ushered into Welles' office and told that he would receive a contract to have the novel craft built. The US Navy had decided to take one of the most important gambles it would ever take.

Time was on the Confederate side, however. They had made a huge leap ahead in building the *Virginia*, and now the US Navy had to catch up. Ericsson's plans were so detailed and exact that Naval officials decided to have the ship built piecemeal by different companies, as they could produce their respective components quicker than if they had to assemble the entire boat. Thomas F. Rowland's Continental Iron Works, in Greenpoint, Long Island, would build the hull, while the turret would come from the Novelty Iron Works in New York. The iron plating would come from several rolling mills, and the rivets and bar iron for the pilot house would come from the Rensselaer Iron Works of Troy, New York. The unusual port stoppers, heavy sheets of iron pulled over the gun ports like window shutters while the guns were being loaded, were to come from Charles D. De Lancy &

Company across the state in Buffalo. Ericsson's contract called for the *Monitor* to be in the water in 100 days.

Ericsson launched into a whirlwind of activity, overseeing every aspect of the boat's building. He even specified the expensive furniture and drapes installed in the captain's salon, and the fine furniture and monogrammed silverware and dinnerware used in the officer's wardroom. Indeed, visitors were surprised how comfortable the officers' quarters were. First Lieutenant Hiram Sickles, an officer in the 17th Independent Battery of New York Light Artillery, visited the *Monitor* when she was in Washington in November, and later wrote to his wife that she would 'be surprised to find her comfortable and the staterooms and accommodations there well-lighted and aired'.[7] The bustle of designing and building activity kept the inventor from reading the local newspapers, many of which disparaged the entire project as 'Ericsson's folly'.

However, once the US Navy became involved in the boat's construction, Ericsson did not do all the design work alone. Chief Engineer Alban C. Stimers, who had joined the Navy as a third assistant engineer in 1849, was appointed Inspector of Ironclads in November 1861 and ordered to New York to serve directly as 'construction superintendent of the John Ericsson Battery'. He actually contributed improvements to the designs for the magazine, living quarters and shell room. When the vessel was partly built, Navy officials also sent Commander David D. Porter to examine the boat and submit his opinion as to her ability to fight another ironclad successfully. Convinced by the plans and what he saw on the docks, he telegraphed back: 'This is the strongest fighting vessel in the world and can whip anything afloat'. Yet when he returned to Washington a Navy official he regarded as 'clever' laughed at his opinion. 'Why, man,' the official said, 'John Lenthall predicts that Ericsson's vessel will sink as soon as she is launched.'[8] Obviously many people still regarded the design as a gamble, and a poor one at that.

Ericsson's ship was launched on 30 January 1862, ahead of the *Virginia*, and many in the crowds watching her slip into the East River were betting that the 'iron coffin' would slip right under the water. They lost their bets; with Ericsson himself standing on her deck, she bobbed and then steadied herself, floating within three inches of where Ericsson had said her waterline would be.

Engineer Stimers, who went on her sea trials as a 'technical passenger' because her roster called for only an assistant engineer among her officers, described the ship to his father in a letter dated 5 May 1862:

When equipped and manned ready for sea she was only 20 inches out of the water. This gives her the most singular appearance. I could not for some time get over being impressed with the idea that she was sinking when I would return after a short absence while she was lying off the Navy Yard here. At the distance of half a mile you cannot see the hull of the vessel at all unless you are elevated, and the turret looks as if it sat upon the water by itself. People in Hampton Roads said she looked like "a wash-tub on a raft", "a cheese box on a plank", "a hat on a shingle" etc., etc.[9]

There was still a great of work for him and Ericsson to do once the boat was actually afloat. A faulty valve setting caused her main engine to work in reverse. Lack of understanding of Ericsson's complex system for absorbing the recoil on the guns resulted in both guns being simultaneously disabled during their trials. At least one sailor learned the importance of using the seacock on the toilets properly when a geyser of water slammed him in the face after he flushed. The steering mechanism was out of balance, making her hard to control. After she rammed a dock the Navy wanted to replace her rudder, but Ericsson said he could solve the problem without taking the month required to replace the rudder. That was just as well, because time was running out. The Confederate monster in Virginia was now ready to be launched. On 25 February *Monitor* was taken into commission under the command of Lieutenant John L. Worden, with Lieutenant S. Dana Greene as executive officer. Greene, a recent naval academy graduate, was much bothered by the lack of sails and spars on his new ship.

On 6 March the *Monitor* set out to sea, off to Hampton Roads to do battle with the *Virginia*. From the first day, the waves of the open sea proved to be a problem for the men serving aboard her. Water washed across her decks. 'The berth-deck hatch leaked in spite of all we could do, and the water came down under the turret like a waterfall,' Greene wrote. 'It would strike the pilot-house with such force as to knock the helmsman completely round from the wheel.'[10] Ericsson later blamed this on a design modification that enlarged the viewing slit.

The builders had placed air pipes over shot-proof gratings for ventilation, but these proved inadequate. According to Engineer Stimers:

These ought to have been higher, for when it blew at the strongest a little water came down these and wet our blower belts – this caused them to break. We had two and they mended one while the other was running but, on one occasion, they did not quite get one in operation before the other snapped, and with no blower running there could be no draught to the boilers. The first burned with a sickly blaze out of the ash pan doors, converting all the air in the engine and fire rooms into carbonic acid gas – a few inhalations of which are sufficient to destroy animal life.

Engineers commenced to stagger and the men to tumble down. I sent them all out and remained awhile alone trying to get the blower going, but I soon began to find myself getting very limber in the legs, so I started also for the top of the turret, which I managed to reach just as my strength gave out and I tumbled over upon the turret deck at full length.

Brave sailors led by the ship's paymaster, William Keeler, re-entered the engine compartment for short periods, and within four hours got the blowers working again and ventilated the dangerous area below the deck. None the less, it was only when calm waters were reached that the crew could get back to work and completely ventilate below decks. Shortly afterwards the boat hit another patch of rough water, and kept her men up fighting leaks and passing filled buckets up through the turret to be emptied overboard and returned for refilling.

On 8 March at 4 p.m., as the craft was passing Cape Henry, the officers and men heard the firing of heavy guns ahead. Rightly figuring that the Confederate ironclad, their objective, had been launched and was even then engaged with Federal ships, Worden ordered the boat stripped of her sea-rig and prepared for action. This included covering the deck lights, so the only light below came from flickering oil lamps. The deck hatches were battened down, and the smokestacks and vent stacks were removed. Earlier, he had had white marks painted on the deck immediately below the turret to indicate port and starboard, bow and stern, to the men in the turret, whose vision was severely limited in action.

When the small boat entered Hampton Roads, the men who had a chance to get on deck saw bright fires flickering over the sunken wreck of the USS *Congress*. A pilot came aboard the *Monitor* and announced that the *Virginia* had indeed paid them a visit, sinking the *Cumberland* and the *Congress*. Only the onset of night had saved the *Roanoke* and the *Minnesota*, and the latter ship had run aground. The next day could well bring disaster to the Federal fleet and the lifting of the blockade. That day would see whether the Navy's gamble on Ericsson's plan would pay off.

The tiny *Monitor*'s arrival at Hampton Roads did not wholly cheer up a navy that had seen crushing defeats with the sinking of two of its ships the day before. As Engineer Stimers, who visited the captain of the *Roanoke* when he arrived, later wrote: 'Our arrival gave but little confidence as we were only an experimental text of an untried invention, the name of the inventor of which was only familiar to the present generation of naval officers through the gigantic failure of the caloric engine to propel ships better than steam'.[11] Executive Officer Greene agreed: 'An atmosphere of gloom pervaded the fleet, and the pygmy aspect of the newcomer did not inspire confidence among those who had witnessed the destruction of the day before'.[12]

That night was a long one. As the off-duty officers and men were preparing to turn in, the officer of the deck was hailed from the *Minnesota* with a message that the wooden ship was getting afloat. Since the *Monitor* was directly in her channel, protecting her, she would have to move. The crew was roused and the ironclad moved to a spot to one side of the channel. It was about 5:30 a.m. when most of the officers and men managed to get back to bed, and then they were roused for a 7 a.m. breakfast. Men already exhausted from a trying trip from New York would now go into battle deprived of normal sleep.

The Federals were jealous of the men on the *Virginia*, who they thought had had a fairly easy day the day before, followed by a good night's sleep. In fact the southern crew had been up much of the night repairing the damage sustained by their own ironclad the previous day. Two of her guns had their muzzles shot off, and the ram, in which they had put so much trust, had broken off when she rammed the *Cumberland*. Federal shot had swept off railings, stanchions, boat davits and steam pipes, and her smokestack had been riddled, making her draught poor. The men even had to put up a boarding pike to replace the flag staff, which had been shot off.

US Navy officers and men crowded to the top of the turret to watch as the *Virginia*, accompanied by a small squadron including the *Jamestown*, *Yorktown* and several other smaller vessels, approached. At first the Confederate ship's pilot seemed not to notice the small Union ironclad, heading instead directly for the *Minnesota*. Frantic crewmen aboard the wooden-walled ship raised signal flags calling for the Union ironclad to attack the *Virginia*. Others helped toss everything from dufflebags to ship's stores overboard, sometimes missing the ship's boats and watching them bob away in the river waters. Several southern cannon roared, their balls smashing through the wooden timbers of the Union ship while the *Monitor's* crew struggled to raise her anchor. Finally, with her anchor stowed in its container, the Union ironclad headed towards the *Virginia*. The officers and men scrambled down from the top of the turret, shot was brought up into the turret, and her giant guns were loaded and run out. Then the crews stood there, silently awaiting the test of the turret's armour. 'The most profound silence reigned,' wrote the boat's paymaster, who stopped in the turret after being ordered off its top. 'If there had been a coward heart there its throb would have been audible, so *intense* was the stillness.'[13]

Worden had her steered straight towards the Confederate ship and, when within short range, changed her course to come alongside. He then gave the command to stop the engine and commence firing. The *Monitor* fired first, her shot doing no damage to the Confederate ironclad. Indeed, one of the *Virginia's* officers, who was convinced the odd floating object in the river was a ship's boiler being removed for repair on a barge, thought the boiler had simply exploded.

Others of the Confederate crew had sized up the new enemy on the water. The larger southern ship slowly turned and made to engage the *Monitor*. The world's first battle of ironclads, the gamble of an unproved design against a more conventional one, was under way.

The first Confederate shots struck the turret with a resounding crash, but the steel walls held. Excited gunners called to the lieutenant in the turret and pointed out where the enemy round had hit. Greene looked it over and then called over to Stimers to see if the turret was still safe. Stimers looked over the guns to the slight bulge in the turret armour. 'Did the shot come through?' he asked.

'No, sir, it didn't come through, but it made a big dent,' was the reply. 'Just look there sir!'

'A big dent?' Stimers replied, 'Of course it made a big dent. That is just what we expected, but what do you care about that as long as it keeps out the shot?'

'Oh,' was the reply from the comforted sailor, 'It's all right then of course sir.'[14] According to Greene, when the sailors realised that they were well protected within the iron walls of the turret, 'A look of confidence passed over the men's faces, and we believed the *Merrimac* would not repeat the work she had accomplished the day before'.[15]

Stimers remained in the turret a while longer, actually being thrown to the deck when a round struck the armour just as he was leaning an arm against the turret. He was able to leap up immediately, however, while two others near him, who had been leaning more on the turret armour, were stunned and had to be taken below to sick bay. They came to later, and after a couple of hours were also able to return to duty. The only other injuries felt in the turret came when Confederate fire knocked some of the nuts off their bolts. They flew around, luckily doing no great damage, though they could have done had they hit any of the crews' faces. Indeed, the worst problem was the noise, both from Confederate balls crashing off the armour and from the Union guns being fired. 'The din inside the turret was something terrific,' wrote an officer who had been inside it. 'The noise of every solid ball that hit fell upon our ears with a crash that deafened us.'[16]

As with the shakedown cruise, however, not everything was going wholly according to Ericsson's plans. The pilot house became an obstacle for the Federal guns. The area of the bow became a dead space, because not only could the Federal guns not fire directly ahead, for fear of hitting the pilot house, but they could not even fire within several points of the bow. They felt in the turret that the blast of the huge guns could injure the captain, the pilot and the quartermaster at the boat's wheel; as many people as could fit in the iron box.

The speaking tube between the turret and the pilot house soon gave way, so Worden assigned two men to pass messages between the two points. Unfortunately the only two available for the job were landsmen with little sea experience, and they failed to understand or pass on all the technical jargon the experienced officers were wont to use.

The turret machinery did not allow exact movement. Once the turret was started on its circular path it was difficult to stop it exactly where desired. Moreover, Greene, commanding in the turret, had a view of the outside world that was limited to what he could see through the gun ports, and these were covered by the heavy ports when the guns were being loaded. Greene would ask through the messenger chain where the enemy lay, receive this information, then try to mark it by the white marks on the deck below the turret. However, the combination of revolving turret and uncertainty of target made accurate, planned firing impossible. Finally, Greene simply had his crews watch for the enemy as the turret revolved and, when the target came within view, fire away. But, to be sure that the shot would pass the pilot house harmlessly, Greene insisted on pulling each lanyard to fire each gun personally. In this manner they got off a round every seven or eight minutes.

Although it was unplanned, the random turret movement proved a blessing, since the guns would be fired when they faced the enemy and then, as the turret slowly continued on its revolution, they could be safely reloaded without having to stop to close the heavy, difficult port covers. The Confederate gunners could not adopt the usual tactic of firing at the enemy's gun ports to disable her guns. Indeed, one of the *Virginia*'s officers wrote: 'We never got sight of her guns except when they were about to fire into us'.[17]

One gun crew watched in dismay as she fired a 180lb shot that smashed right into the *Virginia*'s armour at relatively close range, only to bounce off, apparently doing no harm. Navy ordnance men in Washington, recalling the explosion of the gun on the *Princeton* years before, forbade the use of the normal 30lb charge, limiting the charges used on the *Monitor* to only 15lb. If only he could have used normal charges, Greene felt, 'it is probable that this shot would have penetrated her armour'.[18] Yet two shots at close range from the Union craft did real damage to the *Virginia*, as one of her officers recalled:

Both shots struck about halfway up the shield, abreast of the after pivot, and the impact forced the side in bodily two or three inches. All the crews of the after guns were knocked over by the concussion, and bled from the nose or ears. Another shot at the same place would have penetrated.[19]

Those aboard the *Virginia* had no way of knowing the problems faced by the men on the *Monitor*. The Confederate sailors knew only that they were taking a pounding, as the crashing of every shot on their ship's side echoed inside the smoke-filled gundeck. At the same time they saw most of their shots miss the small target and splash in the water many yards away. The draught through the oft-holed smokestack was taking effect, and the *Virginia*'s chief engineer reported that it was hard to keep up steam. Moreover, the deep draught of the *Virginia*'s hull kept her in the main channels, while the *Monitor*, with its 12-foot draught, was able to dance around her.

After about two hours of battle the *Virginia* became stuck fast. The *Monitor* took advantage to close and circle the trapped, turtle-like warship, firing shot after shot at her armour. Southern engine-room workers poured on what little remained of her coal to build up enough pressure to get the screw to free her. They also added anything that would burn hot and fast, ranging from wood splinters to oiled cotton waste, to get the fire hotter. The chief engineer tied down the steam safety valves designed to prevent the boiler from building up enough pressure to blow up. Suddenly the men on the gun deck, who had been ordered to stand easy and not return the Federal fire while stuck, staggered to one side as the ship pulled free.

The cannon were then ordered to resume fire. While passing along her gun deck, the *Virginia's* executive officer noticed a division of the ship's guns standing at ease. 'Why are you not firing, Mr Eggleston?', the lieutenant asked.

'Why, our powder is very precious,' came the reply, 'and after two hours' incessant firing I find that I can do her about as much damage by snapping my thumb at her every two minutes and a half.'[20]

The *Virginia's* captain then tried to ram the nimble Union boat, but as he lumbered towards her the *Monitor's* captain skipped his boat away, receiving but a glancing blow. Moreover, fearing her shaky ram, the *Virginia's* commander ordered her engines at half speed at the last moment, so that the blow was not delivered at full speed and did no harm. The blow did spring a leak at the bow of the Confederate ship, but her pumps were able to keep it under control.

Boarders were armed on the Confederate ironclad, but again her captain was unable to close sufficiently to send them away. They might not have been very successful had they reached the *Monitor's* decks. Prepared for such a move, Worden ordered the guns loaded with canister that could have swept the decks clean. Furthermore, the Confederates would have had to cross the decks while the defenders in the turret and pilot house harried them with grenades, thoughtfully placed there before the battle for just such an event.

Some fifteen minutes of firing between the two ships apparently did no harm, and the ammunition in the *Monitor's* turret had been expended. Greene passed word to Worden that there was no ammunition left in the turret, and Worden pulled his boat back, out of action, so that the turret could be stopped to allow replenishment. In the meantime, the captain scrambled through a gun port on to the flat deck to see the *Virginia* better than he could from the pilot house. The surgeon went to the spirit room and then walked through the ship, passing out a half-gill of whisky to every man aboard.

When the turret was again supplied with ammunition, Worden climbed back through the gun port and went down to his post, ordering the ship to return to action. Again he brought the ironclad close to the enemy and the two boats exchanged shots. Inside the *Virginia*, the gunners had changed their strategy. They had been told that, as they could do no apparent damage to the turret, they should concentrate their fire on the more vulnerable pilot house. Finally, about noon, a lucky Confederate shot fired at close range smashed directly on to the slit of the pilot house. Pieces of iron and powder blasted on Worden, who had been staring out of the slit as the ball hit. Blinded, and with blood pouring from his face, he staggered back and ordered his boat to sheer off.

Greene was sent for, scrambled down from the turret and ran forward to find Worden standing at the bottom of the ladder to the pilot house. 'He was a ghastly sight, with his eyes closed and the blood apparently rushing from every pore in the upper part of his face. He told me that he was seriously wounded, and directed me to take command.'[21] Greene helped the stricken officer to his leather-covered couch in his salon and called for the doctor. Then, after telling Worden that the job was done and the *Minnesota* safe, he made his way back to the pilot house. About half an hour had passed since the *Virginia*'s shot had hit the pilot house.

The pilot house was a shambles. The top had been partly blown open, and the iron log that had taken the direct hit was broken. But the steering gear was intact, and Greene, although he was aware that another such shot would bring certain death and perhaps make the boat unmanageable, had no desire to give up the fight. He brought the boat back towards the *Virginia*. By then, however, the *Virginia*'s commander had had enough, and saw that the *Monitor* had withdrawn to a point where the southern ship's deep draught would not permit pursuit. The Confederates also noted that the tide was falling, and soon they would have even less water under them. Were their ship to become stuck, it would be all over. The *Virginia*'s captain therefore gave the order to steam back towards Sewell's Point, and from there to the dockyard at Norfolk. The battle was over.

Both sides claimed a victory. Certainly the *Virginia* was victorious in the first day's action, before the *Monitor* arrived. She sunk several major Union warships and proved the efficacy of her design, even if not the dependability of her engines, material and workmanship. The *Monitor*, on that day, had the sole task of protecting the *Minnesota*, and this she did. Beyond that, however, the *Monitor* had to justify John Ericsson's very unusual design, and prove that the gamble taken by the entire US Navy in building her, against the wishes of the leading marine architect and engineer of that service, was a winning one. John Worden and his crew proved that it was.

Notes

1 Welles, Gideon, 'The First Iron-Clad Monitor', *The Annals of the War*, Philadelphia, 1878, pp.19-20.
2 Sloan, Edward William, III, *Benjamin Franklin Isherwood, Naval Engineer*, Annapolis, Maryland, 1965, p.50.
3 Miller, Edward M., *USS Monitor, the Ship that Launched a Modern Navy*, Annapolis, Maryland, 1978, p.22.
4 Davis, William C., *Duel Between the First Ironclads*, New York, 1975, p.15.
5 Welles, Gideon, *op. cit.*, p.19.
6 Davis, William C., *op. cit.*, p.20.
7 Maryniak, B. R., 'A Rare Account From Aboard The Monitor,' Newsletter of the Buffalo Civil War Round Table, no date or page number given.
8 Porter, David D., *Naval History of the Civil War*, Secaucus, New Jersey, 1984, p.121.
9 Maryniak, B. R., *op. cit.*
10 Greene, S. Dana, 'In The "Monitor" Turret', *B&L*, Vol. I., p.720.
11 Maryniak, B. R., *op. cit.*
12 Greene, S. Dana, *op. cit.*, p.722.
13 Davis, William C., Daly, Roberts, ed., *Aboard the USS Monitor: 1862*, Annapolis, Maryland, 1964, p.34.
14 Maryniak, B. R., *op. cit.*
15 Greene, S. Dana, *op. cit.*, p.723.
16 Davis, William C., *op. cit.*, p.129.
17 Davis, William C., *ibid.*, p.121.
18 Greene, S. Dana, *op. cit.*, p.725.
19 Wood, John Taylor, 'The First Fight of Iron-clads', *B&L*, Vol. I, p.702.
20 Wood, John Taylor, *ibid.*, p.702.
21 Greene, S. Dana, *op. cit.*, p.727.

A GAMBLE AT THE BRIGADE LEVEL
J. E. B. Stuart Rides Around McClellan

THE GAMBLE: *that a Confederate cavalry brigade riding around the flank of the entire Union Army of the Potomac, which may cut off its return, can continue all the way around the Union force despite heavy rains and swollen streams, returning safely to its starting point.*

The objective of the United States forces in the east in 1861 was clear. Richmond, Virginia, the political and manufacturing centre of the southern states, had to be captured. But, to quote the lyrics of a popular song of the time, 'Richmond was a hard road to travel'. Major General Irvin McDowell, pressured by the pleadings of newspapers and the demands of politicians, was the first to try. He led an unprepared, untrained and unready army directly south from Washington along the main roads to Richmond, where he was met by an equally untrained army under General P. G. T. Beauregard, whose main advantages were fighting on the defence and some able subordinates, such as 'Stonewall' Jackson. There, at the first battle of Bull Run, the first northern drive to take Richmond was turned back – decisively.

McDowell, who some in his army thought sent messages to his opponents via the oddly shaped hat he wore, was dismissed. He was replaced by Major General George B. McClellan, a brilliant young engineer officer who had been singled out for success after the Mexican War, only to retire to accept a position as president of a railroad. Recommissioned when the war began, McClellan won some early victories in West Virginia. He was quickly brought east to make order out of the chaos that was the Union Army of the Potomac around Washington.

President Abraham Lincoln could not have picked a better man to organise his army. McClellan was one of the best organisers and morale builders. He obtained new warm clothing for his men for the winter, he drilled them until they could 'by file left, march' in their sleep, and he held parade after parade and review after review.

However, he had one characteristic that Lincoln did not like. He refused to put his beloved army in harm's way. Lincoln finally issued an order, obviously aimed at McClellan, for an overall Union advance on Washington's birthday in March. Even after receiving such a direct order, McClellan refused to leave the warm camps his men had so patiently built.

But even someone with the personal popularity of a McClellan could not avoid moving for ever. After all, the army was being paid to go south and defeat the Confederate forces there, and bring those states back into the Union. That was something they could not do from the Washington camps.

Lincoln urged McClellan to advance along the same route that McDowell had used earlier. McClellan made a counter-proposal. He would load his entire army of well over 100,000 men on to ships, sail down the Atlantic coast and land near Fort Monroe, where a peninsula led from Richmond to the west directly into the ocean. This peninsula would become his road to Richmond. The distance would be much shorter than the overland route, and his flanks would be protected by the James and York rivers; rivers that would be controlled by ships of the US Navy, which were virtually unstoppable by the small Confederate flotilla there. His supply lines would be totally secure.

Lincoln agreed, with one proviso that became of utmost importance in McClellan's mind. At least a corps would have to be retained around Washington to protect the north's capital city. McClellan was forced to accept the proviso, but it would eventually become an excuse for his failure, as he also claimed to believe the wildly overblown estimate of Confederate troops counted for him by his amateur intelligence chief, civilian railroad detective Allen Pinkerton.

Besides faulty intelligence, other things began to go wrong in McClellan's mind from the outset. He had believed that the US Navy could protect him along both rivers, but just before his landing the Confederate Navy played its ace card in the form of the CSS *Virginia*. Although she had been stopped by the *Monitor* and had been obliged to withdraw back up the James River towards Richmond, she still posed a threat and effectively made that river unusable for offensive action. At the same time, well-placed batteries along the York River at Gloucester Point made it impossible for McClellan to bring his troops further along the Peninsula than Yorktown to land.

So McClellan landed below Yorktown, where Confederates had erected a line of fortifications. Already mentally beaten by all the problems he believed he faced, he called for a formal siege. Throughout April McClellan's army dug in before the Confederate troops at Yorktown. The Federals brought up heavy artillery, both large-bored siege guns and mortars.

Eventually even George McClellan had to commit his army to battle. On 3 May, just before the Federals were due to open up their guns on the Confederates, the Confederates finally fell back. Magruder's bluff had bought them the time they needed to consolidate and reinforce their troops on the Peninsula before Richmond. The overall commander on the scene, General Joseph Johnston, had moved out just in time to avoid the massive shelling McClellan had planned, and now slowly withdrew, seeking a better spot from which to confront the pursuing Union troops.

Rains that turned the roads into mud baths delayed both armies, but the Federals came on, constantly skirmishing with the southern cavalry rear guard led by another young officer, Brigadier General James Ewell Brown ('Jeb') Stuart. Stuart, then 29 years old, was a graduate of the US Military Academy in the class of 1854. He had been a professional soldier all of his life, serving mostly with the 1st US Cavalry Regiment on the Kansas frontier, where he had almost been killed in a skirmish with Indians. When Virginia left the Union and joined the young southern Confederacy he was a lieutenant in the US Army, but, being a native Virginian, he quickly resigned his commission and returned home to receive the appointment of colonel of the 1st Virginia Cavalry Regiment. He led this regiment in a charge against the New York Fire Zouaves at the first major battle of the war, the First Bull Run, and this brought him the popular praise that he had sought all his life.

Stuart was an odd mixture. He was most obviously vain, taken to wearing elaborate uniforms with much gold lace and plumes. He was extremely anxious to be recognised as a brilliant soldier and brave warrior, and shaded all his writings, both personal letters and official reports, to show this. Yet he was a faithful Episcopalian who had been converted in adult life and was so active in the church that he was a representative at one of that church's national conventions. He never drank alcoholic beverages, following a pledge to his mother to remain a teetotaller. But he surrounded himself with young, fun-loving staff officers and orderlies orderlies, even having a banjo player accompany them in the field, so that almost every evening in his headquarters was a party. Finally, he could inspire men to do their best.

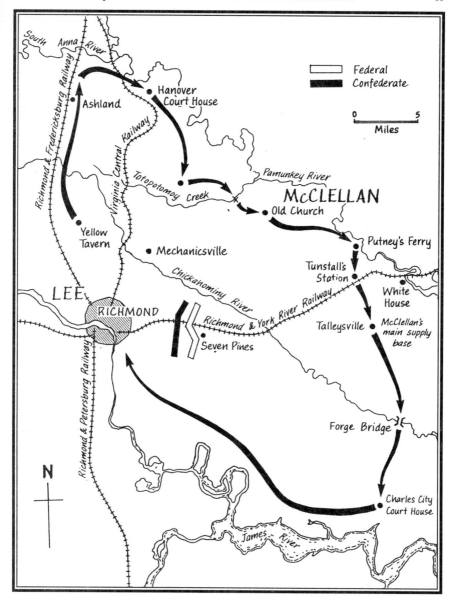

Stuart was promoted to brigadier general on 24 September 1861 and given command of the army's cavalry brigade. It was this brigade that covered the retreat of the Confederate army back towards Richmond. But no matter how it was described, the march was a retreat that yielded southern soil, and even McClellan managed to plod along after the Confederates. Finally, on 31 May, Johnston saw a chance to inflict a blow on McClellan, and sent his troops against the Federals at Seven Pines. The attackers were badly mauled, losing almost a third of their men, including the commanding general, who was wounded in the action. General Robert E. Lee, like McClellan a noted officer of Engineers in the pre-war US Army, was appointed in Johnston's place.

The new officer was not very well thought of by many of his men. His first campaign, in West Virginia, had been a failure, and many in his new army thought Lee incapable of offensive action. Stuart, on learning of the appointment, wrote: 'with profound personal regard for Gen'l Lee, he has disappointed me as a general'.[1] Stuart and his fellow soldiers of what Lee now called 'The Army of Northern Virginia' were wrong. Lee was indeed a fighter.

Lee spent a short time becoming familiar with his new command. Then, in early June, he summoned his cavalry commander to his headquarters. The two talked for a time about Lee's intentions; his plans for ridding the capital of the Union threat. Then, on 11 June, he gave Stuart his orders.

Essentially, he called for Stuart to scout the rear of the enemy along the Chickahominy River, burning supply wagons as he found them. Lee wanted to know how deep the Union lines were spread, how many men manned them, and from what commands they were drawn. Stuart, Lee warned, must 'remember that one of the chief objects of your expedition is to gain intelligence for the guidance of future movements'. Battle was not one of Stuart's objectives.

At the same time, Lee was concerned that Stuart would act impetuously and get into trouble. Lee warned him that: 'The utmost vigilance on your part will be necessary to prevent any surprise to yourself, and the greatest caution must be practised in keeping well in your front and flanks reliable scouts to give you information'. Indeed, Stuart was 'not to hazard unnecessarily our command'. Therefore, said Lee: 'Should you find, upon investigation, that the enemy is moving to his right, or is so strongly posted as to make your expedition inopportune, you will, after gaining all the information you can, resume your former position'.[2] In other words, Stuart would take his cavalry well around the Union right flank, find out what was there, and immediately return to his original camp.

Stuart ordered his command to move out on the morning of the 12th. Each man was to carry three days' worth of rations and 60 rounds of ammunition for each pistol and carbine. The weather was foul, with a steady rain falling. Stuart had flares fired off to alert the men, reasoning that flares would be less noticeable to out-of-sight Federals than the blowing of bugles. 'It was 2.00 on the morning of the 12th,' wrote one of his staff officers, Heros von Borcke, 'and we were fast asleep, when General Stuart's sonorous voice awakened us with the words, "Gentlemen, in ten minutes everyone has to be in the saddle". In a few moments we were dressed, the horses saddled, and the given period scarcely past, when we reached the general ...'3

Stuart led some 1,200 cavalry in four regiments, the 1st, 4th, and 9th Virginia Cavalry Regiments and the Jeff Davis Legion, and a section of artillery. As they moved out, the adjutant of the 9th Virginia heard one of his men call back to those who had to remain in camp, 'Goodbye boys; we are going to help old Jack [i.e. Stonewall Jackson] drive those Yanks into the Potomac'.4 Another officer called out to Stuart, asking when he and his men would be back. 'It may be for years, it may be forever,' the general gaily shouted back.5

With the 9th Virginia in the lead, Stuart's men headed north along the Brook turnpike, travelling some 22 miles from Richmond by the evening. They camped on Winston's Farm, near Taylorsville Station. The rain kept the men cold that night, for they were forbidden to light fires and had to maintain strict silence.

Next morning they mounted up again. Scouts sent out during the night returned with the word that the road to Old Church was clear of enemy troops. Stuart therefore headed his men eastwards and slightly south of Taylorsville Station, towards Hanover Court House. They arrived at this small county seat at about 9.00 a.m., finding Union cavalrymen lounging around the brick buildings. Stuart sent a skirmish line straight ahead, and sent most of his men around the right to try to cut them off from the rear, but a few of the hard-pressed and outnumbered Union cavalrymen managed to mount up and ride off before his troopers could get in place. Others, including a sergeant from the 6th US Cavalry Regiment, a regular army unit, were captured.

A scouting party of the 5th US Cavalry, on a routine patrol of Hanover Court House, arrived at about 11.00 and saw the victorious Confederates in the town. The Confederates charged them. 'The enemy broke into wild flight with the first shock,' wrote von Borcke, 'then began a daring and exciting chase of nearly three miles. Both sides were soon enveloped in thick clouds of dust, through which the shots flashed and the shells whistled to and fro.'6

Finally, most of the Union troops managed to break away and return to their picket posts at Hawes' Shop. While waiting there for the Confederates, they sent a courier back to their main camp at Old Church with news of the loose southern cavalry approaching the Federal rear. Poor communications, however, hurt the Federal defenders. The original note about the Confederates was so poorly written that many precious minutes were lost while its receiver tried to decipher the bad handwriting. Moreover, the message indicated that the Confederate column included infantry. The commander at Old Church ordered the scouts to continue falling back, all the way back to his camp.

In the meantime, Stuart, not wanting to lose time at Hanover Court House, remounted his men after a quick drink of water and headed east by Taliaferro's Mill and Enon Church to Hawes' Shop. From there it was a straight ride east to the Federal camp at Old Church. However, the Totopotomoy Creek, which flowed northward into the Pamunkey River, had to be crossed first. It was there that the Union pickets who had fled at Stuart's arrival drew up a defensive line.

'The road here,' wrote Major H. B. McClellan, an assistant adjutant general on Stuart's staff, 'passes through a deep ravine, whose steep banks are fringed with laurel and pine, the narrow road permitting a direct attack only in column of fours.' In such a situation, the superior numbers of the Confederate cavalry would be overcome, and the Union cavalrymen could rake the column with carbine and pistol fire as it attacked. The 9th Virginia commander, Colonel W. H. F. Lee, sent out flanking parties who worked their way through the dense woods and across the stream. They soon came in contact with the Federal forces. The Union cavalrymen, dismounted and firing their carbines, fought well, but were greatly outnumbered and had to withdraw, falling back to a crossroads. There, joined by the main body of Union cavalrymen (still no more than a company), they halted, still mounted, with drawn pistols, ready to receive an attack.

The 9th sent forward a squadron with drawn sabres in fours at a full charge. The Union troops lacked carbines, being armed only with sabres and short-ranged pistols that failed to stop the surge of mounted men. In the lead, Captain Latanè, commanding Company F of the 9th, sabred the Union commander, Captain William B. Royall, but in turn received the full blast of his pistol at close range. Latanè was hit by five bullets and killed instantly, the only fatality of the charge. Royall reeled in his saddle, but managed to get back to the Federal camp, weak from loss of blood.

A Confederate later recalled:

I remember passing a Dutch [German] cavalryman who was writhing with a bullet through the breast, and biting and tearing up the ground. He called for water, and I directed a servant at a house nearby to bring him some. The last I saw of him, a destitute cavalryman was taking off his spurs as he was dying. War is a hard trade.[7]

The Federals fell back, then wheeled back into line to receive another charge. The Confederates pressed on and quickly broke this second line. A third line was made and again broken before the Federals finally fled the field, back to Old Church, where the blue-coated troopers made a final defensive line.

Fighting was fierce as the Confederates hit this final line. 'To shoot or to cut us down was the aim of every Federal as he neared us, but we did what we could to defend ourselves,' wrote the adjutant of the 9th Virginia. 'Every one of my comrades was shot or cut down, and I alone escaped unhurt. After having been borne along by the retreating enemy for perhaps a quarter of a mile, I leaped my horse over a fence into the field and so got away.'[8] Most of the wounds were cuts or bruises from the dull sabre blades, indicating the close quarters of the fighting.

The 9th, exhausted by its hard riding and fighting, halted to send pickets out to guard their flanks while the rest gathered their prisoners. The 1st Virginia now passed them, pressing on, aiming at the Union line with drawn sabres at a full charge. The Federals turned and fled before the charge hit their line, back to their main body of troops, leaving the Confederates in charge of Old Church. Von Borcke recalled:

When we reached their camp, the work of destruction began. Everyone tried to gather up as many luxurious articles as he could, but only a few succeeded, or, in accordance with the well-laid plan of our leader, flames soon blazed up, and in a very few minutes the entire camp was enveloped. Hundreds of tents burning together presented a wonderfully beautiful spectacle.[9]

Many civilians who lived in the area, overjoyed to see their own men driving off the Federals, came out with offerings of food, which was much appreciated and quickly disappeared into saddlebags. Some of the women pressed bouquets of flowers into the hands of passing officers.

In the meantime, a Federal cavalry lieutenant who had been among the fleeing Union troopers reached the headquarters of the Army of the Potomac's cavalry in the late afternoon. Here he told Union cavalry commander Brigadier General P. St George Cooke that his unit had been overpowered and he had managed to escape through the woods. Moreover, he indicated that the enemy was right behind him. Cooke ordered his nearby troops of the 5th and 6th US Cavalry Regiments to mount up immediately, and sent them towards where the pickets had been driven off. Cooke had been given to understand that the Confederate force was a large one of some 3,000 to 5,000 men, complete with as many as five regiments of infantry and artillery, as well as cavalry. He therefore gathered the rest of his units slowly, making sure he would have his maximum strength available for the coming battle. As it transpired, the bugle call 'to horse' that Cooke had sounded at his headquarters was not repeated in many of the unit camps. Much more time was wasted because many troopers did not hear that the movement order.

Cooke himself went off to look for two of his missing units, the 1st US Cavalry and 6th Pennsylvania Cavalry ('Rush's Lancers'), and then proceeded to his commander's headquarters to arrange for infantry to join the pursuing force. Finally he rejoined his brigade, which was on the road, moving towards Stuart's last reported position. The 6th Pennsylvania and the 1st US also moved up and joined the brigade around sunset. Then the 6th's commander realised that the unit had not brought any rations, and obtained permission to return to camp to get forage and rations before rejoining the brigade. As a result, the Federal high command did not get effectively on the move until the next morning, although Stuart did not know it.

Stuart's men were now directly north of the Federals in Old Harbor and along the Chickahominy River, which flows roughly parallel to the Pamunkey in the north and the James in the south, at New Bridge. Stuart had reached his objective, and had gathered much vital intelligence. His scouts had shown that the Federal infantry was not posted on its right towards Hanover Court House. Lee would be free to strike from that direction. It was time to leave and get that information to Lee.

But how? 'We now found ourselves in the heart of the enemy army,' von Borcke later wrote. Union troops could block their route back to Lee's army in any direction, and word of their presence had surely been passed on by the escaping Union cavalrymen.

'Here was the turning point of the expedition,' Stuart wrote in his offi-cial report. 'Two routes were before me – the one to return by Hanover Court House, the other to pass around through New Kent, taking the chances of having to swim the Chickahominy and make a bold effort to cut the enemy's lines of communication.'[10]

As one of his staff officers later wrote:

How was he to return? He could not cross the Pamunkey, and make a circuit back; he had no pontoons. He could not return over the route by which he had advanced. As events afterward showed, the alarm had been given, and an overpowering force of infantry, cavalry, and artillery had been rapidly moved in that direction to intercept the daring raider. Capture stared him in the face, on both of these routes –– across the Pamunkey, or back as he came; he must find some other loophole of escape.[11]

The obvious route, the one Lee expected them to take, was that along which they had come in the first place, back west to Hanover Court House and then south to Richmond. But that would be obvious to the Federals as well, who would now be streaming in that direction like bees from a disturbed hive. Moreover, Stuart could only cross at a regular ford of any major river, because of recent rains. He could turn a bit east and north and cross the Pamunkey at Piping Tree Ferry and then head east, leaving the river to pro-tect him. But he knew that, once he was on that side, Federal cavalry could block him at any one of the mere handful of crossings west of Piping Tree. He also knew that large bodies of Federal infantry were camped only a few miles away both west and south of him and, led by their cavalry, they could probably be in Hanover Court House before him. He knew there would be trouble to the east because the main Federal supply depot, guarded by navy gunboats and a 600-man garrison including a squadron of the 11th Penn-sylvania Cavalry, was located almost due east of him at White House on the Pamunkey.

Indeed, troopers of the 5th and 6th US Cavalry and 6th Pennsylvania Cavalry, the only regiment of lancers in the Federal army, were already on the move, although slowly and indecisively, to cut Stuart off at the Totopo-tomoy Creek.

So, which way to go? The conservative options were to go north, across the Pamunkey, and then recross the river to the west, or to move back the way he had come as quickly as possible, trusting that the battle-tested troopers could cut their way out of any trap.

But Stuart decided to gamble. He would move faster than the Federals gathering behind him, going first east, then south, and then west along the James River, a ride that would take him and his men completely around the huge army of George B. McClellan. There were some valid reasons for his taking this gamble, but Stuart had an emotional one as well. He wanted to hurt the enemy, especially their cavalry, which was commanded by his father-in-law. He reported: 'the hope of striking a serious blow at a boastful and insolent foe, which would make him tremble in his shoes, made more agreeable the alternative I chose'.[12]

One of his officers wrote:

> We were now at Old Church, where Stuart was to be guided in his further movements by circumstances. I looked at him; he was evidently reflecting. In a moment he turned round to me and said: "Tell Fitz Lee to come along, I'm going to move on with my column". These words terminated my doubt, and I understood in an instant that the General had decided on the bold and hazardous plan of passing entirely round McClellan's army.[13]

Stuart first disclosed his plan to his officers, many of whom were less than thrilled by the idea of moving right around the enemy force. None the less, all of them assured Stuart of their full support. Stuart then gathered a picked group of scouts, told them his plans to encircle the Federal forces, and started them on their way. Many of the scouts he chose were local men who were quite familiar with the territory the Confederates would have to cover. Indeed, Stuart trusted the advance of his men from Old Church east to Tunstall's Station to one such local man, Private Richard E. Frayser, a member of the New Kent company of the 3rd Virginia Cavalry. For his scouting work Frayser was later appointed a captain in the signal corps and assigned to Stuart's staff.

Tunstall's Station was vital for the Confederates. Here the railroad ran between White House, the main Union supply base, and the Union lines outside Richmond. 'Here was our point of danger,' wrote Colonel Robins of the 9th Virginia. 'Once across the railroad, we were comparatively safe. But in possession of the railroad, with its rolling-stock, the enemy could easily throw troops along its line to any given point.'[14]

Garlick's Landing, a small docking area on a creek just off the Pamunkey, stood between Stuart and Tunstall's Station. A fourteen-wagon supply train and three schooners filled with forage were at Garlick's Landing, defended by a lieutenant and nine men of the 1st Cavalry who were expecting no trouble. They had set up a small camp, unsaddled their horses and were lounging around eating when they were first spotted by Stuart's scouts. Stuart halted his men and sent forward a dismounted skirmish line through the woods to discover the defender's strength. When they saw how few Union troopers there were, and their nonchalant behaviour, the Confederates came out of the woods, opening fire.

The shots drove off the Union horses, and the Union cavalry grabbed their weapons, organised themselves, and fell into a small firing line. Their return shots appeared to hit several Confederate troopers as the grey-clad line fell back to the trees. The Confederates then remounted and charged the Union defenders, who fled into the woods, leaving the wagons and boats behind.

One of the wagons was filled with much-needed Colt revolvers, something many Confederate cavalrymen still lacked. Stuart halted his men long enough to loot and then burn the schooners and wagons. It must have been one of the few times in military history when cavalry captured boats.

While this destruction was going on, a group of Union cavalrymen came round the bend in the road and were confronted by the scene. After several seconds of confusion, while both sides simply stared at each other, the Federals turned and fled. One of them, dashing through Tunstall's Station as quickly as his spurs could drive his horse, passed a lounging infantryman there. 'What's to pay?' the infantryman called out.

'Hell's to pay,' the mounted man replied, as he pressed on as quickly as he could.

A band of Confederates mounted up and started after him, soon reaching the railroad station. Robins, who was leading the Confederates, later recalled:

We could see the enemy scattered about the [station] building and lounging around before we charged them. The greater part scattered for cover, and were pursued by our people. Only one of them seemed disposed to show fight. He ran to the platform where the muskets were stacked, and, seizing one of them, began to load. Before he could ram his cartridge home, a sweep of the sabre, in close proximity to his head, made him throw down his gun, and, jumping into a ditch, he dodged under the bridge over the railroad and made his escape.[15]

The other infantrymen, around a dozen including their captain, quickly surrendered.

The Confederates then set to work to block the tracks. First they tried to switch the points, so that any incoming trains would be shunted to a dead-end line at the station. Unfortunately they had rusted shut too firmly to be budged. Several men then took axes and began chopping down a tree alongside the tracks, so that it would fall across them. Others put an oak log about a foot square and fourteen feet long near the fallen tree.

Before they could do any more, however, a train came down from the north. Its engineer, seeing the debris on the tracks and the grey-clad troopers on either side of the tracks, put on as much steam as possible. With a smashing blow, the engine's cow-catcher struck the tree and log, tossing them aside easily as Confederates dashed for safety. The train had not even slowed down.

Von Borcke wrote:

General Stuart quickly posted a portion of his men on both sides of the embankment, with orders to fire on the train if it did not stop at the station. Slowly it steamed towards us, and soon we could see that it was filled with troops, most of whom were in open cars. Not only was the order to stop disregarded, but, on the contrary, the train's speed was accelerated, so the firing began along our entire line.[16]

Confederate fire toppled a couple of men on board the train and wounded eight more. Several Union soldiers jumped from the train as it was moving, fearing that it would be derailed, and were quickly disarmed and captured. Von Borcke recalled:

A battle of the strangest description developed. [Some of] the soldiers on the train returned our fire, others jumped out of the cars to save themselves by flight, while others lay down flat on the bottom [of the cars]. The train, though its speed had increased, was not going so fast that we could not keep up with it by galloping hard. And so our men engaged themselves in a wild pursuit, while others maintained a constant fire along our half-mile-long line. I had become so highly excited myself, having already had my hat almost knocked off my head, that I did not even heed our own fire, and my horse sprang over the embankment as I discharged all five rounds of my revolver into the face of the enemy.[17]

The train escaped to bring word of Stuart's location to the main Union army. Stuart could not afford to dawdle at the station, since he was within only a few miles of troops on either side. None the less, his men took the time needed to destroy telegraph poles for some distance along the tracks, as well as the railroad bridge over Black Creek.

By then it was dark, and many of the men were hungry, having eaten whatever food they had brought at the start of the first night. Moreover, they had been moving so rapidly that they had not had a chance to use the typical cavalryman's resupply method of foraging off civilians. So they searched the buildings and captured wagons at the station for things to eat, and the search was successful. 'Champagne and Rhine wine flowed copiously,' one of the scouts wrote.[18]

Even though he knew his men were hungry and tired, Stuart felt they could not waste time at a spot where by now they were known to be. If it was not enough that the train had escaped to take word of their position to the main Federal army, the flames from the bridge and wagons leapt high in the sky, pinpointing their position for miles. As one of his staff officers later wrote:

> The question was, should he go back and attack the White House, where enormous stores were piled up? It was tempting, and he afterwards told me he could scarcely resist it. But a considerable force of infantry was posted there; the firing had doubtless given them the alarm; and the attempt was too hazardous. The best thing for that grey column was to set their faces toward home, and "keep moving," well closed up both day and night, for the lower Chickahominy. So Stuart pushed on.[19]

Stuart ordered his men back in the saddle without taking a pause to rest. At least the rain stopped; the clouds raced on east, and pale moonlight now lit the troopers' way. One Union officer later wrote that, by midnight, 'the moon [was] shining brightly, making any kind of movements for ourselves or the enemy as easy as in daylight'.[20]

Stuart's men again headed west, led by First Lieutenant Jones Christian, another New Kent County member of the 3rd Virginia. They turned south, however, before reaching New Kent Court House, not far from the Pamunkey, and instead made for Talleysville. On the way the advance guard had the good luck to find a small store well equipped by its northern owner with delicacies such as canned fruits, sardines and crackers. The advance guard took a few moments to sack the shop completely before moving on, leaving little for their friends in the main body.

Behind them, the first Union forces entered Tunstall's Station cautiously shortly after midnight. They found fires still raging and several dead bodies, and halted to extinguish the fires and wait for the rest of the Union cavalry. It did not arrive until about 2.00 a.m.

The still-moving Confederates arrived at the sleepy Virginia town of Talleysville well after dark. There the men took a three-hour break, allowing them time to cook some dinner while waiting for scattered detachments to rejoin the main body. It was hard to build fires with woodthat was soaked by the rain that had fallen since they had first mounted up for the raid. At about 11.00 p.m. they remounted and started for the Chickahominy Creek, where they planned to cross at a little-known ford near Forge Bridge, some eight miles to the east and south of Talleysville. Federals were close behind, their first scouts reaching Talleysville about 2.00 a.m. There, the Federals, who had not been able to determine exactly where Stuart was nor the strength of his force, called it a night, allowing him precious time to make good his escape.

Unfortunately, when the Confederates arrived at about 5.00 a.m. they found the river flooded more than many of the local men had ever seen. 'The banks were overflowed,' McClellan wrote, 'and an immense volume of water rushed madly on, as if mocking the weary horsemen who stood upon the bank.'[21]

Colonel W. H. F. Lee, leading his men of the 9th Virginia, was one of the first on the scene. One of Stuart's staff officers found him staring at the rushing waters. 'What do you think of the situation, Colonel?' he asked.

'Well, Captain,' Lee replied, in his habitual tone of cheerful courtesy, 'I think we are caught.'[22]

After this brief discussion, Lee splashed his horse into the rough water. A couple of his cavalrymen followed. It was hard going. The water in the middle of the river was some 15ft above the river bank, and the current was rapid in the narrow river bed. Several of the horses got their hoofs tangled in branches of trees that had been tossed about on the river. Lee did reach the other side and the entrapped horses were freed, but only after hard, slow travel. It was obvious that an entire command, complete with artillery, could not cross there.

Returning to the north bank, Lee ordered his men to begin chopping down trees to make a temporary bridge. But every time a soldier tried to get a tree set up in the river, the swift current ripped it out of the riverbed and bore it downstream.

Stuart arrived on the scene in time to witness this abortive attempt at pioneer work. 'Every face showed anxious care,' McClellan wrote, 'save that of Stuart himself, who sat upon his horse, stroking his long beard, as was his custom in moments of serious thought.'[23] As he was thinking, a courier from the rear guard he had left behind arrived with a note reporting that an entire division of Federal cavalry was not far behind them.

Finally, Stuart called one of his couriers to his side and scribbled a note for the corporal to take across the river to the main Confederate Army, to its commander General R. E. Lee. In it, Stuart told Lee of his location and the situation there, and asked Lee if he could create an infantry diversion on the Charles City Road to keep the Union troops busy while Stuart extricated his men. As the corporal rode off, a local man told Stuart about the remains of an old bridge where the road between Charles City Court House, near the James River in the south, and New Kent Court House in the north crossed the Chickahominy. It had not been used for years and had largely fallen apart, the man said, so Stuart rode out to see for himself.

What he found were solid foundations still standing in the 30ft-wide river, and a large abandoned warehouse nearby. Stuart immediately ordered his men to the new location, and put them to work tearing down the wooden warehouse and rebuilding the bridge. Very soon there was enough of a bridge to allow each cavalryman to cross, leading his horse by its reins while it swam the river alongside the bridge. Others continued to work as the cavalry crossed, and by 1.00 p.m. a strong enough bridge had been made to allow the artillery to pass over the raging river. Stuart's men had done it. The last across piled fence rails on the bridge and set them alight. It was about 2.45 p.m.

On the other side of the fog of war, at about 8.00 a.m. a Confederate deserter surrendered to Federals. He gave them the first concrete information on the size of the Confederate raid, setting their number at some four regiments of cavalry and a battery of artillery. At the same time, scouts of the 6th found the trail left by hundreds of Confederate horseshoe marks in the wet soil. The regiment, now armed with information on the actual size of the force, got under way with more determination that had been the case earlier the pursuit.

Soldiers of the 6th Pennsylvania, who had almost caught up with Stuart's men as they were trying to cross the river, spotted the column of smoke. The nervous commander sent forward eight troopers under command of the unit's Major Robert Morris, Jnr. As they came through the woods they spotted the burning bridge and five Confederates on the other side. One of the troopers fired a single shot from his carbine. The rearguard commander recalled:

> I was seated under a tree on the bank of the river, and at the moment that the hissing of the burning timbers of the bridge let me know that it had fallen into the water, a rifle-shot rang out from the other side, and the whistling bullet cut off a small limb over my head, which fell into my lap. The shot was probably fired by some scout who had been following us, but who was afraid until the bridge was gone. With a thankful heart for his bad aim, I at once withdrew the men, and pushed on after the column.[24]

Although they all breathed large sighs of relief, with the raging river between them and their pursuers, they were still 25 miles from Richmond and 20 miles behind the Union Army's front lines. Moreover, much of this land was swampland, almost impossible to bring mounted men through, let alone artillery. The men were becoming exhausted from the combination of sleeplessness, hard work and constant tension. 'Until now I had not felt fatigued,' wrote von Borcke, 'but after this strenuous work in the water, I felt it settling heavily in all my limbs.'[25]

Remounted, Stuart's men pressed due south, across a swollen branch of the Chickahominy. There they could cross without having to build a bridge, although the pole of one of the artillery limbers was broken in the process. With no time to effect a repair, the cannoneers abandoned the limber.

After some 36 hours in the saddle without sleep, Stuart's men arrived in Charles City Court House that evening. There they halted to make dinner from food found nearby by foraging parties, and to try to get some much-needed rest. The horses were set to feed in a field of clover. Stuart himself decided to press on to Richmond with the information required by Lee, and handed command to Colonel Fitz Lee with orders to get the men up, in the saddle, and moving east to Richmond at 11.00 that night.

It was 30 miles across country roads, deep in enemy territory, from Charles City Court House to Richmond. Stuart, accompanied by a scout and a courier, rode all night, luckily without encountering a single Federal soldier on the way. About halfway there the three stopped and lit a small fire to brew up some coffee. Otherwise they spent the entire time in the saddle, reaching Lee's headquarters before sunrise on the 15th.

Stuart's men started shortly after the general's departure, having had only the briefest catnaps. A southern officer wrote:

Although in the saddle and in motion, and aware that the safety of the expedition depended on great vigilance in case the enemy should be encountered, it was hard to keep awake. I was constantly falling asleep, and awaking with a start when almost off my horse. This was the condition of every man in the column. Not one had closed his eyes in sleep for forty-eight hours.[26]

Early next morning the column was halted by the happy sight of a Confederate picket from the 10th Virginia Cavalry. They had reached Confederate lines, bringing with them 165 Union prisoners and 260 captured mules and horses, which arrived a short time later. They had lost only one man killed. The information gathered by Stuart allowed Lee to launch his attack against the Army of the Potomac which became known as the Seven Days, and drove off the threat against Richmond. Stuart's gamble had paid off.

Notes
1 Thomason, John, *Jeb Stuart*, New York, 1930, p.138.
2 McClellan, H. B., *The Campaigns of Stuart's Cavalry*, Secaucus, NJ, 1993, pp.52-53.
3 Wright, Stuart, ed, 'The Prussian Remembers', *Civil War Times Illustrated*, March 1981, p.44.
4 Robins, W. T., 'Stuart's Ride Around McClellan', *B&L*, Vol. II, p.271.
5 Mosby, John S., *The Memoirs of John S. Mosby*, Bloomington, Indiana, 1959, p.112.
6 Wright, Stuart, *op. cit.*, p.44.
7 Cooke, John Esten, *Wearing of the Gray*, New York, 1969, p.169.
8 Robins, W. T., *op. cit.*, p.272.
9 Wright, Stuart, *op. cit.*, p.45.
10 *ORs*, Series I, Vol. XI, Part I, p.1037.
11 Cooke, John Esten, *op. cit.*, p170.
12 *ORs*, Series I, Vol. XI, Part I, p.1038.
13 Cooke, John Esten, *op. cit.*, pp.169-170.

14 Robins, W. T., *op. cit.*, pp.272-273.

15 Robins, W. T., *ibid.*, p.273.

16 Wright, Stuart, *op. cit.*, p.45.

17 Wright, Stuart, *ibid.*, p.45.

18 Mosby, John S., *op. cit.*, p.116.

19 Cooke, John Esten, *op. cit.*, p.174.

20 *ORs*, *op. cit.*, p.1030.

21 McClellan, *op. cit.*, p.63.

22 Cooke, John Esten, *op. cit.*, p.177.

23 McClellan, *ibid.*, p.64.

24 Robins, W. T., *op. cit.*, pp.274-275.

25 Wright, Stuart, *op. cit.*, p.46.

26 Robins, W. T., *op. cit.*, p.275.

A GAMBLE AT THE BRIGADE LEVEL
Mulligan Defends Lexington

THE GAMBLE: *that a brigade, short of supplies and lacking fighting experience, can stand off a greatly superior force and defend a town until reinforcements arrive.*

From the beginning, both sides understood that the so-called border states, in which slavery existed alongside pro-Union sentiment, were vital to the success of either side. These states included Maryland, in which the national capital city of Washington was located, Kentucky, and Missouri. Of these states, Missouri was quite possibly the biggest powder keg.

Missouri was also one of the most important of all the border states. St Louis was not only its largest city, it was also one of the largest cities in the United States, even at that early stage in its history. St Louis was also important to both sides in the short run, because the Army arsenal there contained some 34,000 small-arms, along with a number of cannon and a great deal of accoutrements and ammunition. It was protected by only a handful of US Army soldiers commanded by a pro-southern officer. Many of the city's residents were Germans who had seen military action in the liberal revolutions of 1848 and had come to the United States for political reasons. They would be strongly anti-slavery and pro-Union.

On the whole, however, Missouri's population fell into one of four political camps: violently pro-southern men who favoured secession and attachment to the new Confederacy, equally violent pro-Union men, and moderates on either side. The scales tended to tip slightly in favour of the Union. Although it is often the hotheads who prevail, in Missouri the moderates maintained an uneasy peace during the turbulent months after South Carolina's secession through the firing on Fort Sumter. Yet the newly elected Missouri Governor, Claiborne F. Jackson, favoured the south and called for a state convention so that the pro-southern people of the state could convince the Federal government that they would not fight against the south. His effort was in vain, for, on 18 February, the day that Jefferson Davis was inaugurated as President of the Confederate States, Missouri voters elected a pro-Union convention. The convention met in Jefferson City on 28 February and picked former Governor Sterling Price, a moderately pro-Union man, as its president. It then adjourned to St Louis, in an effort to avoid pressure from local pro-southern groups.

Price, born in 1809, was not a young man. A lawyer, he had served in the state legislature and US Congress, resigning to take a commission as colonel of the 1st Missouri Volunteers in the Mexican War. He had received a commission as brigadier general of volunteers for his efforts there, and had been the military governor of New Mexico.

Congressman Francis P. Blair, newly appointed Chairman of the Military Affairs Committee of the US House of Representatives and head of the state's Republican party, represented the opposite end of the spectrum from Jackson. Considering Jackson a 'traitor', Blair worked long hours trying to get Washington to authorise the US Army's Department of the West to organise troops in Missouri. With these troops, Blair argued, Missouri could 'take care of ourselves if authorised to raise a sufficient force within the state'.[1] Jackson, on the other hand, did not raise any troops to support his political views.

Blair was aided in his efforts by Captain Nathaniel Lyon, commander of a company of troops of the 2nd US Infantry Regiment which arrived in St Louis on 6 February to bolster defence of its arsenal. Lyon, a Connecticut native and rabid abolitionist, visited Blair shortly after arriving. Delighted by the presence of a fellow Union man with some authority, Blair asked him to organise St Louis' many German marching and gymnast clubs into volunteer infantry companies. Lyon happily accepted the job, and soon had them guarding the city and its arsenal.

On 6 May the city's police commissioners asked Lyon to remove his troops from the various buildings in the city that they were guarding. Lyon flatly refused.

At the same time as Lyon was turning athletes into soldiers, the pro-slavery force began organising their own state militia in St Louis. They organised the 2nd Regiment of State Guard Infantry there in February 1861. Called the 'Minute Men', the regiment was specifically raised 'for the defence of Missouri'.[2] Several St Louis volunteer companies, especially the Missouri Dragoons, withdrew from the official state militia as a result, while others, including the Mounted Rifles, City Guard, and Union Riflemen, composed of Swiss immigrants, simply disbanded to avoid being forced into a pro-southern force. None the less, the men of the 2nd felt strong enough to raise a Confederate flag over the Berthold mansion in St Louis on the day Lincoln was inaugurated in Washington. News of this event concerned the Lincoln government, which quickly sent Lyon a promotion to the rank of brigadier general of volunteers and appointed him to the post of commander of the newly created Department of the West.

By early May enough State Guard troops had been enlisted to fill a small camp in Lindell's Grove, near western St Louis. In the city it was said that the camp was a hotbed of secessionism, with the company streets named for southern heroes such as Davis and Beauregard. They also received weapons, including mortars, which supposedly arrived in boxes marked 'marble'. According to the camp commander, General D. M. Frost, the organisation would demobilise on 11 May. But Lyon feared that, instead of a peaceful demobilisation, the troops there would continue to grow in number and would eventually come to capture the arsenal. He decided to strike first, capturing the men in the camp because of their 'unscrupulous conduct, and their evident design ...'[3]

Early on the morning of the 10th, Lyon led his men, along with his newly trained Germans, a total of as many as 7,000 men, to surround the pro-southern camp. The State Guardsmen, of whom there were about 700, surrendered without firing a shot at the overwhelming numbers brought against them, and Lyon brought his prisoners under guard back to the arsenal. As they passed along the streets of St Louis, thronged by crowds, a scuffle broke out between pro- and anti-southern sympathizers and shots were fired. By the end of the riot, in which mobs dashed through the city's streets for two days, 36 people were dead. One was a small child, an innocent lost in a time of loss of innocence. Federal General William S. Harney, who had been replaced by Lyon on 21 April, returned to take command of the arsenal and try to calm things down. He succeeded, and St Louis remained in the Union.

For a time there was an uneasy stalemate in the state. On 21 May Price and Harney agreed that state troops would be used to keep the peace in Missouri, and that no Federal troops would be brought into the state as long as peace was maintained. However, officials in Washington, hearing reports of mistreatment of pro-Union sympathizers, mistrusted Price and his men and, as a result, Harney. He was replaced by Lyon on 31 May. This truce came totally to an end, however, when Lincoln requested troops of Missouri to put down the rebellion in the southern states. On 17 April 1861 Jackson wrote to the Secretary of War in Washington:

> Your dispatch of the 15th instant, making a call on Missouri for four regiments of men for immediate service, has been received. There can be, I apprehend, no doubt but the men are intended to form a part of the President's army to make war on the people of the seceded States. Your requisition, in my judgment, is illegal, unconstitutional, and revolutionary in its object, inhuman and diabolical, and cannot be complied with. Not one man will the State of Missouri furnish to carry on any such unholy crusade.[4]

Jackson then called a special session of the state legislature, and called up the state militia for duty. Jackson named Price commander of the state militia in May, as well. However, the politics of the day had largely destroyed the old militia system, such as it was. Many years had passed since 1847, when Missouri quietly abandoned its old enrolled militia system. Since then, a loose confederation of uniformed volunteer companies assigned to a paperwork structure of divisions and brigades had made up all there was of a militia system. According to legislation, volunteers were to serve seven-year enlistments, but the units chose their own uniforms and enforced their own discipline, as the state did neither. However, the state did provide weapons to uniformed volunteer militia companies on request.

On 10 June Jackson issued a proclamation of 50,000 militia to repel a Federal invasion. The next day Jackson and Price met with Blair and Lyon. The governor was astonished when Lyon demanded that Missouri submit to Federal laws and proclamations, such as the requisition of troops, unconditionally. By this time Lyon had a number of volunteer companies to back him up. 'This means war,' Lyon said after the meeting, adding that he would see all Missourians 'under the sod' before the state dictated terms to Federal officers.[5]

Jackson also refused to submit, and the two pro-southerners left St Louis for their temporary state capital of Jefferson City. The next day, Jackson issued an additional call for Missourians to enlist in a new State Guard, commanded by Price, 'for the defence of their most sacred rights and dearest liberties'.[6] Beyond that, Jackson had his militia detailed to watch the St Louis Arsenal, and at the same time wrote to the new Confederate government in Montgomery, Alabama, asking for artillery for his Minute Men.

With this artillery the pro-southern forces could capture the arsenal. In the meantime, they went ahead and captured a small arsenal at Liberty, just above Kansas City, where they found 1,500 small-arms and four cannon. The governor also saw to the destruction of a number of bridges over which Federal troops would have to march to enter the state.

As a result, the US War Department, in response to urging from Blair, authorised Lyon to muster four local regiments, made up of his volunteer companies, into Federal service. It also asked the Governor of Illinois to send several regiments to St Louis to protect the arsenal. The request fell on sympathetic ears: 'We want to be fully ready to take the starch out of the Missouri secession chivalry,' Illinois Governor Richard Yates telegraphed Washington.[7]

Lyon mustered in his men, gave them some last-minute training, and then headed out to destroy the Confederate forces in the state. On 15 June they captured Jackson's capital city, then pressed on after the retreating governor and his forces. On 17 June they captured Booneville after a brief skirmish, and Jackson and his followers were forced to fall back to the southwestern part of the state. There, near Carthage on 5 July, the Confederates were confronted by a German force led by Franz Sigel. After some heavy fighting, which resulted in some 170 Confederate casualties and some 42 Union casualties, the Union troops were beaten back. They marched to join Lyon at Springfield while Jackson marched south to join the troops under Price. The days that followed were filled with minor skirmishes.

By then the pro-Union forces controlled so much of the state that the State Convention called by Jackson declared that he was no longer governor. In his place they elected Hamilton R. Gamble, a pro-Union man, who was inaugurated on 31 July. In the meantime Lyon had advanced as far south as Dug Springs. There, on 5 August, he heard that Jackson had been reinforced and was advancing, and retreated to Springfield. The Confederates came within a short distance of Springfield, to a spot along a small river called Wilson's Creek. Lyon advanced to meet them and, on 10 August, in a battle of amateur forces, he was killed and the Federals withdrew to Rolla, southwest of St Louis. The tide was turning in Missouri.

Lyon's overall commander, Major General John Charles Frèmont, was in St Louis, where he declared martial law. He also closed down two pro-southern newspapers. But he was worried about the growing southern strength, and telegraphed Washington for more troops. On 30 August, as a desperate measure, Frèmont proclaimed that he would confiscate all the property of 'those who shall take up arms against the United States,' adding, 'their slaves, if any they have, are hereby declared free men'. Men taken with guns would be tried by court martial and, if found guilty, would be shot.[8] Shocked, Lincoln asked Frèmont to tone down his language and alter the proclamation to eliminate the emancipation policy. He was worried that the proclamation 'will alarm our Southern Union friends, and turn them against us -- perhaps ruin our rather fair prospect for Kentucky'.[9]

But Lincoln's concern came too late to stop the pro-southern tide resulting from Price's victory at Wilson's Creek and Frèmont's proclamation. Price decided to go on the march and win back Missouri. He had four possible targets; Jefferson City, Booneville, Kansas City and Lexington. Lexington appeared to be the most promising of the four. A commercial centre, it was the largest city on the river between Kansas City and St Louis, so it would be an excellent place to resupply his forces. Moreover, additional supplies would be forthcoming from the nearby countryside, which was rich. The large population would provide additional recruits from among anti-Union sympathizers, and, finally, it did not appear to be well defended.

Price wanted to bring the Confederate troops, under Brigadier General Ben McCulloch, with him in his invasion of the state, but McCulloch refused to go. He excused himself with orders that his troops protect the Indian Territory and Arkansas from Union troops in Kansas. In fact he appears to have wanted to disassociate himself from the Missourians, for whom he had little regard. Price's column started towards Lexington on 25 August. They brushed aside troops of the Union's Kansas Brigade on 2 September, just east of Fort Scott, Kansas.

In the meantime, Brigadier General Jefferson C. Davis (no relation to the Confederate president) summoned one of his colonels, James E. Mulligan, commander of the 23rd Illinois, and ordered him to take his regiment out to the defence of Lexington. Mulligan, a 32-year-old rising politician from Chicago, had raised the 23rd, which he called the 'Irish Brigade', from among his constituents there. The regiment had been mustered on 15 June and had performed garrison duty in St Louis and Jefferson City. It was as yet unblooded. Davis told Mulligan to gather Missouri troops on the way to Lexington. One of these units was Colonel Thomas A. Marshall's cavalry regiment, which Davis believed to be besieged by Confederates at Tipton, Missouri. If necessary, Davis was to fight his way into Tipton and then bring Marshall's troopers out with him on the way to Lexington.

One of the most important duties assigned to Mulligan while he was in Lexington was to save the funds in the banks, to prevent them falling into southern hands. Depriving the south of money to pay troops and buy equipment was vital to northern success.

In fact, Davis' information was inaccurate. When the 23rd reached Tipton it found neither Marshall's cavalrymen nor Confederates. So, after a short rest, the regiment continued its march to Lexington. On 9 September they reached their destination, where they found Marshall's regiment along with other local units. After marching north through the town they camped on the campus of the Masonic College on the river bluffs. The college, founded in the 1840s, was centred on a three-storey brick building with white pillars surrounding its front porch. A boarding house lay some 50 yards west of the college, and a three-storey brick home belonging to Dr Oliver Anderson lay west of that. Down below the college, on the river bank, were a hemp warehouse and dock.

On 1 September a breathless messenger brought a letter from Colonel Everett Peabody of the 13th Missouri Home Guards, stating that Price's men, some 10,000 strong, were on the way from Warrensburg. Peabody's men had been sent there to seize bank funds, in accordance with orders from Frèmont, and were retreating in the face of overwhelming odds. They burned bridges behind them.

The colonels present in Lexington gathered in a candlelit room in the college building to discuss what to do. In addition to Mulligan of the 23rd, there were the commanders of troops from the 8th, 25th and 27th Missouri Volunteers, the 13th and 14th Missouri Home Guards, Berry's and Van Horn's Missouri Cavalry, and the 1st Cavalry. In all, the force totalled some 2,780 men and seven cannon. None of them was prepared for lengthy fighting, the troops having only the standard 40 rounds of ammunition contained in the issue cartridge box, and a haversack filled with several days' supply of rations. Mulligan, who had the senior commission and hence command of the entire garrison, had little use for the Missouri troops, who he described as 'in peace invincible; in war invisible'.[10]

Price obviously had more men and guns. The Missouri officers strongly urged Mulligan to abandon the city. Two boats, a ferry and a steamboat, were docked below the college. They could carry the men in the garrison and allow a safe retreat. It was the only sensible thing to do, the officers argued. Mulligan, however, had been ordered, in his words, to 'go to Lexington, and hold it at all hazards'.[11] He had been assured that he would be

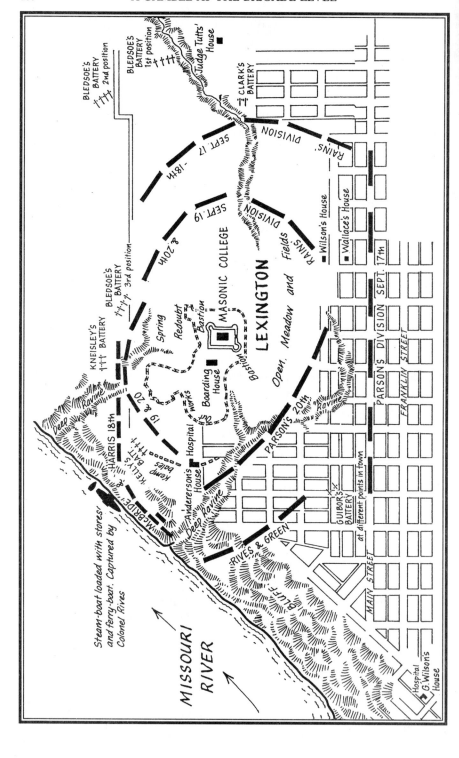

reinforced if Price attacked the town. After hearing the advice of his subordinates, who were unanimously in favour of retreat, he announced his intentions. He would not do the safe, conventional thing and retreat. He would gamble that his men could hold on long enough, despite short supplies and untrained troops, to be reinforced. 'We'll fight 'em,' he said.[12]

Mulligan sent a courier to Jefferson City, Davis' headquarters, announcing his plans to stay and urgently requesting reinforcements or, if that were not possible, at least rations to last through a siege. 'Strengthen us; we will require it,' he wrote to Davis, who received the message on the 12th.[13] Davis forwarded the message to his headquarters in St Louis. Back came orders that Davis send two of his regiments towards Lexington. He was also to have troops under Brigadier General Samuel D. Sturgis at Mexico, Missouri, and others under Brigadier General John Pope in north-central Missouri, start marching to Lexington. Then word was sent to Mulligan that help would arrive by the 18th. Meanwhile, the Lexington garrison went to work, throwing up defences and digging entrenchments on College Hill. A native of the town described their efforts:

> The college is on a bluff about 200 feet above the lower water-mark and from 15 to 30 feet higher than on North or Main street. Third street runs along the top of the bluff. Close to and surrounding the college building was a rectangular fort of sods and earth about 12 feet thick and 12 feet high; with bastions at the angles and embrasures for guns. At a distance of 200 to 800 feet was an irregular line of earthworks protected by numerous traverses, occasional redoubts, a good ditch, trous-de-loup, wires, etc., etc. Still farther to the west and north were rifle-pits. The works would have required 10,000 or 15,000 men to occupy them fully. All the ground from the fortifications to the river was then covered with scattering timber. The spring just north and outside of fortifications was in a deep wooded ravine, and was the scene of some sharp skirmishing at night owing to the attempts of the garrison to get water there when their cisterns gave out.[14]

In all, the fortifications covered some 15 acres of ground.

Mulligan turned the Anderson house, some 80 yards outside his entrenchments, into the garrison hospital. Regimental surgeons set up tables for operations, and hospital stewards laid out what medicine they had and gathered water for washing wounds.

While most of Mulligan's men turned labourers and dug out entrenchments, a handful went through the town, trying to find all the food they could. Their mission, however, was largely a failure. The men would have to live on the small amount of hard tack and meat they had brought in their haversacks. Mulligan also had the money he did get out of the town bank buried in a hole under his tent floor.

At the same time, Mulligan sent out two 6lb cannon and some troops under Peabody to take up position near the covered bridge south of the town, where he expected the Confederates to arrive. That night passed slowly. 'It was a night of fearful anxiety,' Mulligan wrote, 'none knew at what moment the enemy would be upon our devoted little band, and the hours passed in silence.'[15]

In the afternoon of 12 September, a stormy day that made marching hard and restricted visibility, Price's advance troops came into contact with Federal cavalry. Peabody immediately sent back a messenger to Mulligan's headquarters in the college. 'Colonel, the enemy are pushing across the bridge in overwhelming force,' he announced.[16] Mulligan ran to the top of the building and peered south through his field glasses. He could see them clearly, even to a mounted officer he believed to be Price, who was riding up and down his lines and ordering his men on.

The cavalry fell back, and the Confederates came on. Mulligan ordered Company K of his own regiment and two companies of the 13th to the bridge, where they halted Price's cavalry. He next saw Price bring his men round the flank of the Union position, and ordered his Illinois cavalry and the last six companies of the 13th to positions among the tombstones of a cemetery. The Federals there surprised and pushed back Price's men before Confederate artillery could get into action. The rest of Mulligan's men continued their gigantic building project.

At about 3 p.m. the Confederate artillery arrived and immediately went into line of battle. Its opening shots were aimed at a group of Federal officers watching from right outside the rising breastworks, and did no real harm. Federal artillery returned fire. A lucky shot hit one Confederate gun, knocking it over and blowing up a caisson filled with artillery ammunition in a spectacular explosion. The Federals held fast. Although Price's men continued to press until dusk, they got nowhere.

Price, a bit surprised by the Federal strength, retired to the town fairgrounds, some two miles south of town. There he decided to wait for all of his infantry before attacking further. During the night it rained even harder than the day before, and the weather was miserable on the morning of the 13th. Trenches began to fill with water, and shovels loaded with heavy, wet dirt were heavier than they had been with dry dirt. Wool uniforms soaked up the rain like sponges. Men lucky enough to have black slick rubberised ponchos and raincoats sweated under them. Others just got wet. The luckiest Union troops were those assigned to take powder that Mulligan's foragers had found in the area and make cartridges for the artillery. This operation took place in the basement of the college building, so the men were dry and comfortable. Others built a foundry and began casting shot for the cannon. In all, they cast balls for some 150 rounds of canister; shotgun-like rounds that had a deadly effect on closely packed infantry formations.

Price held off on Friday the 13th, happily for his more superstitious troops if not for many of his more eager subordinates, who wanted to attack immediately, and over the weekend as well. Within the growing entrenchments around the college, many of Mulligan's men rested from their labours for a brief time on Sunday to hear mass celebrated by the regimental chaplain of the 23rd, Father Thaddeus J. Butler. As the priest was reciting the ancient words of the mass, however, his words were punctuated by the rifle-fire of pickets on both sides.

At least one Confederate sharpshooter was a civilian from the Lexington area. He spent the nights at home, coming out every morning with a carefully packed lunch, a rifle, and ammunition. He would fire away all morning, then retire to a safe position at noon to eat his lunch. That done, he would return to the front lines to fire until the rest of his ammunition ran out, or darkness made rifle-sighting difficult. Then he would go home for a comfortable rest in his own bed, returning the next day.

The Confederate forces, meanwhile, gradually extended their lines so that they entirely surrounded the Federal position. Confederate artillery went into position and began firing on the Federals, and especially on the college building itself. Confederate battery commander Captain Hiram M. Bledsoe had a fire built near his guns so that he could heat solid iron cannonballs. His guns then fired these red-hot balls at the college building in an effort to burn it to the ground, much as sailors fired heated cannonballs at wooden ships to destroy them.

One of his first successful shots penetrated a wall and rolled to rest on the floor. Colonel C. R. Van Horn noticed smoke rising from the charring wood around the ball. He grabbed a shovel and scooped up the ball, tossing it out of a window to the ground, where it sizzled harmlessly on the earth below. A young soldier saw Van Horn's action and told him, 'I can do that'. Almost as he spoke, another of Bledsoe's 'hot shots' crashed through a wall and rolled to a stop on the floor. The youngster took the shovel from Van Horn, scooped up the ball and dropped this one, too, out of the window. Van Horn gave the young man the permanent job of 'hot shot scooper', showing him where to hide to be protected from enemy shot while watching for the flash from Bledsoe's battery that indicated a hot ball was on the way, so he could be ready to scoop it up after it had come to rest. Catching a slowly rolling cannonball was a temptation that had hospitalised many men with broken limbs. The soldier spent the rest of the bombardment removing hot shot from the college building. Bledsoe's efforts were all in vain.[17]

Mulligan expected the Confederates to launch their attack early on the morning of Monday the 16th, so he got his troops up early and had them ready. But no attack came. Price was still feeling out the Federal position.

Not until the morning of the 18th was Price ready to make his move. His reserve ammunition train had finally caught up with him, having been left behind in the rapid march his men had made to reach Lexington. His men were now largely rested after that hard march. Price moved out. He sent two regiments under Colonel Benjamin Rives to a point west of Mulligan's entrenchments, along the river bank. These troops captured the two boats on the river and locked Mulligan's men in Lexington as safely as if they were in a prison. Mulligan now had no choice; he would have to fight or surrender.

Then Price's men came on directly at Mulligan's lines. Mulligan wrote:

> They came as one dark moving mass, their guns beaming in the sun, their banners waving, and their drums beating – everywhere, as far as we could see, were men, men, men, approaching grandly. Our men stood firm behind the breastworks, none trembled or paled, and a solemn silence prevailed. As Father Butler went round among them, they asked his blessing, received it with uncovered heads, then turned and sternly cocked their muskets.[18]

Father Butler then went to the hospital in the Anderson house to wait for the anticipated wounded.

All of the cannon on the Confederate side opened up, to be answered by the Federal guns. Confederate infantry quickly swarmed around the Anderson house and occupied it, the Federal medical personnel, the wounded and Father Butler being taken prisoner. The troops then climbed the stairs to the third floor and began firing into Federal entrenchments from the windows, while other Confederates swung out on to the roof to take even more commanding firing positions. Their accurate fire began to take its toll in the unprotected trenches, where the Federals huddled as close to the ground as possible for protection.

Mulligan dashed out to where his troops were taking casualties and ordered the nearest company, a Missouri Home Guard unit, to attack the brick building, but the men refused to move from the relative safety of the trenches. It was the same with the men of the next company he found, one of the 14th Missouri. Finally he came to the company commander of one of his own companies, a company called 'The Montgomery Guards', and ordered them to attack. Mulligan reported:

> Their captain admonished them to uphold the gallant name they bore, and the order was given to charge. They started; at first quick, then double-quick, then on a run, then faster. Still the deadly fire poured into their ranks. But on they went; a wild line of steel, and, what is better than steel, irresistible human will. They reached the hospital, burst open the door, without shot or shout, until they encountered the enemy within, whom they hurled out and sent flying down the hill.[19]

No quarter was given to the Confederates within, whom the Federals assumed had violated the unwritten rules of warfare by firing from a hospital. The fighting was hand-to-hand and desperate, but in a short time the Federals had cleared the building. Such an important key to the Federal defence could not remain free of southern attention for long, however. At about 8.00 p.m. Price ordered yet another attack on the building, and this time took it once and for all. Then he put his men to work digging entrenchments on either side of the building to make it even safer from attack. Other Confederates brought up a number of bales of hemp they had found nearby, part of the inventory of local ropemaking factories, and laid them in a line, forming a wall around the house. Before rolling some of the heavy bales up the hill into position, the troops soaked them in the river so that they would not catch fire from enemy bullets. Alternatively, they soaked dry bales once they were placed in position.

A Confederate colonel wrote:

These portable hemp-bales were extended, like the wings of a par-
tridge net, so as to cover and protect several hundred men at a time,
and a most terrible and galling and deadly fire was kept up from them
upon the works of the enemy by my men. I divided my forces into
reliefs and kept some three hundred of them pouring in a heavy fire
incessantly upon the enemy, supplying the places of weary with fresh
troops.[20]

By then it was getting dark, and Price, satisfied with the progress his men
had made that day, called off the attack. His men settled down in the positions they occupied at the end of the day's fighting.

That night was especially hard on the Federals. Dead horses just outside
and within their lines were putrefying, and their smell drifted across the
trench lines. An even a more pressing problem, however, was lack of water.
Owing to the shortage of able-bodied workmen, Mulligan had ruled
against digging wells before the siege began. There were two cisterns at the
college, but the cavalry had earlier watered their horses there, and little
water was left. There were two springs at the foot of the bluffs, one on the
north and one on the south, but the Confederates captured them early in
the siege and had them well within their guarded lines. River water was no
longer available, thanks to Price's earlier move of sending his two regiments
to capture the two boats.

That evening Mulligan saw the straits his men were in for want of water:
'Our supply of water had given out and the scenes in the hospital were fearful to witness, wounded men suffering agonies from thirst and in their
frenzy wrestling for the water in which the wounded had bathed,' he wrote.
He added that his fighting men also suffered, because 'all day long they
fought without water, their parched lips cracking, their tongues swollen,
and the blood running down their chins when they bit their cartridges and
the saltpetre entered their blistered lips'.[21]

The men received some relief when rain began to fall. 'On the morning
of the 19th it rained heavily for about two hours, saturating our blankets,
which we wrung out into our canteens for drinking,' a Federal soldier
wrote.[22] Other soldiers put out their hats upside down, frying pans, bowls
from the college, and waterproof blankets to catch as much water as they
could in the downpour.

The men looked for additional relief on the 19th, as they had been
promised that reinforcements would arrive on that day. The relief column

was on the way. Sturgis waited at the Hannibal and St Joseph Railroad depot at Utica, some 40 miles from Lexington, until he had gathered enough wagons to carry his supplies. Then, on the morning of the 18th, he set off for the river. From there he planned to head directly towards Lexington. Unfortunately for the Union cause, Price's men had intercepted the message coming to Mulligan to advise him of the relief column. Price, in this instance surely a better general than Sturgis, quickly detached some 3,000 of his men and placed them under the command of Brigadier General Monroe M. Parsons, giving him orders to meet and beat the Federal column.

By the evening of the 18th Sturgis, who was greatly concerned by reports of the size of Price's force, began to hear gunfire from Lexington, some 15 miles distant. He decided that his forces could not beat Price's, and that he would be unable to lift the siege. He turned the head of his column away from Lexington, heading to Fort Leavenworth, Kansas. On the way he told one of his aides to listen to the number of dogs barking continuously on the other side of the river, a sure sign, he said, of a huge force of men there. He was convinced that only luck and rapid marching allowed his column to reach the upper ferries and cross the river into the safety of Kansas without loss.

Parsons, in the meantime, saw that Sturgis' men presented no threat and returned to his original position, having left some scouts to make sure that Sturgis had left the area. There would be no relief for the garrison at Lexington. Sturgis' retreat ensured that Mulligan would lose his gamble, unless the Federals were to gather another, stronger relief column – and quickly.

Mulligan, however, did not know that. The Union troops continued exchanging shots with the Confederates who, with part of their force up the river preparing to halt Mulligan's reinforcements, chose not to renew their attack that day. As evening fell, the Federals sent a flag of truce, asking if they could remove the wounded and sick from within their lines to the relative safety of the city. The two sides negotiated before they ceased fire and allowed the Federals to bring out 122 patients, complete with their surgeons. The Federal patients were met by a number of local doctors who were Union sympathizers and helped the army surgeons.

The next dawn revealed a cloudy but cool day. That morning a Confederate officer, whose name is lost to history but who surely must have had some formal military training, looked out over the entire scene. In a typical siege of the period, the besieging force pushed ever closer to the enemy's lines by rolling large wicker baskets called *gabions* in front of the diggers of trenches, towards the enemy's fortifications. The *gabions* protected the workmen behind them so that new trenches could be dug closer to the besieged fortifications. Something in this officer's mind suddenly clicked; the hemp bales piled up as a wall around the Anderson house were in effect ready-made *gabions*. Soaked wet so they would not catch fire, they could be rolled towards the Union lines, protecting the attacking force behind them as the Confederates neared the Union position.

Hurriedly he passed on his suggestion, and it was eagerly accepted. Men ran to the river, returned with filled pails and splashed water over the hemp bales. Then some men started rolling the bales towards the Union line, while others followed with loaded muskets with fixed bayonets. Above them all waved Price's colours. Every few yards the Confederates would halt, poke their muskets over the tops of the bales and fire. Some would provide covering fire for others who were rolling their bales forward. These would then halt a bit ahead of their protectors and fire while the men in the rear rolled their bales to a new position ahead of the men now firing.

The Union soldiers watched in horror for a second, then opened their heaviest fire yet on the rolling wall of hemp bales. 'All our efforts could not retard the advance of these bales,' Mulligan wrote. 'Round-shot and bullets were poured against them, but they would only rock a little and then settle back. Heated shot were fired with the hope of setting them on fire, but they had been soaked and would not burn.'[23] The slow Confederate advance proceeded throughout the morning hours.

In the meantime, another group of Confederates charged a small redoubt built around a single cannon on the north-west corner of Mulligan's lines. The Federal infantry, eager to get close to their enemy, leaped over the earth walls and charged right into the advancing Confederates. After several minutes of hand-to-hand combat both sides fell back, leaving several dead and wounded Federals to mark where they had fought. A Federal in this outpost, looking back and seeing his wounded comrades, raised a white piece of material and stepped over the redoubt walls. He was met by a Confederate, of whom he asked permission to bring the wounded back. This was granted, and a ceasefire began at this point on the field.

Combatants elsewhere on the field noticed the white flag over the Federal redoubt and the lack of firing there. They assumed that a general truce was in effect, and the firing slowly began to cease. Other white flags appeared elsewhere on the field. Price, thinking the Federals might be surrendering, sent a note to Mulligan, asking him the reason for the white flags and lack of firing.

'General,' Mulligan wrote on the back of Price's note, 'I hardly know, unless you have surrendered.'[24] Price assured him that this was not the case, and the commanders on both sides prepared for yet more killing.

But Mulligan's troops were weary of it all. As he looked on, he noticed that yet another of his regiments had raised a white flag, so he ordered his commanders to another council of war in the college. Mulligan summed up the situation: 'Our ammunition was about gone. We were out of rations and had been without water for days, and many of the men felt like giving up the post, which it seemed impossible to hold longer.'[25] Even so, when the vote was taken on fighting or surrendering, there were two Federal officers in favour of holding out, against four in favour of surrendering. This time Mulligan bowed to popular opinion. He sent word to Price that he would negotiate a surrender.

Colonel Thomas L. Snead, of Price's staff, was sent into the Federal lines to negotiate with Mulligan's representative, Colonel Marshall. Snead wrote:

Of course I demanded the unconditional surrender of the post, with its officers and men and material of war. Colonel Marshall hesitated, and at last said that he would have to submit the matter to Colonel Mulligan. As we knew that reinforcements were on the way to Mulligan, and as I feared that Mulligan was only practising a ruse in order to gain time, I said to Colonel Marshall that if the terms which I offered were not accepted within ten minutes, I should return to our lines and order fire to be reopened. He left me, but returned just as the ten minutes were expiring, and said that the surrender would be made as demanded.[26]

Price was now master of some 3,500 men with 3,000 stand of arms, five cannon, two mortars and some 750 horses. Union casualties were 39 dead and 120 wounded, compared with Confederate losses of 25 killed and 72 wounded out of a total force of 18,000. Price also took over the $900,000 that Mulligan had hidden beneath his tent floor, along with some state records and the Missouri Great Seal. Price met Mulligan and his officers, saying: 'You gentlemen have fought so bravely that it would be wrong to deprive you of your swords. Keep them. Orders to parole you and your men will be issued, Colonel Mulligan, without unnecessary delay.'[27]

In fact, Mulligan was not immediately paroled, but was sent south as a prisoner until his release on 30 October. He would return to battle only to die in combat at the Battle of Winchester on 24 July 1864.

Notes

1 Anders, Leslie, *The Eighteenth Missouri*, Indianapolis, Indiana, 1968, p.2.
2 Todd, Frederick P., *American Military Equipage 1851–1872*, Vol. II, New York, 1983, p.949.
3 Long, E. B., *The Civil War Day by Day*, New York, 1971, p.72.
4 *ORs, op. cit.*, Series III, Vol. I, pp.82–83.
5 Long, E. B., *op. cit.*, p.84.
6 Anders, Leslie, *op. cit.*, p.2.
7 *ORs, op. cit.*, p.272.
8 Long, E. B., *op. cit.*, p.112.
9 Long, E. B., *ibid.*, p.114.
10 Hicken, Victor, *Illinois in the Civil War*, Urbana, Illinois, 1991, p.18.
11 Mulligan, Colonel James A., 'The Siege of Lexington, Mo.', *B&L, op. cit.*, Vol. 1, p.307.
12 Smith, Harold F., 'The 1861 Struggle for Lexington, Missouri', *Civil War History*, June 1961, p.159.
13 Smith, Harold F., *ibid.*, p.161.
14 Mulligan, James A., *op. cit.*, p.309.
15 Mulligan, James A., *ibid.*, p.308.
16 Mulligan, James A., *ibid.*, p.308.
17 Smith, Harold F., *op. cit.*, p.105.
18 Mulligan, James A., *op. cit.*, pp.309–310.
19 Mulligan, James A., *ibid.*, pp.310–311.
20 Mulligan, James A., *ibid.*, p.312.
21 Mulligan, James A., *ibid.*, p.311.
22 Mulligan, James A., *ibid.*, p.311
23 Mulligan, James A., *ibid.*, p.312.
24 Mulligan, James A., *ibid.*, p.312.
25 Mulligan, James A., *ibid.*, p.312.
26 Mulligan, James A., *ibid.*, p.313.
27 Mulligan, James A., *ibid.*, p.313.

A GAMBLE AT THE DIVISION LEVEL
The Battle of Port Gibson

THE GAMBLE: *that a Confederate force significantly smaller than an attacking Union force can defeat the Union troops and stall any assault on Vicksburg.*

With the fall of New Orleans in the south and Memphis in the north, the Mississippi River, which cut like a knife north to south, dividing the Confederacy in half, stood in danger of falling entirely into Union hands. The last major position the Confederates held on the river was the fortress town of Vicksburg, Mississippi, which linked the western and eastern Confederacy. In October 1862 Lieutenant General John C. Pemberton was named commander of the Department of Mississippi and East Louisiana, and given the overall job of defending Vicksburg and the Mississippi River.

Opposing him was Major General Ulysses S. Grant, fresh from his hard-fought victory at Shiloh. He had been shelved temporarily after that battle, but on 16 October 1862 he was given command of the Department of Tennessee by President Lincoln, who trusted Grant's fighting abilities. Grant immediately began planning to take Vicksburg.

In fact, the job of taking Vicksburg first went to Major General John A. McClernand, who had been appointed commander of the Army of the Mississippi. McClernand was no soldier by trade, but had been a politician before the war. He had gained his appointment because Lincoln was keen to place important members of his opposition party in positions of power to show a unified front in pursuing the war. Some of these political generals performed acceptably, and won grudging respect from the professional, West Point trained generals who made up most of the high command. McClernand was not one of these: 'I doubted McClernand's fitness,' Grant later wrote.[1] McClernand was routinely disregarded by virtually all professional soldiers, including Grant, who was none the less aware of his presence. But Grant took a telegraph from Washington saying that he was to command all the troops sent to his department, and that he could fight the enemy wherever he pleased, with authority to take over McClernand's army if it came near his. Finally, on 18 December, Grant was ordered to divide his command into four corps, of which McClernand was to command one.

Grant's first idea, the obvious one, was to proceed south towards Vicksburg and take the city from that direction. That way he would maintain his supply and communication lines, via the railroad lines that ran down from northern points. 'Up to this time,' Grant later explained, 'it had been regarded as an axiom in war that large bodies of troops must operate from a base of supplies which they always covered and guarded in all forward movements.'[2]

He first moved via the Mississippi Central Railroad to where Pemberton had dispatched troops to entrenched positions along the Tallahatchie River, north of Oxford, Mississippi. As the Union troops dug in, General Braxton Bragg, then preparing for the Murfreesboro campaign, helped Pemberton by sending cavalry under brilliant cavalry commander Major General N. B. Forrest to destroy Grant's supply lines.

On December 11 Forrest's cavalry moved out, and in a short time had destroyed large sections of the Tennessee railroad. Forrest also threatened the important railhead at Columbus, Kentucky, where vast quantities of supplies were kept and forwarded to Grant's army. Grant wrote:

> This cut me off from all communication with the north for more than a week, and it was more than two weeks before rations or forage could be issued from stores obtained in the regular way. This demonstrated the impossibility of maintaining so long a line of road over which to draw supplies for an army moving in an enemy's country.[3]

Grant's response was to switch his supply base to Memphis. From there equipment would reach his men by going east on the Memphis & Charleston Railroad to Grand Junction. On 20 December Major General Earl Van Dorn, Pemberton's commander on the scene, sent his cavalry, some 3,500 strong, from Grenada, south of Grant's lines, to attack the important Union supply base at Holly Springs. Southern raiders burned over $1 1/2 million dollars' worth of equipment, ammunition and food. Federal cavalry chased Van Dorn's men unsuccessfully, as the southern troopers easily reached the safety of their own lines after the burning.

In the meantime, Pemberton withdrew his men to Vicksburg, just as Major General William T. Sherman approached the city's defensive line.

Sherman went ahead and ordered an attack on Vicksburg's defences. 'The front was very narrow, and immediately opposite, at the base of the hills about three hundred yards from the bayou, was a rebel battery supported by an infantry force posted on the spurs of the hill behind.'[4] Sherman's attack was a failure, some 500 men being left behind, wounded or taken prisoner.

Sherman withdrew, but dug in around the site. His scouts brought reports of reinforcements arriving in Vicksburg, as well as information that McClernand was in the area. Sherman reported to McClernand and discovered that Grant had retreated after the Holly Springs disaster. The two decided that Vicksburg was invincible for a time.

On 17 January Grant arrived at McClernand's headquarters. There he found that 'both the army and navy were so distrustful of McClernand's fitness to command that, while they would do all they could to ensure success, this distrust was an element of weakness. It would have been criminal to send troops under these circumstances into such danger.'[5] Grant decided to assume command of the entire expedition himself, much to McClernand's displeasure.

Grant recalled:

The real work of the campaign and siege of Vicksburg now began. The problem was to secure a footing upon dry ground on the east side of the river from which the troops could operate against Vicksburg. The Mississippi River, from Cairo [Illinois] south, runs through a rich alluvial valley of many miles in width, bound on the east by land running from eighty up to two or more hundred feet above the river. On the west side the highest land, except in a few places, is but little above the highest water. Through this valley the river meanders in the most tortuous way, varying in direction to all points of the compass. At places it runs to the very foot of the bluffs. After leaving Memphis, there are no such highlands coming to the water's edge on the east short until Vicksburg is reached.

The intervening land is cut up by bayous filled from the river in high water – many of them navigable for steamers. All of them would be, except for overhanging trees, narrowness and tortuous course, making it impossible to turn the bends with vessels of any considerable length. Marching across this country in the face of an enemy was impossible ...[6]

Rather than try again from the north, Grant decided to cross the river in the south, below Vicksburg, and come up on the town from the south. He first tried to have a canal cut to transport his troops south past the southern batteries which dotted the riverbanks, but a sudden rise in the river washed out a dam on 7 March, and the useless canal filled up with water before it could be finished. This failure was followed by other attempts to gain a proper foothold, all of which failed. But Grant, known for his stubborn ways, persisted, and, while northern newspapers were writing off the entire expedition as a failure, managed to get McClernand's XIII Corps to New Carthage at the end of March. The XIII Corps was named the army's right wing, and its men began working on roads to get the entire army moving.

By 27 April McClernand's Corps, followed by Major General James Birdseye McPherson's XVII Corps, was at Hard Times. From there Grant had determined to cross the river to the east quickly. On the morning of the 29th he ordered McClernand to get as many of his men as possible into the transports and barges available and be ready cross to the other side. The US Navy, in the meantime, went against Confederate positions in Grand Gulf to clear away the enemy there, after which McClernand's men would cross.

Some 10,000 soldiers huddled in the rag-tag fleet as the Navy's boats bombarded the Confederate position for about $5^{1}/_{2}$ hours. Not a single Confederate gun fell silent, and finally the Navy admitted its failure and withdrew. Grant then determined to land his men at Rodney, Mississippi. However, an escaped slave convinced him that Bruinsburg would be a better point, and on 30 April both corps crossed to that point.

Grant later wrote:

When this was effected I felt a degree of relief scarcely ever equalled since. Vicksburg was not yet taken it is true, nor were its defenders demoralised by any of our previous moves. I was now in the enemy's country, with a vast river and the stronghold of Vicksburg between me and my base of supplies. But I was on dry ground on the same side of the river with the enemy. All the campaigns, labours, hardships and exposures from the month of December previous to this time that had been made and endured, were for the accomplishment of this one object.[7]

In all, Grant had some 33,000 men, while he understood that Pemberton's command numbered some 60,000 men. None the less, Grant went immediately on the offensive in what one historian referred to as 'Grant's Mississippi Gamble'.[8]

His first move was to capture Grand Gulf, and for that reason he ordered McClernand to move on that town. McClernand issued two days' worth of rations and ammunition to his men and then moved out.

To get to Grand Gulf, McClernand's men would first have to pass through Port Gibson, a small town about 10 1/2 miles east of the Mississippi and 22 miles south-west of Vicksburg. It lay near the only bridge that crossed Bayou Pierre, a swampy lowland. Although McClernand's men moved at a reasonably rapid pace, they were not the first to get into the town. The first were Confederate troops sent by the commander of the Grand Gulf defences, Brigadier General John S. Bowen.

Bowen, a graduate of the West Point class of 1853, had been an architect in St Louis, Missouri, before the war. A captain of Missouri militia, he had formed the 1st Missouri Infantry Regiment, and served as its colonel until receiving the wreath of a general on 14 March 1862. He was wounded at Shiloh, but had had little chance to gain glory thereafter. Now would be his chance, but only if he gambled successfully that his smaller force could hold off the Federal force until reinforcements from Pemberton could arrive. It was a gamble that many thought unlikely to succeed, if pure numbers counted for anything. According to *Harper's Weekly*, the small number of troops Bowen could muster 'made victory for him impossible, for Grant almost inevitable'.[9]

Bowen himself realised that the defence of Port Gibson required 'from 15 to 20 thousand men to ensure our success'.[10] As it was, he had 6,300 men available with which to stop a Federal force numbering 23,000. He did not realise that there was such a tremendous difference in numbers in the early hours, although he knew that his force was outnumbered. Still, Bowen did choose to gamble, and to advance to meet Grant's men. Indeed, he even considered attacking the Federals before they could deploy. He telegraphed Pemberton in Vicksburg: 'I have prepared for defence on both sides of Bayou Pierre. The country and the jaded condition of Tracy's and Baldwin's men forbid an advance. If it can be done today, I will do it.'[11]

When word of the Union advance reached Bowen, he ordered his troops out to meet the Federals at Port Gibson. He first sent a brigade of 5,164 men under Brigadier General Martin E. Green on 30 April to do just that. Green was not a professional soldier; a steam sawmill operator, he was not even especially well educated. None the less, he was elected colonel of

Green's Missouri Cavalry Regiment at the war's outbreak, and served so well at the battles of Lexington, Pea Ridge, Iuka and Corinth that he was commissioned a brigadier 21 July 1862.

Bowen had picked good defensive ground for Green's troops. Grant wrote:

> The country in this part of Mississippi stands on edge, as it were, the roads running along the ridges except when they occasionally pass from one ridge to another. Where there are no clearings the sides of the hills are covered with a very heavy growth of timber and with undergrowth, and the ravines are filled with vines and canebrakes, almost impenetrable.

This was quite true at the point where Green placed his men, near where:

> ... the road to Port Gibson divides, taking two ridges which do not diverge more than a mile or two at the widest point. These roads unite just outside the town. This made it necessary for McClernand to divide his force. It was not only divided, but it was separated by a deep ravine of the character above described. One flank could not reinforce the other except by marching back to the junction of the roads.[12]

Moreover, the heavy brush would help equalise forces by breaking up Union formations.

The Federal troops set off for Port Gibson at 5.30 p.m., with the 21st Iowa in the lead. The going was hard in the darkness, over unfamiliar roads. 'In many places the road seems to end abruptly, but when we come to the place we find it turning at right angles, passing through narrow valleys, sometimes through hills, and presenting the best opportunity for the Rebels for defence if they had but known our purpose,' wrote Sergeant Charles A. Hobbs of the 99th Illinois.[13]

The first skirmishers came in contact at about 3.00 a.m. on 1 May, gunshots ringing out in the humid early morning darkness. The only things that could be seen in the inky blackness were the sharp red flares of gunfire. The Federals stopped where they were, to wait until they could see what they faced. When the first Federals took some return fire from pickets, with an exchange of shots, McClernand halted to see what the dawn would reveal. He found in the morning light that the Confederates had a

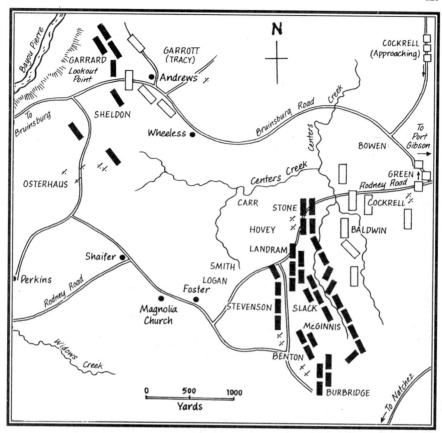

strong natural position. Little did he know that his two divisions were opposed by only some 450 men. As the early morning grey light disclosed the scene, firing became more widespread, and company volleys were heard.

Green's line was drawn up across the southern road at Magnolia Church, about three-quarters of a mile from the town of Port Gibson itself. His regiments included the 6th Mississippi on the right, the 12th Arkansas Sharpshooter Battalion across the road, and the 15th and 21st Arkansas on the left. Five Arkansas sharpshooters were posted in the Shaifer house where Green made his headquarters, 600 yards to the left of the four-gun-strong Pettus Flying Artillery Battery.

While Federal scouts tried to reconnoitre the Confederate positions in the dark, Bowen ordered forward another brigade made up of some 1,500 men from Alabama, under Brigadier General Edward D. Tracy, a 29-year-old lawyer by trade with no military experience before the war, and the

Botetourt Artillery, a Virginia battery, late on 30 April. Battery sergeant James L. Burks recalled their difficult trip into position:

> We reached Big Black about 12 o'clock at night and were engaged from that time until daylight marching about one mile. We had to pass through mud in which the guns would sink up to the axle-trees and the horses mired so deep that they couldn't pull out at all and had to be taken out.
>
> The guns and caissons had to be pulled out by hand, having to take the ammunition chest off before they could be moved at all. We finished ferrying our battery over about daylight on the morning of the 30th and then moved on towards Grand Gulf without stopping to feed the horses.[14]

Tracy's Brigade, which reached the front at about 10.00 a.m., had been posted on the northern road, with a defensive line nearer the spot where the roads forked. Tracy arranged his troops from the left to right, with the 23rd, 31st, 30th and 20th Alabama in line, the centre held by the Botetourt Artillery. In the early morning, as the sun finally rose at about 5.00 a.m., the Federals hit, first on Tracy's line. Lieutenant John S. Bell of the Arkansas sharpshooters recalled:

> We could hear the enemy forming, and it was so still we could hear every command given. Our men had orders not to fire until word was given. Soon we could see their line of skirmishers coming down the road and could hear them say there was no one here, it was only a cavalry scout. When they were within 50 yards the word "fire" was given.[15]

The volley stopped the Federals, who then pulled their troops into line of battle. Their officers placed the 7th Michigan Battery on the road, where they could fire against the Botetourt Artillery. While these shells burst, two brigades of infantry from Indiana, Kentucky and Ohio moved out against the brigades of Green and Tracy, their formations rapidly falling apart in the heavy brush. The men tried to keep their line by watching the silk national and regimental colours in the centre of each regiment bobbing through the brush.

Green's and Tracy's brigades withstood assault after assault, the first hitting them at about 5.30 a.m. Hard pressed, Green sent an urgent message to Tracy asking for a section of artillery and an infantry regiment. Running low of ammunition, Green thought that 'he could not sustain his position on the left fifteen minutes unless reinforced'. He was also worried that a collapse of the Confederate left would trap the troops on the right.[16] Tracy forwarded two 12lb howitzers of the Botetourt Artillery, which soon found themselves in the midst of a hot artillery counterbattery fight with Union 10lb Rodman rifles. In the meantime, Union sharpshooters worked their way round the flanks of Tracy's lines and began picking off artillery horses. Cannoneers began to beg Tracy to be allowed to withdraw their caissons while they had enough horses to do the job. Tracy refused.

At about 8.00 a.m. (the exact time differs in various accounts because most observers were apparently too busy to keep accurate notes), Sergeant Francis G. Obenchain of the Botetourt Artillery approached Tracy with a second request to pull back the battery's caissons. While they were speaking, recalled the sergeant, 'a ball struck him on the back of the neck, passing through. He fell with great force on his face and in falling cried "O Lord!". He was dead when I stooped to him.'[17]

Colonel Isham W. Garrott, commander of the 30th Alabama and another pre-war lawyer with no military experience, assumed command of the brigade's survivors. After the battle, First Lieutenant Calvin Smith, 31st Tennessee Infantry, recorded in his dairy that 'Colonel Garrott of the 23rd Alabama was seen to fall from his horse and was taken prisoner but made his escape which gave glorious news as he was a brave officer and an accomplished gentleman'.[18]

When he first heard firing, Bowen rode towards the front line, arriving there to take personal command at about 8.00 a.m. He reached the battlefront not long after Tracy's death. Quickly assessing the situation, he realised that the Magnolia Church ridge was the commanding point on the field, the key to victory, and ordered the Arkansas sharpshooters to be ready to take the ridge when the Union artillery was silenced. Then, drawing his sabre, he dashed in front of the 6th Alabama and 23rd Mississippi, yelling: 'Follow me! Let's take that battery!'

The Confederates lowered their muskets and ran after him bravely enough, but they just could not take the battery, which was defended by infantry on either side. 'As we went back,' recalled Captain William C. Thompson of the 6th Mississippi, 'we were amazed and shocked to see how many of our men were lying dead or wounded in the path of our advance.'[19]

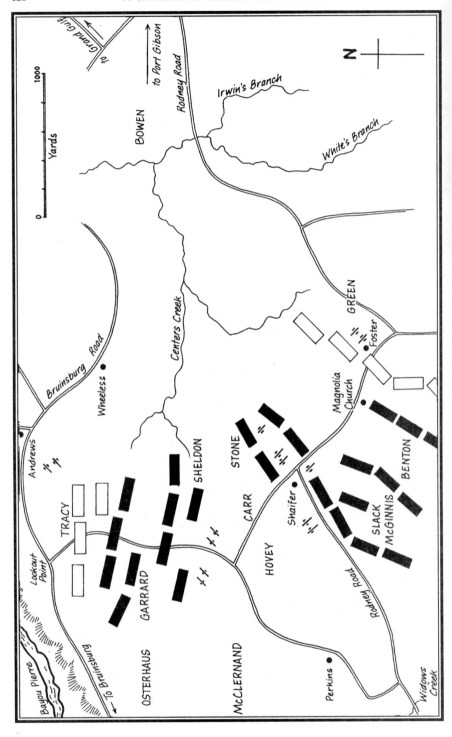

Above: The Federal army advances to the front at the First Bull Run. (*Frank Leslie's Illustrated Newspaper*)

Below: The Confederate line, under Brigadier General Bernard Bee, rallies at the First Bull Run. The flag at the right is a Georgia flag. (*B&L*)

Above: The 1st Virginia Cavalry charges the 11th New York Infantry, which was supporting the Federal artillery on Henry House Hill. Although the cavalry left the infantry relatively intact, the New Yorkers fell back behind the guns, allowing the 33rd Virginia to make its desperate charge. (*Harper's Weekly*)

Left: Colonel Joshua L. Chamberlain, seen here later as a brigadier general, gambled that a bayonet charge would drive off a superior enemy and save the Union left flank at Gettysburg. (National Archives)

Top: The view from the top of Little Round Top. Plum Run lies in the valley below. (*Harper's Weekly*)

Above: The *Arkansas* passes through the Federal fleet on its way south to Vicksburg. (*Frank Leslie's Illustrated Newspaper*)

Right: Lieutenant Commanding Isaac N. Brown, who gambled that he could take the CSS *Arkansas*, despite her weak armour and decrepit engines, all the way to the Gulf of Mexico from far north on the Mississippi River, through an enemy fleet.

Left: Commander John L. Worden, who gambled that inventor John Ericsson's calculations were right, and the USS *Monitor* would not only float but also stand off an ironclad enemy vessel. (Author's collection)

Below: The USS *Monitor* in calm water. In action, the structures on her deck would be removed, save for the pilot house at the bow, allowing her guns full range. (*Harper's Weekly*)

Bottom: The *Monitor* attacks the *Virginia* in the first clash of ironclads, a battle that revolutionised naval warfare. (*B&L*)

Above: Serving inside the turret of the *Monitor* was an unusual experience for seamen of the period. They were comforted when the first direct southern hit on the turret's walls left only a dent. (*B&L*)

Right: Major General J. E. B. Stuart, who gambled that he could ride his brigade all round the huge Army of the Potomac on the Peninsula without significant loss. (Library of Congress)

Above: In a throwback to the old days of knights in armour, a Federal and a Confederate meet in single combat while their friends watch during Stuart's ride around McClellan. (*B&L*)

Left: Colonel James E. Mulligan gambled that he could defend Lexington, Missouri, successfully while waiting to be reinforced in time to save the town. (*Harper's Weekly*)

ove: The scene behind the Union
tifications at the siege of Lexington,
ssouri. (*Harper's Weekly*)

Below: Mulligan's own 23rd Illinois Infantry
charges over the fortifications at Lexington to
recover the hospital area. (*Harper's Weekly*)

ght: Confederates advance
wards the Union position at
xington, Missouri, behind
e protection of dampened
tton bales. (*B&L*)

Above: Union troops advance on Port Gibson. (*Harper's Pictorial History of the Civil War*)

Left: Lieutenant General Thomas J. 'Stonewall' Jackson gambled that he could destroy the Federal army piecemeal at Cedar Mountain. (*Library of Congress*)

Top right: Cedar Mountain is at the left of this scene, drawn from the Union lines.(*B&L*)

Centre right: The scene from the Union lines at the Battle of Cedar Mountain shows how that mountain, centre and left, commanded the battlefield. (*Harper's Weekly*)

Right: Federal troops sweep through the woods on the Confederate right, which had been poorly reconnoitred before the action began, smashing the famed Stonewall Brigade and almost losing Jackson the battle. (*Frank Leslie's Illustrated Newspaper*)

Above: Federal troops assault the fortifications at Secessionville, South Carolina. (*Frank Leslie's Illustrated Newspaper*)

Below: Lieutenant Colonel David Morrison, 79th New York Infantry, reaches the top of the Confederate works at Secessionville and fires his revolver into the Confederates in their fort. Moments later the colonel was shot in the head. (*Frank Leslie's Illustrated Newspaper*)

Right: Major General Lewis Wallace, who gambled to buy time to build up Washington's defences by fighting the Battle of Monocacy. (*Harper's Weekly*)

Below: Major General John B. Magruder fortified Yorktown, centre, and the line south across the Peninsula, then gambled that he could defend that line with his small force of troops. This sketch of the Confederate works was supposedly made by a Federal officer of Topographical Engineers. (*Harper's Weekly*)

Top left: Magruder used such ic ploys as wooden non and stuffed dummies luff the Union army. (*B&L*)

ntre left: A view from the deral line towards the nfederate works near rktown. (*Harper's Weekly*)

ttom left: Despite the use tethered balloons for aerial servation, McClellan's army led to discover Magruder's uff at Yorktown. (*Harper's eekly*)

bove: McClellan halted his rive on Richmond in order to uild these fortifications and et siege to an army that was ctually much smaller than his t Yorktown. (*B&L*)

Right: Major General William . Sherman gambled that he could safely take an nsupplied army completely through enemy territory. (Author's collection)

Bottom right: Sherman's men became adept at rapidly destroying long sections of railroad lines; lines that the poorly industrialised south was unable to repair. (*B&L*)

Left: Apart from food carried by Sherman's men, most of the food eaten by the army was acquired by its 'bummers', infantrymen mounted on captured horses and mules who ranged the countryside looking for hidden foodstuffs. (*Frank Leslie's Illustrated Newspaper*)

Centre left: Federal troops destroyed wherever they went. This was the state prison at Milledgeville, which Sherman's men destroyed. The Union troops recruited a prisoner company there for their service. (*Frank Leslie's Illustrated Newspaper*)

Below: Federal troops on the edges of the huge column made by Sherman's army not only acquired their food, but looted widely. Southerners buried their worldly goods to save them, but African Americans often revealed the hiding places.

Right: Thousands of newly freed slaves, along with the comical group of lame and halt, followed Sherman's army as it headed towards Savannah. (*Harper's Weekly*)

Centre right: Captain David Farragut, who gambled that he could bring a Union fleet past a line of Confederate gunboats, passive defences and forts along the Mississippi to capture New Orleans. (*Author's collection*)

Below: On the left is Fort Jackson, while in front of the Union ships lies the chain of hulks designed to prevent an attack on the city. (*Frank Leslie's Illustrated Newspaper*)

Top: The second division of Farragut's fleet enters the channel between the forts. The *Manassas*, a turtle-backed ironclad, attacks from the left. (*Frank Leslie's Illustrated Newspaper*)

Above: Fire rafts, which the Confederates set alight and let drift into the Federal fleet, posed a threat, so the USS *Westfield* was assigned the job of extinguishing them. (*Frank Leslie's Illustrated Newspaper*)

Right: Someone unfamiliar with the design of the *Manassas* drew this picture of the Confederate ironclad with a fire raft hitting Farragut's flagship, the USS *Hartford*. Yet the picture captures the desperation of the moment. (*Frank Leslie's Illustrated Newspaper*)

Garrott's new command fell back to their original position, and there they hung on, but Union pressure increased and the Confederate line slowly began to fall back. By 11.00 a.m., however, the Federal troops, under Brigadier General Peter J. Osterhaus, had only pushed the Alabama brigade back about a thousand yards, past Magnolia Church. In the process the Alabamians had lost two cannon of the Botetourt Artillery to the 11th Indiana Regiment, whose men grimly swung the captured guns around and then opened up on the retreating Confederates.

Help came with the arrival of another brigade that Bowen had ordered up, troops from Mississippi and Louisiana led by Brigadier General William E. Baldwin. Baldwin was yet another non-professional among the ranks of the Confederate generals. He had been a book and stationery seller in South Carolina before the war, although he had been interested in military affairs and had served in a volunteer militia company for many years before entering the Confederate service. This made him probably the most experienced of the amateur Confederate generals who had taken up their trade since the war began, compared with many of their Federal counterparts, who had long years of service in the regular Army of the United States in addition to US Military Academy training.

Bowen may not have been a professional, but even he realised that the amount of firing along his lines that morning meant that he had to bolster his line. He called for troops from Grand Gulf to move up immediately, although that post was also threatened. William Chambers of the 46th Mississippi Infantry was among the reinforcements passing through the town of Port Gibson, where civilians realised they would soon be in the way of a battle. He wrote:

In the streets all was confusion. Men with pale faces were running hither and thither, some with arms and seeking a command, women sobbing on every side, children in open-eyed wonder clinging to their weeping mothers not understanding the meaning of it all, and negroes with eyes protruding like open cotton bolls were jostling each other and everybody else and continuously asking about "dem Yankees".
The ladies cheered us through their tears and besought us to drive the invaders from their homes. One lady while she prayed Heaven to protect us, said we felt as near to her as though we were her own sons going forth to battle. The wounded, too, were meeting us, some in vehicles and some on litters, and many a poor fellow with a shattered

limb or a gaping wound would wildly hurrah for the "brave Mississippians".[20]

Baldwin's troops were weary, having just marched the 44 miles from Vicksburg at quick time. The entire march had taken 27 hours. At first, wrote one man of the 46th Mississippi:

> The men were wonderfully elated. Again and again we made the echoes ring with our shouts. Jest and repartee were heard on every side. But physical fatigue will dampen the ardour of the most elastic spirit, and as the long hours dragged by with no orders save "close up!" the enthusiasm seemed to die away and a great weariness of limb overtook us.[21]

Bowen left one regiment on the Grand Gulf River front, while other troops of the Missouri Brigade were stationed along the bluffs of Grand Gulf as a reserve. The 1st and 4th Missouri Infantry Regiments, with a battery, were sent to serve as guards for a crossing on the Bayou Pierre, north-west of Port Gibson. The 3rd, 5th and 6th Missouri Regiments, with a section of Landis' battery and another Missouri battery, Guibor's, rushed as reinforcements to Port Gibson itself.

Baldwin's brigade arrived just as Bowen's charge failed and he reinforced Garrott's line with the 6th Missouri, which was positioned on the left of a new line posted along Willow Creek, to extend the line and prevent Federals working their way round the flank.

On the Union side, Grant himself arrived on the field at about 10.00 a.m. and took a quick ride along the line. 'On the right the enemy, if not being pressed back, was at least not repulsing our advance. On the left, however, Osterhaus was not faring so well. He had been repulsed with some loss.'[22]

On the Confederate side, Green's brigade continued to take heavy losses. Federals dashed forward and, despite heavy casualties, broke into their line. The Pettus Flying Artillery managed to limber up and retire intact. At first the Botetourt Artillery kept the Federals at bay by firing double canister, but soon blue-coated infantrymen were wielding their musket butts like clubs among the southern guns. Most of the guns were captured at that point. The Federals left the road, worked their way through and pushed the southerners back to a second line astride the Rodney Road. There they were reinforced by Baldwin's troops and the regiments from Missouri under Colonel

Francis M. Cockrell. Bowen assigned command of the new line to Baldwin and ordered Green to go personally and take command from Garrott. Men with time to glance at their pocket watches saw that it was about 10,00 a.m.

Garrott needed help. Grant recalled:

As soon as the road could be cleared of McClernand's troops I ordered up McPherson, who was close upon the rear of the 13th corps, with two brigades of Logan's division. This was about noon. I ordered him to send one Brigade (General John E. Smith's was selected) to support Osterhaus, and to move to the left and flank the enemy out of his position.[23]

The additional Federal troops, in particular the 120th Ohio Infantry, now assaulted the right line of the Alabama brigade. 'This is hot,' remarked the commander of the section of the Botetourt Artillery to Sergeant Obenchain.[24] Cannoneer after cannoneer fell, badly wounded or dead. 'Lieutenants Peters and Douthat [were] killed by the same shell,' a battery member recalled, 'Lieutenant Peters having upper front part of his head and Douthat back part of his head carried away.'[25] Men along the Confederate line could see more Union colours in the distance, and mounted officers were also able to see long columns of blue coated troops, indicating that large numbers of enemy reinforcements were on their way.

The remaining guns of the Botetourt Artillery, now commanded by Sergeant Obenchain, were quickly hooked to their limbers and brought back to a post half a mile behind the Confederate line. The Union success threatened to smash the line on Bowen's right flank. If they moved quickly along the northern road they could capture the bridges over Bayou Pierre and cut Bowen's troops off from Vicksburg. The capture of Bowen's command would greatly reduce Pemberton's defensive forces.

Bowen telegraphed back to Pemberton:

We have been engaged in a furious battle since daylight, losses very heavy. General Tracy is killed... We are out of ammunition for cannon and small-arms, the ordnance train of the reinforcements not being here. They outnumber us trebly. There are three divisions against us. My whole force is engaged, except three regiments on Big Black, Bayou Pierre, and Grand Gulf.

Pemberton, who made no real effort to help his subordinate, said that he had ordered up two brigades from Jackson for additional reinforcements, but 'it may be some time, as the distance is great. You had better whip them before he [Brigadier General William Loring, brigade commander] reaches you.' Bowen's reply, sent to Pemberton at 3.00 p.m., was: 'I still hold my position. We have fought 20,000 men since dawn, besides skirmishing last night. They are pressing me hard on the right. My centre is firm; the left is weak. When can Loring get here?' There was silence from the Vicksburg end of the telegraph line.[26]

The colonel commanding the 6th Missouri, Eugene Erwin, sized up the situation. 'It was apparent,' he said, 'that unless some assistance was afforded them [the Alabama troops under Green] they would be driven from their position. I therefore felt that a prompt action was necessary.'[27] Taking advantage of the fluid situation, Erwin ordered his men to fix bayonets and then ordered his line 'Forward, march'. His troops caught the Federal forces at their most vulnerable, as they were coming up in column and had yet to deploy into line. Some Federals turned the cannon they had captured earlier on the advancing 6th, but in vain. The Confederates soon overran the battery, whose horses had been shot, preventing the guns being limbered up and withdrawn. The colour bearer of the 6th fell, shot, and Private William E. Franklin scooped up the colour and dashed forward with the rest of the regiment.

In a matter of minutes the Missouri troops had pushed the Federals back into the tangled underbrush of tall magnolias, briar and cane patches, and cypress draped with Spanish moss. But Erwin, overcome with the heat of battle, did not halt his troops. He led them on through the brush, his bright sword swinging. In what the brigade historian calls a 'most audacious gamble', the regiment charged on. 'With one regiment I charged the whole left wing of the Federal army,' Erwin later bragged.[28] He also effectively reduced the strength of that part of the Confederate line by one regiment -- some 400 men -- who were greatly needed to help defend the overall position. Erwin's move was a gamble, but it was ill-conceived.

What remained of the regiment's formation after its charge and fighting amidst the captured battery fell completely apart in the ravines and heavy underbrush. It virtually ceased to exist as a fighting unit owing to Erwin's blunder. The right division, or wing, lost contact with the colour company and the left. The left, personally directed by Erwin, pressed on after the retreating Federals through the bushes and vines. The right, commanded by the regiment's major, Stephen Cooper, slowed down as Cooper tried to keep in control of his company commanders. Finally, Cooper, having no word of the rest of the regiment, told his wing to work their way back to where they had started from. Heading eastward, he eventually reached higher ground with his wing fairly intact, and linked up with one of the other battle lines still engaged. Still others from the regiment straggled off and were not seen again during the battle.

Eventually, Erwin's wing of the 6th emerged into an open field at the bottom of a hill just south of the Bruinsburg Road, in the gap between Green's and Tracy's brigades. Hardly had they reached this position when they came under fire from the 49th Indiana, which formed up and charged towards the top of the hill on which stood the Wheeless House. Realising that if the Federals took the house his men would be downhill and exposed to fire from a protected force, Erwin, too, ordered his men to double-time up the hill and take the house. According to the colonel of the Indiana troops: 'We were about one minute too fast for them'.[29] Erwin had made yet another mistake, as his men now came under fire from the Federals all around the house, outbuildings and fences. Falling on all sides, his men ran to re-form behind an adjacent ridge, apparently west of the house.

There they ducked behind trees and the ridge itself and opened fire on the pursuing Federals. 'We held them in check for an hour and a half, they on one side of a very narrow ridge and we on the other, within 10 or 20 yards of each other.'[30] Erwin sent a messenger back to the main line, asking for reinforcements to hold his position. The messenger apparently fell on the way, because Bowen did not even know that the 6th had got so badly out of position and was in such a terrible situation. Not only did reinforcements not arrive, therefore, but the order which surely would have come had the general known of the 6th's plight, instructing them to withdraw as quickly as possible, did not come. Meanwhile, the hard-pressed soldiers of the 6th steadily fired away their last rounds of ammunition.

Even had he known of the plight of the 6th, Bowen could not have sent reinforcements. His entire front was hard pressed as the Union commanders threw more and more troops at the grey line, and the Confederates were becoming exhausted after eight hours of steady fighting in the hot sun. William Pitt Chambers of the 46th Mississippi had just been formed into line along the left of the road, with a small stream in front of him, when he saw one of those odd incidents that happen from time to time:

Esterling being weak from his recent illness, had been unable to keep up in our forced march. Coming up a little later utterly exhausted, he sat down by a tree. When the bullets began to whistle about us he took his gun by the muzzle to draw it to him. The hammer struck the tree, the cap exploding and the whole charge struck his right arm, literally tearing it to fragments from the waist to above the elbow. Never will I forget the horror-stricken face as he cried, "Oh! Pitt, I have ruined my arm!". Seeing his clothes burning I asked Crawford who stood near him to extinguish the flame. Asking for water, he fell fainting as I reached him, but revived as the water was placed to his lips. He was placed on a litter, borne to the rear and I never saw him again.[31]

Bowen had only two regiments, the 3rd and 5th Missouri Regiments, in reserve, and at about 1.00 p.m. he sent them with a section of artillery to the heavy underbrush at the Irwin Branch of Center's Creek. It was a move that one historian of the battle has called 'a long-shot gamble'.[32] The historian of the Missouri Brigade agrees, calling it 'a desperate gamble'. Their mission was to turn the right flank of the Federal forces. As their historian noted in the brigade history:

On few occasions in the Civil War had so few troops on either side been given a more desperate assignment than Colonel Cockrell's two regiments. General Bowen realised that probably neither he nor many of his Missourians would survive the gamble to win time and salvage an improbable victory from the jaws of defeat.[33]

The two regiments moved off along a watershed covered in brush. Even so they were spotted and their movement reported to the Federal general commanding that flank. As the Confederates slogged on through heavy timber, the Federals prepared their line and waited for the Missourians to emerge. One advantage the Federals had, although they did not know it, was that Bowen had underestimated the length of the Federal line. Indeed, the spot where the regiments were to attack was not on the far Union right at all, but closer to the Union centre. Finally the 700 Confederates halted, dressed their lines as much as possible in a thick canebrake, fixed bayonets and prepared for what a sergeant in their ranks later called 'one of the most desperate charges of the war'.[34] Bowen himself drew his sword and, mounted, led his second attack of the day.

The thick canebrake not only broke up the Confederate linear formation; it also helped them by hiding their attack until they burst out of it only ninety yards from the Federal line. The 29th Wisconsin, the regiment directly in the path of the assault, lost ten killed and 65 wounded that day, most of them at this moment. The 56th Ohio and 47th Indiana were also overrun, their survivors running back in disarray. In fact, the charge hit the flank of a Federal brigade which rapidly gave some ground before the brigade commander shifted two regiments to refuse his flank. But greater Union numbers and superior firepower began to tell. Federal reinforcements filled the gaps in the line and caught the two Missouri regiments in their musket sights. Infantry traded volleys at distances of no more than 20 yards. 'The continuous roll of small guns was appalling, almost drowning the fierce discharge of the artillery,' recalled Colonel Robert S. Bevier of the 5th Missouri. 'The noise was so incessant that no order could be heard.'[35] Federal artillery, some 24 massed guns in all, opened large holes in the Confederate line.

The Confederate attack, Bowen's last gamble, stalled and fell apart. Finally the 5th Missouri fell back into a ravine running parallel with White Branch, from where they returned the Federal fire. Then the 3rd Missouri did the same; two regiments fighting what Bowen estimated as at least twelve Union regiments. Indeed, there were so many Federals arranged against the Confederates that, wrote one, 'the slope in their side was soon covered, it seemed about as thick as they could stand'. A southern journalist wrote: 'The gallant charge of the two regiments of this brigade upon three brigades of the enemy [and] their success in preventing a further advance, or a flank movement of the enemy, I witnessed, and regard as one of the most daring deeds of the war'.[36]

'I did not suspect that *any* of you would get away,' Bowen told the survivors of the charge, 'but the charge *had* to be made, or my little army was lost.'[37]

A few officers of the 5th Missouri tried to rouse their men for another charge, and some of them dashed again at the 29th Wisconsin. Again overwhelming Federal fire forced them back to their defensive line along the canebrake. Bowen called on Baldwin to bring his three regiments forward in another attempt, but Federal artillery broke up their formations before they could get fully aligned. Bowen's final charge was a failure, and now his last reserve was pinned down by overwhelming Federal fire. The front along the Missourian's position turned into a fire-fight, both sides trading shots for almost two hours.

Bowen had made his last play. The Federals now held all the cards. A whole new division under Major General John A. Logan arrived shortly after 4.00 p.m. and deployed immediately into line to bolster the Federal attacks. The Union troops advanced into a 'dense and impenetrable growth of cane' and finally began turning the Confederate right flank.[38] Logan's men rushed into the fight and the Confederate line began to dissolve. The Federals made a concentrated push against both wings of the Confederate line, being successful on the north road, where the Confederate defence fell apart. As Confederate troops began to stream towards the rear, Bowen ordered a general retreat.

Bevier recalled:

By signs only could the retreat be *sounded*. All semblance of organisation was lost. The rush to the rear was active and speedy; and over the low brow of the hill, for fifty feet sheer down, the two regiments tumbled, each man ploughing his individual furrow through the canebrake, to the sore distress of his person and his uniform.

At the very place where we lay so long in the cornfield, our flags were again unfolded and the rallying point established. Out of the three hundred and fifty men that went into the fight, we lost over one hundred. The remnant promptly rallied round the flag. Here we remained until near sundown, the enemy not seeming disposed to follow us up or push their advantage. We retired slowly, and with precision.[39]

Many of the Confederate units maintained good order, leaving behind a skirmish line to protect their columns as they pulled away. The 46th Mississippi, for example, marched the three miles back to town from their final position in column, although at a quick step – minus Company C of the regiment, which had been deployed as skirmishers. Only seven volunteers remained as skirmishers behind the 5th Missouri, and they 'held in check the advance of a whole Fed[eral] Div[ision] after their Regiment had fallen back, expending all their ammunition,' recalled one Confederate officer.[40] All managed to escape without even being wounded.

In the meantime, Colonel Erwin of the forgotten men of the 6th Missouri finally realised his position. 'Gentlemen,' he told his assembled officers as the sun began to sink and the sounds of gunfire grew further away from their position, 'it is necessary to fall out of this. We are being surrounded and are in danger of being captured. We must fall back.'[41] It was a statement he should have made some hours earlier.

Seeing no help around, Erwin briefed his officers on his plan to escape. His men would prepare to file out to the left when he had distracted the enemy. Then he stood up and called out: 'Attention, battalion! Fix bayonets! Forward, double quick, march!' The Federals, many of them only ten yards away, prepared for a charge. In fact the Confederates fled to the left. A lieutenant noted in his diary: 'our regiment made a very narrow escape we had to extricate ourselves by taking to our heels, and moving off by the left flank, under a severe fire'.[42]

Luckily the terrain provided a perfect escape route, Erwin's survivors descending one of the deep ravines that cut the area, even though they were fired upon. However, there were more Federals on what had now become their front, so the men of the 6th halted, gave them a volley and headed towards a gap in their line at the double quick. Many fell as they ran through a cornfield under fire, while another 50 were captured. The survivors dashed between Union units like pinballs in a pinball machine. Erwin was wounded, but finally led his remaining men towards the Bayou Pierre bridges in the evening hours. They were the last Confederates to withdraw from the right wing that day.

The regiment had lost 82 men. Garrott had suffered 272 casualties among the 1,400 troops he had brought into the fight, but he had held out for 11 hours against some 5,000 Federals, inflicting about as many casualties on them as he had taken himself. In all, the Confederates had 68 killed, 380 wounded and 384 missing and presumed captured out of some 7,000 men they had had on the field. The Federal tally was 131 killed, 719 wounded and 25 missing out of 24,000 men.

The Confederates fell back through Port Gibson. Colonel Bevier recalled:

The social festivities of Port Gibson had endeared it to us. The elegant hospitality of its people had constituted the place as an oasis in the desert of our military career. It was, therefore, with sad hearts that the remnants of our regiments slowly, and for the last time, marched through the streets. Again the terrified friends were out to greet us, with tearful eyes and pale faces, wishing us God speed and apprehending the worst of fates in their own future.[43]

Rations for the troops had been sent to Port Gibson, and the civilians cooked a meal for what they hoped would be their victorious army. As it turned out, the Confederate troops fell back so rapidly through the town that they did not eat there. Pitt Chambers of the 46th Mississippi gave a black man by the roadside $5 for three hens, which he fried when the unit finally halted.

Bowen rallied his men at Bayou Pierre's north bank, which they reached at about midnight. 'I am falling back across Bayou Pierre,' he notified Pemberton. 'I will endeavour to hold that position until reinforcements arrive.'[44] Additional reinforcements, too late for the battle even if their small numbers could have done much good, finally reached him there. All night, men crossed over into the Confederate lines, having been cut off from their units during the fight. Bowen waited until all the Confederates who were likely to reach his lines had done so, and then, at about 2.30 a.m., he ordered the suspension bridge burned and withdrew towards Vicksburg. 'We marched back that night to camp and felt thankful that we had escaped as well as we had,' concluded one Confederate lieutenant.[45]

Notes

1 Grant, U. S., *Personal Memoirs*, New York, 1952, p.224.
2 Grant, U. S., *ibid.*, p.220.
3 Grant, U. S., *ibid.*, p.225.
4 Sherman, William T., *Memoirs of William T. Sherman*, New York, 1990, p.314.
5 Grant, U. S., *op. cit.*, p.229.
6 Grant, U. S., *ibid.*, pp.230-231.
7 Grant, U. S., *ibid.*, p.252.
8 Goodman, Al W., Jr., 'Grant's Mississippi Gamble', *America's Civil War*, July 1994, p.51
9 Carter, Samuel, III, *The Final Fortress: The Campaign for Vicksburg 1862-1863*, New York, 1980, p.184.
10 Tucker, Phillip Thomas, *The South's Finest*, Shippensburg, Pennsylvania, 1993, p.126.
11 Goodman, A. W., Jr., *op. cit.*, p.53.
12 Grant, U. S., *op. cit.*, p.253.
13 Winschel, Terrence J., 'Grant's Beachhead For The Vicksburg Campaign', *Blue & Gray Magazine*, February 1994, p.15.
14 Winschel, Terrence J., *ibid.*, p.16.
15 Winschel, Terrence J., *ibid.*, p.19.
16 Winschel, Terrence J., *ibid.*, p.20.
17 Winschel, Terrence J., *ibid.*, p.21.
18 Carnes, F. G., "We Can Hold Our Ground," Calvin Smith's Diary', *Civil War Times Illustrated*, April 1985, p.27.
19 Goodman, A. W., Jr., *op. cit.*, p.54.
20 Carter, Samuel, *op. cit.*, pp.183-184.
21 Goodman, A. W., Jr., *op. cit.*, p.53

22 Grant, U. S., *op. cit.*, p.254.
23 Grant, U. S., *op. cit.*, p.254.
24 Winschel, Terrence J., *op. cit.*, p.49.
25 Winschel, Terrence J., *ibid.*, p.50.
26 Goodman, A. W., Jr., *op. cit.*, p.55.
27 Tucker, Phillip Thomas, *op. cit.*, p.129.
28 Tucker, Phillip Thomas, *ibid.*, p.130.
29 Tucker, Phillip Thomas, *ibid.*, p.131.
30 Tucker, Phillip Thomas, *ibid.*, p.132.
31 Chambers, William Pitt, *Blood & Sacrifice*, Huntington, West Virginia, 1994, p.64.
32 Goodman, A. W., Jr., *op. cit.*, pp.55-56.
33 Tucker, Phillip Thomas, *op. cit.*, p.135.
34 Tucker, Phillip Thomas, *ibid.*, p.137.
35 Goodman, A. W. Jr., *op. cit.*, p.56.
36 Tucker, Phillip Thomas, *op. cit.*, p.139.
37 Winschel, Terrence J., *op. cit.*, p.53.
38 Roberts, Bobby, and Moneyhon, Carl, *Portraits of Conflict, a Photographic History of Mississippi in the Civil War*, Fayetteville, Arkansas, 1993, p.228.
39 Wheeler, Richard, *The Siege of Vicksburg*, New York, 1991, p.125.
40 Tucker, Phillip Thomas, *op. cit.*, p.141.
41 Tucker, Phillip Thomas, *ibid.*, p.142.
42 Tucker, Phillip Thomas, *ibid.*, p.143.
43 Wheeler, Richard, *op. cit.*, p.125.
44 Goodman, A. W., Jr., *op. cit.*, p.56.
45 Tucker, Phillip Thomas, *op. cit.*, p.145.

A GAMBLE AT THE DIVISION LEVEL
Wallace Buys Time at Monocacy

THE GAMBLE: *that a relatively small force, which had never served together as a unit and contained a number of troops who had never seen combat, could hold back a larger force of seasoned combat veterans long enough for reinforcements to fill the fortifications around Washington before the Confederates could take the city.*

All through the spring of 1864, Robert E. Lee's invincible Army of Northern Virginia had been tied down, constantly fighting the Army of the Potomac. Lee had been unable to manoeuvre freely, instead having to react to Union moves. His freedom of action was apparently limited to anticipating what Grant would do next. This was not his style at all; Lee liked to be able to move around, to find weak points and attack, not merely to try and reach the next defensive position first.

Even as Lee studied the maps of his own front, trying to figure out Grant's next move, he kept an eye on maps of the Valley of Virginia, the Shenandoah Valley, the source for much of the food his men and animals ate as well as a gateway to the north. Once, in 1862, Stonewall Jackson's brilliant campaign in that Valley, halting three separate Union armies, had panicked Washington. Lincoln halted troops due to join McClellan's Peninsula Campaign, an excuse McClellan used to fail in that campaign.

On 6 June 1864 Lee wrote to Jefferson Davis:

I think some good officer should be sent into the Valley at once to take command there and collect all the forces, regulars, locals and reserves, and endeavour to drive the enemy out. It is apparent that if Grant cannot be successfully resisted here we cannot hold the Valley. If he is defeated it can be recovered. But unless a sufficient force can be had in that country to restrain the movements of the enemy, he will do us great evil and in that event I think it would be better to restore General Breckinridge the troops drawn from him.[1]

Major General John C. Breckinridge, who had commanded in the Valley, was earlier ordered to Hanover Junction in support of Lee's hard-pressed forces. This left only a small cavalry force, under Brigadier General W. E. Jones, in the Valley.

If the Valley was a knife pointed at the heart of Pennsylvania, it also led back into Virginia. It was natural that Federal troops should want to take it, even more so because many of Virginia's foodstuffs were grown there. That year the US government put together a large force for the purpose of conquering the Valley once and for all, placing it under the command of Major General David Hunter with orders to head south once again. Breckinridge was sent into the Valley to protect it.

But Lee had even bigger plans. He hatched yet another offensive plot, one that would send an entire corps of the Army of Northern Virginia through the Valley, defeating the Federals there, then up into Maryland as he had done in 1862 and again in 1863, and towards Washington. Twice before he had taken the war to the enemy in this manner, and twice before his manoeuvres had given relief to Virginia, allowing farmers to get their crops in peacefully, and caused northern troops to hasten to their own capital's defence. Now it was time to make just such a move once again.

Lee picked his Second Corps, commanded by Lieutenant General Jubal A. Early, to do the job. Early, a West Pointer with much active service, had been a lawyer for years before the war. He had fought well in earlier campaigns and had commanded A. P. Hill's Corps for a time during the Wilderness Campaign. He had been promoted to the rank of lieutenant general on 31 May, just in time to receive command of the Second Corps.

On 12 June Lee called Early to his headquarters to discuss his plans for another northern invasion through the Valley. According to Early, in memoirs written years after the war, when the event was history, Lee made it clear that the raid would simply threaten Washington. Years after the war, probably to silence critics who felt he should have taken the city, Early wrote that he asked whether he should go ahead and capture the place if it were possible. He wrote that Lee replied no, adding that such a move would be impossible.[2] Lee then told Early to pick two additional artillery battalions and, with the rest of his corps, be ready to move into the Valley. In all, including troops already in the Valley that would join Early, the force would number some 18,900 men, 13,500 of whom were infantry.[3]

Early recalled:

After dark, on the same day, written instructions were given me by General Lee, by which I was directed to move, with the force designated at 3 o'clock next morning, for the Valley, by way of Louisa Court-House and Charlottesville, and through Brown's or Swift Run Gap in the Blue Ridge, as I might find most advisable; to strike Hunter's force in the rear, and, if possible destroy it; then move down the Valley, cross the Potomac near Leesburg in Loudon County, or at or above Harper's Ferry, as I might find most practicable, and threaten Washington City. I was further directed to communicate with General Breckinridge, who would co-operate with me in the attack on Hunter and the expedition into Maryland.[4]

The very short time that Lee allowed Early to pack up the baggage of an entire corps and move out − less than one night − certainly indicates the importance he placed on this raid, and on making it quickly. So it was that Private John Worsham, 21st Virginia Infantry, recalled that, on 12 June, 'We were aroused about midnight and formed into line'. There they endured the infantryman's traditional stand and wait for several hours. Finally, 'Before day we marched out of the woods on to a road leading toward Mechanicsville'.[5] Early remembered that the Second Corps was all on the road by 2.00 a.m., an hour earlier than required. If his men moved as rapidly in the rest of the campaign, the Confederates had a good chance of fulfilling their mission.

At Lynchburg Early's men joined the 11,000 troops of Breckinridge, and the combined force confronted a Federal force under Major General David Hunter. On the 17th Early received a telegraph sent to him by Lee on the 16th: 'Grant is in front of Petersburg. Will be opposed there. Strike as quick as you can, and, if circumstances authorise, carry out the original plan, or move upon Petersburg without delay.'[6] Early's men probed the Union position the next day, only to discover that Hunter's troops had stolen away in the night.

Early's men followed the trail of the Federals back towards the West Virginia mountains, and the Confederates caught up with them near Salem. Their attack there ended in Hunter suffering a number of casualties and the loss of eight cannon, plus the loss of his troops' confidence in their commanding general. Although Hunter wired Washington from his post in the hills of West Virginia on 28 June, saying that his move in the Valley had been 'extremely successful, inflicting great injury upon the enemy,' and that his men were in 'excellent heart and health' and would be able to attack again after resting, he was plainly eliminated from the rest of the Valley campaign.[7]

While Hunter was giving overly optimistic news to his superiors in Washington, Early had made a victorious march up the Valley. Early himself reached Staunton on the 26th, while the rest of his troops arrived during the following 24 hours. There the force camped and reorganised for the rest of the raid. The artillery was reduced by a number of damaged guns and spent horses. A survey showed that about half of his 10,000 men were barefoot, and his quartermasters sent requisitions for shoes to Richmond. Commissary officers also went to work obtaining rations from local sources as well as from Richmond.

While there, Early received a telegraph from Lee asking whether, with Hunter being in West Virginia, Early thought the raid should continue as previously planned. Early thought it should, but wanted to make some organisational changes, which he did. He renamed his force 'The Army of the Valley', and gave Breckinridge command of one corps, as well as appointing him second in command of the entire force. Then the force pressed on.

Early's troops entered the city of Winchester, often the site of battle, on 2 July, and were greeted enthusiastically as they halted to forage. Lee telegraphed Early there, as well, ordering him to wait 'until everything was in readiness to cross the Potomac'.[8] Among the things to be done was the threshing of wheat for making bread, as the commissary had no bread or flour to issue. Early later recalled that he was ordered, once he was on the move, to be especially careful to destroy the Baltimore and Ohio Railroad running westward from Harper's Ferry into West Virginia. Then his men were to press on towards Washington, capturing Federal reserves at railroad and supply dumps along the Potomac, including the garrison at Harper's Ferry.

Early was ready on the 3rd, and started his lead troops up towards Leestown. There, stiff Union opposition allowed the Federals to escape largely unharmed, saving much of the government property in the area. From there Early sent troops on to Martinsburg to capture supplies there. They then proceeded to Harper's Ferry, which had been evacuated by prudent Federal forces before the Confederates arrived, the next day. In a short time Early's men had cleared the Valley of Federal forces and arrived at a point where they threatened the capital city of the United States. Federal troops from the Valley had retreated west, towards Ohio, and very few troops of any sort remained between Early's seasoned veterans and Washington.

Grant telegraphed on 5 July: 'If the enemy cross into Maryland, or Pennsylvania I can send an army corps from here to meet them or cut off their return South'.[9] In reality, 28,000 of the 75,000 men in the overall area were under Hunter to the west and north, while 1,100 were in central Pennsylvania. Moreover, it would take at least several days for a corps from the Petersburg area to move into the Washington area. Major General Lew Wallace in Baltimore, with only 7,000 men, was the only force immediately able to deploy between any Confederate advance to Washington and Early's troops. If Early could move quickly, and evidence from the Valley suggested that he could, he would be almost impossible to stop.

Even at this point top Federal officials refused to take the threat seriously. Why would the Confederates try such a raid? Surely their only objective was to retake the Valley. Grant, south of Richmond at City Point and only vaguely aware of the true situation, thought that the Federals who had retreated before Early should sweep around and join the main army at Petersburg. Only John W. Garrett, president of the Baltimore & Ohio, who was always concerned about threats to his precious railroad, saw through the fog of war to determine Early's threat.

By 6 July Early was headquartered across the Potomac in Maryland, near the old battlefield of Sharpsburg, or Antietam as it was known by Federals. But he was not moving as quickly as Jackson would have done. Maryland staff officer Henry Kyd Douglas took advantage of a halt of several days, to receive and issue new shoes, to take 'Early, Breckinridge, Gordon, and Ramseur [generals under Early's command] to my father's house for a brief call and to get a glance at Sharpsburg and the battlefield as we passed through'.[10] It is hard to imagine Stonewall Jackson taking a sightseeing break in the midst of such a raid. Early also sent off his cavalry brigade in an attempt to free prisoners at Point Lookout, a prisoner of war camp between Baltimore and Washington, where the Potomac pours into the Chesapeake Bay, that was understood to be poorly guarded.

To be fair, it should be mentioned that Early's men were also delayed by the need to stop to destroy northern equipment such as the railroads and the Chesapeake and Ohio canal, an aqueduct over the Antietam Creek, and other Northern-owned items that could be said to contribute to the Federal war effort. Drug stores, hatters, shoe stores and the like were especially hard hit. Confederate raiders demanded money from northern township officials, saying that the towns would be burned if the money was not forthcoming. Of course they had to give the officials time to raise the money. The township fathers of Hagerstown, Maryland, were allowed three hours to produce $20,000, and that time was lost for marching on towards Washington. Moreover, Federal cavalrymen, especially the 8th Illinois Cavalry, skilfully fought delaying actions with the Confederates. Their scouting brought information on Early's movements and numbers that proved extremely useful to US Army officials in Washington who were trying to make sense of it all.

Indeed, the 8th, joined by troops of the 3rd Maryland Potomac Home Brigade and a handful of men from both the 159th Ohio Mounted Infantry and the Independent Loudon County Rangers, all of whom were under command of Colonel Charles Gilpin and supported by three cannon, drew up a battle line along the main roads coming from the west towards Frederick City. A ridge line there, which lay between the turnpikes from Hagerstown and Harper's Ferry, gave the Union troops a natural line of defence, and the force stalled the Confederate cavalry ahead of Early's infantry. Colonel David R. Clendenin, commander of the 8th, was delighted to telegraph his overall department commander, Lew Wallace, in Baltimore, that his force was holding. As the Confederates waited for the bulk of their infantry to arrive, Wallace telegraphed the Union troops to 'Endeavour to hold your ground. At 1 p.m. tonight 80,000 veterans will be here.'[11]

It was now up to Indiana native Lew Wallace to hold Early back long enough for that promised corps from Grant's army to arrive in Washington. Wallace's job was not to defend Washington; he was responsible only for Baltimore, which was also a possible target for Early's men. There he could find a number of possible defensive positions along the creeks that ran largely north to south. Moreover, he could be reinforced by troops, largely militia, from Pennsylvania and Delaware.

In the meantime, Washington could take care of itself, given the well-designed forts that ringed that city. Constructed over several years, they had interlinking fields of fire that entirely covered the ground around the city, and were crammed with heavy cannon that had never been fired at an enemy. Unfortunately for the city, however, they were almost unmanned, the heavy artillery regiments that had occupied them for so many years having been called up to reinforce the badly battered Army of the Potomac earlier that year. Only a handful of men now garrisoned the city, and many of them were men of the Veteran Reserve Corps. This organisation was made up of men who were unable, owing to wounds or disease, to take the field. Many of them lacked limbs and were even unable to fire weapons. They were poorly armed with French-made pistols, non-commissioned officers' straight swords and an assortment of smooth-bore and rifled muskets. They had been used mainly to guard prisoners and help out in hospitals, and would certainly present little opposition to Early's men. Wallace was aware of this, and for the most part, therefore, he felt he could only draw on the Baltimore garrison, even though that largely consisted of militia troops with no combat experience.

For example, the 144th Ohio National Guard made up part of the garrison in Baltimore. This regiment had been organised in Ohio in May 1864 for 90 days of duty. The regiment was split up, with one company in Wilmington, two in Baltimore, one at Camp Parole, Maryland, and one at Fort Dix. Its members had seen no combat. Nor had the 149th Ohio National Guard, a unit raised at the same time and place as the 144th for the same length of service, or the 1st and 3rd Maryland Potomac Home Brigade, although the 1st had been in the garrison at Harper's Ferry when it was captured in 1862 and then, having been exchanged, saw some service at Gettysburg. Moreover, one of his most important artillery elements, Alexander's Baltimore Battery, had re-enlisted strictly for the $950-a-man bounty and because they were stationed 'so near home, where we could go three or four times a week, and get a square meal, have a good bath and change clothes, go to the theatre and other amusements'.[12] These artillerymen were not happy to find themselves bouncing around on top of limber chests, breathing in dust from their horses on the road west.

Certainly, if one were to get the best fighting from such troops, conservative judgment would place them behind the great earthen walls of the forts around the city. But Wallace decided to gamble, to buy time by fighting Early's men as long as possible and as far west as he could get.

The 36-year-old Wallace certainly would not have been Grant's choice to try to hold Early back. Although he was a bright man, noted as a lawyer and state politician, and had seen service as a lieutenant in a state regiment in the Mexican-American War, his Civil War service to date was not notable. At Shiloh Grant ordered him to march the division he commanded from Crump's Landing to the battlefield, there to smash into the Confederate left and roll up their line. Instead, due to poor reconnaissance, he marched the division far from where he should have gone. Indeed, not hearing from his troops, Grant even sent further orders having him come up immediately. Even then, his men ended up on the field hours after their arrival would have done any good, after the first day's fighting was over. Wallace claimed that his orders were vague. Grant, however, later wrote: 'I never could see and do not now see why any order was necessary further than to direct him to come to Pittsburg landing, without specifying by what route. His was one of three veteran division that had been in battle, and its absence was severely felt.'[13] Thereafter, as Grant's star rose, Wallace's declined, and he was effectively removed from where Grant thought he could do any harm and given administrative assignments, first in Cincinnati, Ohio, and then in Baltimore.

Such was not the record of a gambler, or even of a general in whom one could have a great deal of confidence. None the less, Wallace was the man on the scene, and he decided to gamble. Instead of falling back to Washington's defensive line he would leave Gilpin's and Clendenin's troops, under the command of Brigadier General Erastus B. Tyler, commander of his First Separate Brigade, where they stood, on elevated ground west of Frederick.

Wallace advanced three companies of the 144th and seven companies of the 149th Ohio National Guards regiments from Monocacy Junction, east of Frederick, to Gilpin's battle line. Wallace himself caught a train to Frederick and then on to the line. Indeed, he left his post in Baltimore without permission from Major General Henry Halleck, the army's chief of staff, or any other superior. Nor did he even try to obtain permission to confront Early's forces with his own smaller numbers. He knew he was taking a gamble that 'might be turned to my serious disadvantage,' since he believed that the army's high command was 'lying in wait for me' to make a mistake.[14] He had taken a double gamble; first, that he could slow down the Confederates enough to allow Washington and Baltimore to be reinforced, and, second, that his superiors would not end his military career for taking that gamble.

The 14th New Jersey Infantry Regiment soon joined Wallace's troops, but it was only Early's slowness and concentration on gathering cattle and other supplies that allowed the Union line to remain intact. None the less, Early's men were on the move, directly to where Wallace's small force waited. Wallace had no idea how many men Early commanded; some reports indicated that there were as many as 30,000 men coming his way. Nor did he know where they were going. Was their target Baltimore, from where they could free prisoners at Point Lookout before heading back south into towards Washington from the north, or did they intend to make a direct attack on Washington?

Finally, Wallace learned that Confederate cavalry had been seen scouting along his southern flank, suggesting that Washington was the target. Even if Wallace, against all odds, were to make a fight west of Washington, he was not in the right place. Early could simply slip to his left and avoid his line altogether, heading directly at Washington. At that point Wallace would have done his job; he would have protected Baltimore. He had no orders to do anything beyond that. Even so, at 8.00 p.m. Wallace telegraphed Washington: 'Breckinridge, with a strong column moving down the Washington pike towards Urbana, is within six miles of that place. I shall withdraw immediately from Frederick City and put myself in position on the road to cover Washington, if necessary.'[15]

Wallace fell back to Monocacy Junction, along the Monocacy River, south of Frederick. The high ground there overlooked the river and the lower ground west of the river, while Early's men would be forced to cross by the railroad bridge right in the centre of the line or at a ford below the bridge that ran directly into a hill. Crum's Ford lay about a mile above the bridge, while another bridge, on the road that ran between Frederick and Baltimore, lay another mile or so above that. The position was naturally strong, but not impregnable. In the meantime, Early's men entered Frederick, to the joy of many of the pro-southern citizens there. Kyd Douglas 'was the first horseman in the town, in recognition of which an enthusiastic citizen – ever since my warm friend – Peter Zahm, presented me with a handsome pair of spurs'.[16]

Although much of what was important in Frederick, including bank money, locomotives and citizens' horses, even those belonging to southern sympathizers, had been sent east beyond the reach of Confederate quartermasters, Early halted to demand a ransom of $200,000. If the money were not in Confederate hands, the city was to be put to the torch. City officials countered that they had not that much money, and other cities were ransomed for less. Negotiations dragged on, finally ending as city officials produced the sum requested. Indeed, the public debt created by the Confederate demand was so large for the time that, with interest growing over the years, it was not finally paid off until 1 October 1951.

But these negations bought Wallace time, and he was buying time for Washington. On 7 July he learned that his line was to receive reinforcements. Finally, too, on 8 July, the first reinforcements, the 10th Vermont Infantry Regiment, from the Army of the Potomac, arrived. Wallace had the regiment marched around and around the same hill to deceive the Confederates into believing that the thin Union line had been strongly reinforced. Wallace also had some of his troops fall back, to lure the Confederates forward. At the same time he sent Clendenin's cavalry to raid around Early's flanks and rear.

Still, Wallace went to sleep that evening worried that most of the reinforcements would not reach him before Early's men clashed with his. A train whistle awoke him, and staff officers rushed in to tell the general that the rest of the Third Division of the veteran VI Corps, which was only a two-brigade division, had arrived from Grant's lines in Petersburg. Soon he was joined by Brigadier General James Ricketts, a professional soldier who commanded the division. Wallace quickly briefed the 47-year-old general, describing all he knew about Early's numbers and intentions and his own numbers and plans. Ricketts then asked for orders and was told: 'I put you across the Washington Pike because it is the post of honour'.[17] The two then shook hands, and Ricketts went off to post his men as Wallace returned to his bedroll.

Ricketts' men filled out their places in line during a shower. They were tired from their all-night race, wet from the rain, and unsure of what the morrow would bring. They were veterans by then, however, and not greatly disheartened. Their arrival must surely have boosted the morale of the green Ohio and Maryland soldiers, who had previously thought they would have to fight alone.

The clouds blew east, and the morning dawned to a clear sky. At about 8.00 a.m. Early sent forward his skirmish lines to feel out the Union numbers and positions. His men found Federals posted all along the line, as Wallace felt he had to have troops at every place where Early could possibly attack, not knowing his foe's plans. The 149th Ohio was positioned on the right, at the Jug Bridge, where three companies had been sent across the bridge to act as skirmishers, while another one of their companies was at Hughes' Ford. The 3rd Maryland Potomac Home Brigade and three companies of the 1st Maryland Potomac Home Brigade were posted along Crum's Ford. Ricketts' men filled in the centre, overlooking the railroad bridge and the covered bridge on the Washington Pike. Wallace also sent two companies of the 1st Maryland Potomac Home Brigade, along with some men of the 10th Vermont, 9th New York Heavy Artillery and two

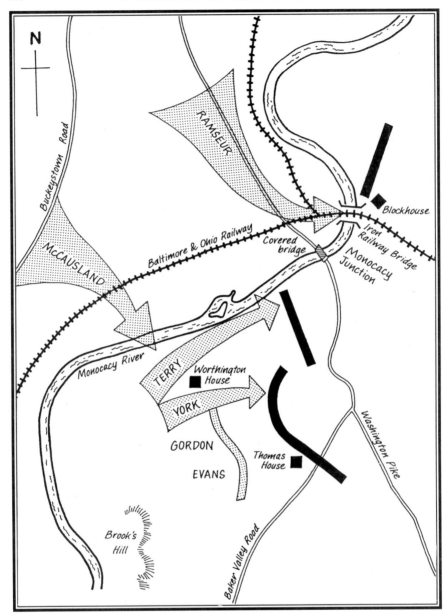

companies of the 106th New York, across the river to form a defensive line around the ways to the two bridges to the Union centre.

Confederate artillery opened up on the railway lines, the first shot landing in the midst of men of the 151st New York who were boiling coffee in their tin pots. Two were killed instantly. The accurate fire forced Wallace to move his headquarters north of the tracks, in the lee of a hill. The Federals replied with their own artillery, including a 24lb howitzer, and infantry small-arms. They fought stubbornly, slowing down the Confederate advance. Early joined his front line, but his information on the area was slight; most of his cavalry from the area was off on a raid towards the Federal prisoner of war camp at Point Lookout. They could have told the southern general about fords he could use to get around Wallace's line quickly, but they were not available.

Early did not want to spend a great deal of time along the Monocacy river. He had already lost too much time in Frederick, and he thought he had only militia in his front. Not wanting to strike directly across the bridges towards the Junction, he rode along the line, reconnoitring. As he rode towards the south he saw about a thousand of his cavalry advance to cross the river at an old farm ford, intending to turn north and strike Wallace's men in the flank. In the meantime, an infantry brigade moved out and aimed directly at the iron railroad bridge at the Monocacy Junction. Defending troops there could take advantage of a blockhouse, manned by men of the 1st Maryland Potomac Home Brigade, which had been built to protect the bridge from southern guerrillas.

The Confederate cavalry ran into a company the omnipresent 8th Illinois Cavalry posted at the ford. The 8th fought well, but was overwhelmed. The rest of the regiment was cut off from Wallace's main body as the grey cavalrymen swarmed across the river. A courier from the 8th found Wallace on some high ground near the Junction and told him of the flanking move. It now seemed as if it were all for naught; Wallace would be unable to buy sufficient time for reinforcements to save Washington. Still, he quickly sent orders to Ricketts to change front and refuse his left. Ricketts, who as a captain had seen his artillery battery overrun in the first major battle of the war, refused to be dismayed. He quickly moved his units around to face this new threat, and soon had stopped a dismounted cavalry charge, inflicting heavy losses.

The July sun now reached its zenith. 'Notwithstanding the attacks received,' Wallace was happy to see that, at noon, 'we were exactly as in the morning'.[18] His troops had already bought six hours of relief to Washington. Their accurate fire had stopped the Confederates virtually along the line. One commander noted a heavy artilleryman, 'a schoolteacher from western New York named Wellon, who stopped and fired each time with great deliberation and excellent effect'.[19]

In one area, in front of the Jug Bridge, Georgia infantrymen drove back Union troops on the Frederick side of the river. Wallace ordered the 149th Ohio to push them back. The attack of the novice soldiers failed, but the general added the three equally amateur companies of the 144th Ohio, and a second try succeeded. Other men of the 149th stopped a probing cavalry drive further north along Hughes' Ford, where the fighting turned into fairly long-range skirmishing for the rest of the day.

Fighting was not as easy at the covered bridge just south of the iron railroad bridge. This old bridge was 250ft long, with two lanes of some 50ft width overall, and was 16ft tall. There, through some confusion, Federal cannoneers spiked one of their howitzers. In the meantime, outnumbered Federal infantry from Vermont and Maryland fought well enough, but the Confederates inched them back a step at a time.

Suddenly the last train in the area, which had been retained to move wounded back to safety, started off as its scared driver found himself under Confederate artillery fire. With him went not only rations, but Wallace's telegrapher. Now Wallace had no way of communicating quickly with his base in Baltimore. Moreover, the 1,000 reinforcements he had expected, which were retained some distance behind him through an error of command, had not arrived. He was beginning to be greatly concerned. Enemy numbers were beginning to tell. At some time in the early afternoon, therefore, he ordered the covered bridge destroyed. Soldiers of the 9th New York Heavy Artillery, pressed into service as infantry, gathered wheat under the bridge roof and set it ablaze. In the dry, hot July air the fire, according to Sergeant Albert Smith, one of its creators, soon 'wrapped the roof in flames like magic'.[20] Although those around the bridge managed to escape easily, other Federals on the other side of the river did not know about the order to burn the bridge, and were cut off. Wallace remembered them and sent a courier to order them back, but he was unable to cross the bridge to reach them. The 10th Vermont and men of the Maryland Potomac Home Brigades had been separated from the main Federal force.

Confederate sharpshooters in a barn made it hot for Federals. A Federal artilleryman wrote:

Our trouble was that we could not locate our enemies for some time until one of our officers noted small puffs of smoke from under the shingles of a barn, a half mile or more away; that barn was filled with sharpshooters, so we directed our attention to them. The second shot burst inside the barn, and so did the third and fourth; the barn was soon on fire and we had the satisfaction of seeing some of them carried away.[21]

On Wallace's left, where the Confederate cavalry had been unable to dislodge Rickett's veterans, there had been a lull in the early afternoon fighting. However, the Confederate commander, 'Tiger John' McCausland, continued to work his Virginia cavalrymen round to the right of his line. Wallace spotted the movement and wrote to Ricketts: 'A line of skirmishers is advancing from the south beyond the cornfield on your left. I suggest you change front in that direction, and advance to the cornfield fence, concealing your men behind it.'[22] Ricketts then adjusted his own line accordingly, just before two lines of southern troops attacked.

An officer of the 14th New Jersey wrote home shortly after the battle:

'Their batteries enfiladed us and did excellent execution, but our boys fought as if they were fighting for their own homes literally[. They] mowed down the first two lines of the rebels who thought they only had to fight 100 day men.' The Federal fire was intense. According to the officer of the 14th: 'there was terrific firing along the whole line ...'[23]

The heavy infantry fire broke up the attack, an eyewitness recalling: '[T]he whole rebel line disappeared as if swallowed up in the earth. Save and except several riderless horses galloping about, and a few mounted officers bravely facing the storm, the attacking force had vanished.' James McChesney of the 14th Virginia was shocked: 'Out of one hundred of our regiment that went into the fight, we had twenty-two men killed and wounded *in less than twenty minutes!*' Another eyewitness thought the survivors looked 'shocked and frightened ... panic stricken by the deadly ambush into which they were unwittingly led'.[24] The survivors ducked to take cover, and the Confederate formations broke up as their soldiers began to move back to the rear.

McClausland rallied his men with difficulty, as they were so badly shaken by the first attack, and led them forward for another try at the Union line. A Federal counterattack on a house between the lines, added to the continued fire, again broke up the Confederate assault. One corporal of the 14th New Jersey, among the counterattackers, recalled how they 'drove them toward the river, killing and capturing many'.[25]

Although the cavalry attack had again been stalled, Early saw an opportunity in the fighting on his right. He ordered a brigade led by Brigadier General John Gordon to follow the cavalry across the river and hit the Union left. At about 2.00 p.m. Gordon's men began to splash across the ford. Each company and regiment had to halt on the other side, first for the men to replace the shoes they had taken off to keep them dry when crossing the ford, and then for the men to fall into correct position in the battle line. While this was happening, Gordon went forward to reconnoitre Rickett's position, where he was seen by Wallace.

With the lack of expected reinforcements and a strong force certain to tip the balance on his left, Wallace finally thought of retreating. His fighting had bought the better part of a day to reinforce Washington's defences. Now it was time to consider retreat. Not yet, suggested Ricketts, as it would take the better part of the night and the next day for Early to get his artillery across the ford and into position. Every hour bought made Washington safer. Wallace agreed. In the meantime, however, he sent couriers to the rear with word that he had been fighting Early's men since dawn and was holding well enough, and that the 18,000 to 20,000-man Confederate force was aimed at Washington.

By 4.00 p.m. Gordon had his men in position for an assault. Then he launched the charge, ordering his men forward *en echelon* by brigades from the right. This would create an attack on Rickett's left with an entire division. The ground was poor for an attack. The fields were broken by fence lines and tall stacks of grain that would break up battle lines, and dotted with farmhouses and outbuildings that provided the Federal troops with ready-made defences.

The Federals fired as rapidly as possible as the Confederates, yelling their bone-chilling 'Rebel yell', came forward at the double-quick. Gordon wrote:

> As we reached the first line of strong and high fencing, and my men began to climb over it, they were met by a tempest of bullets, and many of the brave fellows fell at the first volley. But over they climbed or tumbled, and rushed forward, some of them halting to break down gaps in the fence, so that the mounted officers might ride through. Then came the grain-stacks. Around them and between them they pressed on, with no possibility of maintaining orderly alignment or of returning any effective fire. Deadly missiles from Wallace's ranks were cutting down the line and company officers with their words of cheer

to the men but half spoken. It was one of those fights where success depends largely upon the prowess of the individual soldier. The men were deprived of that support and strength imparted by a compact line, where elbow touch of comrade with comrade gives confidence to each and sends the electric thrill of enthusiasm through all. But nothing could deter them.[26]

Even the private soldiers agreed. 'It was the most exciting time I witnessed during the war,' wrote John Worsham of the 21st Virginia Infantry. He added that the Confederate soldiers 'were perfectly wild when they came in sight of the enemy's column'.[27]

A combination of the broken ground, lack of information on the nature of the Federal forces and excitement may have led Confederate commanders to omit sending out a skirmish line. 'I never saw such a bold move before,' wrote an officer of the 14th New Jersey. 'They evidently thought we were recruits and walked right up to us in this open field without skirmishing, dodging or running as soldiers usually do in the open on a charge.'[28] The Confederates paid for this when the Federals opened fire on their columns of companies.

Great bloody gaps fell all along both lines. Thomas Nichols of the 61st Georgia was hit in the head, the ball slicing his skull open. Sitting up, he wiped his own brains from his forehead and was heard to mutter that he would go straight back to Virginia where he would find a horse to go home, and he would never cross the Potomac again. He lived only 12 hours more. One private of the 21st Virginia Infantry was hit badly, turned and headed back to the road. When he reached the fence he mounted it, breathed his last and fell back, dead. The 12th Georgia lost six colour bearers, the last being shot through the lungs. One survivor figured that only some 800 to 1,000 men out of Clement Evans' Georgia brigade survived the heavy, accurate Federal fire. Evans himself was hit in the left side, the bullet passing through a coat pocket and hitting and driving a number of pins from a folded paper into the general's side. They were so deeply embedded that they were not all removed until years after the war.

Federal losses were almost as heavy. The 146th Ohio lost three colour bearers in succession. An officer of the 14th New Jersey Infantry wrote:

When the enemy at Monocacy first struck us, three lines deep against our single line, his fire was terrific. Our Colour-Sergeant (William B.

Cottrell) while bravely waving his colours in front of his regiment, received a ball which before striking him passed through and severed the flag staff just below his left hand. He fell forward and died upon the flag, his lifeblood staining its folds. Our colours were immediately raised by one of the colour guards; he, also, was almost instantly shot down. Then another raised it up; he was badly wounded and turned it over to the next corporal, who was mortally wounded. These four were killed and disabled in almost the time it has taken me to write it.[29]

Federal senior commanders, such as Lieutenant Colonel Stewart and Major Edward Taft of the 9th New York Heavy Artillery, fell dead or wounded. The lieutenant colonel of the 14th New Jersey left the field with a broken arm, while the regiment's next-ranking officer fell mortally wounded. The next in command was shot through the lungs and was carried from the field. Command passed to another captain, who was killed instantly a few minutes later. At the battle's end the 14th could count only three officers, Captain John Patterson, the new commander, a first lieutenant and the regimental adjutant. Moreover, Federal cannoneers began to run low on ammunition and their firing fell off.

The Federals fell back to a second line of defence. Gordon wrote:

The Union lines stood firmly in this second position, bravely defending the railroad and the highway to Washington. Between the two hostile lines there was a narrow ravine down which ran a small stream of limpid water. In this ravine the battle swayed across the little stream, the dead and wounded of both sides mingling their blood in its waters; and when the struggle was ended a crimsoned current ran toward the river. Nearly one half of my men and large numbers of the Federals fell there.[30]

Gordon called for reinforcements, and a Virginia brigade came forward to assault Rickett's line closer to the river. Although they were hit by the 110th Ohio as they came up, the added Virginia brigade swung the tide. The Confederates, aided by accurate artillery fire, soon drove off the 110th and the 9th New York artillerymen from their positions. Now the Federals began to fall back under pressure from the battle-fired Confederates all along the line and, at 4.00 p.m., Wallace gave the command for a general retreat. 'The men of the Third Division were not whipped,' he later wrote, 'but retired reluctantly, under my orders.'[31] He ordered the blockhouses burned, and, as the log buildings blazed away, the disorganised Federals fled, leaving the field to the Confederates.

The 10th Vermont, cut off, had to double time through rough stubble to reach safety. The colour bearers both fell, exhausted, and their colours were picked up by Corporal Alexander Scott, who would receive the Medal of Honor for his act. Another 10th Vermont Medal of Honor went to First Lieutenant George E. Davis for holding the approach to the covered and iron bridges and then bringing his men over the iron bridge to safety as the Federal line collapsed. The bridge had no railings, and only a narrow foot-path made of boards in its centre. The ties were too far apart for people to use, so the men had to dash across in single file. Wallace himself saw how the lieutenant put his men in a column with no 'crowding or pushing or struggling to pass or yelling' and got them over with but slight losses, all due to enemy small-arms fire. 'Now and then we could see one stop short, let go his musket, throw up his hands and with a splash disappear in the stream beneath,' Wallace remembered.[32]

Davis' men were followed by troops of the 20th North Carolina, who quickly captured the other side of the river. Confederate troops also captured Wallace's field hospital and hundreds of Federals who had become separated from their units in the confusion of the flight. The 10th Vermont, for example, reported only four men killed in the fighting, despite being cut off, but 32 missing in action. By 6.00 p.m. Early's troops were in complete control of the Monocacy battlefield. Fighting continued into darkness as Federals attempted to escape towards Washington and Confederate skirmishers pressed them. 'But the retreat was so rapid that pursuit by infantry was useless and it was soon stopped,' recalled staff officer Kyd Douglas.[33] The Confederates reorganised, ate their meals, gathered up the dead and wounded, and started prisoners on their long walk south. They had finished for the day; they would go no further towards Washington.

Wallace had lost his battle, but he had cost Early a precious day that Grant used to rush the VI Corps into Washington's defences. Moreover, he had frightened Early badly. The Confederate general had thought that he would be able to move so quickly that only militia would stand between him and the capital city. Yet many of the dead and captured of Monocacy bore the Greek Cross cap device of the veteran VI Corps that he knew was in Grant's army at Petersburg. He now would have to move with more caution. One Federal Corps was almost the equal in numbers as well as fighting ability to his force. Early would go on to gunshot range of the fortifications ringing Washington, but he would act cautiously and, in the end, simply return to the Valley without attempting to force his way into the city.

Wallace had won his gamble. He was praised even by Grant, who later wrote that he 'moved with commendable promptitude to meet the enemy at the Monocacy'.[34]

Notes

1 Dowdey, Clifford, and Manarin, Louis H., *The Wartime Papers of R. E. Lee*, New York, 1961, p.767.
2 *B&L, op. cit.*, Vol. 4, p.492.
3 Cooling, B. F., *Jubal Early's Raid on Washington, 1864*, Baltimore, Maryland, 1989, p.23.
4 Early, Jubal A., *Narrative of the War Between the States*, New York, 1989, p.371.
5 Worsham, John H., *One of Jackson's Foot Cavalry*, Jackson, Tennessee, 1964, p.146.
6 Dowdey and Manarin, *op. cit.*, p.791.
7 Cooling, B. F., *op. cit.*, p.13.
8 B. F. Cooling, *op. cit.*, p.24.
9 Cooling, B. F., *op. cit.*, p.38.
10 Douglas, Henry Kyd, *I Rode with Stonewall*, Chapel Hill, North Carolina, 1940, p.293.
11 Cooling, B. F., *op. cit.*, p.45.
12 Cooling, B. F., *ibid.*, p.57.
13 Grant, U. S., *Personal Memoirs*, New York, 1952, pp.173-174.
14 Cooling, B. F., *op. cit.*, p.55.
15 Cooling, B. F., *ibid.*, p.48.
16 Douglas, Henry Kyd, *op. cit.*, p.293.
17 Cooling, B. F., *op. cit.*, p.61.
18 Cooling, B. F., *ibid.*, p.66.
19 Judge, Joseph, *Season of Fire: The Confederate Strike on Washington*, Berryville, Virginia, 1994, p.178.
20 Cooling, B. F., *op. cit.*, p.68.
21 Judge, Joseph, *op. cit.*, pp.180-181.
22 Judge, Joseph, *ibid.*, p.182.
23 Olsen, Bernard A., ed, *Upon the Tented Field*, Red Bank, New Jersey, 1993, p.253.
24 Judge, Joseph, *op. cit.*, p.185.
25 Judge, Joseph, *ibid.*, p.186.
26 Gordon, John B., *Reminiscences of the Civil War*, New York, 1903, pp.311-312.
27 Worsham, John H., *One of Jackson's Foot Cavalry*, Jackson, Tennessee, 1964, p.154.
28 Olsen, Bernard A., ed., *op. cit.*, p.253.
29 Olsen, Bernard A., ed, *ibid.*, p.255.
30 Gordon, John B., *op. cit.*, p.312.
31 Cooling, B. F., *op. cit.*, p.76.
32 Judge, Joseph, *op. cit.*, p.196.
33 Douglas, Henry Kyd, *op. cit.*, p.293.
34 Grant, U. S., *op. cit.*, p.460.

A Gamble at the Corps Level

Jackson Strikes at Cedar Mountain

THE GAMBLE: *that a quick-moving Confederate force can strike a divided Federal force and destroy its separate parts before they can unite.*

By late August 1862, Robert E. Lee, who had fought a driving campaign, the Seven Days, against the Union Army of the Potomac which had been threatening Richmond, was pleased. Although his losses were heavy, the enemy was entirely stopped, driven back to a small, secure area along the river from where it was very likely it would move no further. The Army of Northern Virginia drew up defences around the entrenched Federals and awaited the next move.

This did not set well with one of the war's greatest gamblers, Stonewall Jackson. Jackson had been rewarded with a major general's commission for his performance at the First Manassas. He then went on a rampage in the Valley of Virginia, where he defeated three separate small Union armies and cleared that important agricultural area of Federals. His performance in the Seven Days campaign had admittedly been lacklustre at best, but his spirit was still high. He had lost none of his gambler's instinct.

Hardly had the fighting of the Seven Days died down, and the last dead from Malvern's Hill been buried, when Jackson called on Lee with an idea for a single gamble that he felt could win the war. Jackson wanted to gamble that it would take McClellan so long to reorganise that he could not move against the capital city of Richmond again for some time. There was time enough, indeed, for Lee to move the bulk of his army, some 60,000 men, north to strike at Washington itself. Only a handful of Confederates would be needed to keep McClellan's troops bottled up, Jackson believed.

Lee turned Jackson down flatly. Jackson, in a move only possible in a largely volunteer army, went over Lee's head and presented his plan to an old friend, asking him to bring it to the attention of Confederate president Jefferson Davis. Davis, too, turned down the plan. It was, he felt, too fraught with perils. McClellan's army could easily be reinforced by troops down along the Carolina coast, and, so reinforced, could move south towards Petersburg and cut off the railroad lines from the south. Finally, the Confederate Army of Northern Virginia was, Davis felt, too bloodied by the Seven Days.

In the north, President Abraham Lincoln was not pleased with the results of McClellan's Peninsula campaign. He ordered the creation of a new army from the troops around Washington, the Army of Virginia, under Major General John Pope, who had been successful in the Western Theatre. Pope was to drive directly from the North down towards Richmond. Gathering some 75,000 men from the Washington area, Pope moved southward, reaching the northern side of the Rappahannock River by late August. He moved fairly slowly, however, because he did not as yet have all the troops assigned to him. As Pope began moving his Army of Virginia south, McClellan was ordered to retire north from the Peninsula. Troops from his army would be added to Pope's forces.

Jackson saw that this moment – before McClellan's men could join Pope's – was the south's brief golden opportunity. For once, the two sides would be fairly evenly matched in terms of numbers. Indeed, a quick movement could even mean that the Confederates could bring more men on to the field than the Federals. If the gamble paid off, and he and his men could move quickly enough, Jackson could destroy an entire Federal field army. He begged Lee to let him take his corps up to meet Pope.

Lee again balked at so dividing his army, especially as McClellan's troops numbered some 90,000. However, on 12 July 1862 Lee learned that some Union cavalry, in advance of the rest of Pope's army, had reached the vital spot of Culpeper Court House. This small town was only 27 miles north of Gordonsville, and threatened the line of the Virginia Central Railroad that passed through there. That particular railroad connected Richmond and the lush farmlands of the Shenandoah Valley. Were it to be cut, Lee's army, as well as the citizens of the city, would be on short rations.

Lee therefore let Jackson take his old Stonewall Division and Ewell's Division north. Even so, the objective Lee gave Jackson was quite limited, unlike the free-wheeling assignment of crushing Pope's field army that Jackson wanted. Jackson was simply to move to Gordonsville to defend the rail line there.

As it transpired, Jackson's gamble about McClellan's knowledge of the reduction in the Confederate force that faced him was correct. McClellan, thoroughly unnerved by the battering he had taken during the Seven Days, made no offensive moves. Even when paid a personal visit by the US Army's chief general, Major General Henry Halleck, McClellan did not suggest an immediate move. He still claimed that the Confederates had some 200,000 men positioned nearby. After McClellan's Army of the Potomac had been reinforced, and only then, he said, he should strike south along the James and seize Petersburg. Eventually this same army would do just that, but it would be under another commander, and after two years' of dying. But when Petersburg was so taken, the end of Lee's army was virtually inevitable.

Halleck rejected McClellan's pleas for more men and his approach to winning the war. Instead, he decided to have McClellan evacuate his position, sail around the peninsula and, landing north, march across to reinforce Pope. He told McClellan of this decision on August 3.

On 16 July Jackson's lead elements approached Gordonsville. Pope may not have been the most brilliant officer in a Union army fairly unburdened by intelligence, but he could read a map and he knew the importance of railroads. Moreover, Halleck had ordered Pope to move forward, to keep the Confederates from massing and destroying McClellan as he pulled his men off their Peninsula base. Pope ordered Brigadier General John P. Hatch to take cavalry and dash into Gordonsville, something he could do before Jackson's troops got there. But Hatch was cautious. He slowly gathered infantry and artillery, along with a wagon train of supplies, for the move. In so doing he lost the advantage, and by the time his troops approached Gordonsville he found Jackson's weary foot soldiers already there.

Jackson, however, wanted his 12,000 men to do more than serve as a blocking force, but there were not enough of them to do anything other than that. He sent word back to Lee that he needed more men. Lee, though still cautious about McClellan's troops, saw that Pope's troops presented a real and growing threat, so he sent additional men under Major General A. P. Hill north. Hill's men reached Jackson on 29 July.

By August 7 Lee had also learned that McClellan's troops were gone. Lee hesitated in case McClellan suddenly turned round to strike, out of character though it would have been. In the meantime he authorised Jackson to move against Pope.

Even though Jackson's force now numbered some 21,000 men, he still had less than half as many men as Pope. So he decided to try to get Pope to divide his force, as he had previously found Union units in the Valley divided. He pulled back south, away from Gordonsville. Pope fell for the ploy, telegraphing army headquarters in Washington: 'Within ten days, unless the enemy is heavily reinforced from Richmond, I shall be in possession of Gordonsville and Charlottesville'.[1]

Pope's plan was to move towards Charlottesville so that Jackson would be forced to counter his move and defend the town. He ordered all available forces to converge on Culpeper, an important point because of the roads that meet there. His forces were not well co-ordinated, however, and troops began to dribble into Culpeper piecemeal.

Jackson reacted in this game of cat and mouse by sending his cavalry to drive the Union cavalry back across the Rapidan and then join up with the Confederate infantry at Orange. In the meantime his infantry went off on a march led 'secretly' by his civilian topographical engineer.[2] The next day the two commands would rapidly move on Culpeper and trap the advanced Union troops there. He later wrote that:

> Having received information that only part of General Pope's army was at Culpeper Court-House, and hoping, through the blessing of Providence, to be able to defeat it before reinforcements should arrive there, Ewell's, Hill's, and Jackson's divisions were moved on the 7th in the direction of the enemy from their respective encampments near Gordonsville.[3]

Not only was Jackson a gambler, but he was willing to switch his play in the middle of the game if he saw a greater advantage. He never stuck to a fixed objective, other than that of annihilating the Union forces against him, or to a preconceived plan.

As it turned out, Jackson's men marched only some eight miles towards Culpeper, which was 19 miles away. In the meantime Pope sent some 8,000 men from two infantry divisions and a cavalry command of the corps of Nathaniel P. Banks to reinforce Culpeper. He also sent orders telling Banks to 'assume command of all forces in the front, deploy his skirmishers if the enemy advances, and attack him immediately as he approaches, and be reinforced from here'.[4] This was all that Banks needed. For Banks, whom Jackson had bested in the Valley, and whose nickname in Confederate circles was 'Mr Commissary Banks' because of all the supplies he had lost to southern hands, was itching for revenge. He moved out. Major General James B. Rickett's division, some 9,200 strong, was on the road behind him, as were another division from Fredericksburg and an entire corps from Sperryville.

While most of these men would not reach the attacking Union force in time, the men already there considerably outnumbered Jackson's force. He had ordered up the division commanded by A. P. Hill, but it was yet to arrive. Here again, Jackson reached a point where action meant a gamble. The conservative move would have been to wait for Hill, the gambler's move, to attack. 'He certainly took a very great risk,' one of his staff officers later wrote, 'trusting to gain an advantage by promptness and impetuosity.'[5] It was a greater risk than he realised, as he was not aware how close Banks' infantry was to the main Confederate force. He was aware, however, that Banks commanded the opposite side, and that gave him an added excuse for his gamble. 'Banks is in our front and he is generally willing to fight,' he told his staff surgeon, 'and he generally gets whipped.'[6]

Jackson had advanced one brigade across the Robinson River, up a small valley bounded by a high spot known variously as Cedar or Slaughter Mountain, on 9 August. 'A large body of the enemy's cavalry was drawn up in the plain,' Jackson's topographer wrote in his diary, 'and clouds of dust beyond showed that large bodies of troops were coming to the field.'[7]

Jackson ordered his advanced infantry deployed into line and moved forward carefully. The troops on the right advanced to the top of the crest. There they saw that Union infantry and artillery backed up the cavalry. The Confederates halted and brought up artillery, which they posted around a clump of cedars. The infantry fell back to the reverse side of the slope, out of harm's way. The rough terrain around the mountain made it easily defensible. One northern newspaper correspondent wrote:

> Compared to the bare plain of Waterloo, Cedar Mountain was like the antediluvian world, when surface was broken by volcanic fire into chasms and abysses. In this battle, the Confederate batteries, along the mountain side, were arranged in the form of a crescent, and, when the solid masses charged up the hill, they were butchered by enfilading fires.[8]

Cedar Mountain stood some 550ft above sea level at its highest point.

Jackson was soon on the scene and again, gambling that he had now drawn Banks' force too far away for Pope to reinforce it, decided to attack. In fact he did not take enough time to consider this decision. He did not know how many Union infantrymen were behind the cavalry screen of which he was aware. He did not know the field well at all, especially on the left, through the woods, which had not been reconnoitred sufficiently. Jack-

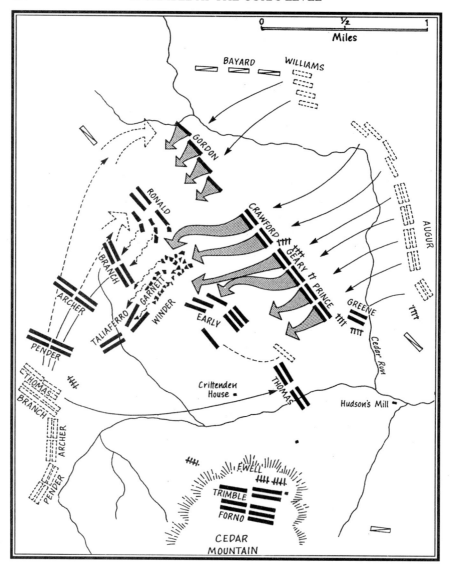

son had not bothered to reconnoitre them at all. He was only vaguely aware
of how the hot weather had contributed to extraordinary straggling in an
army in which straggling was commonplace. Indeed, the leading historian
of the Army of Northern Virginia titled his chapter on Cedar Mountain
'Jackson fumbles at Cedar Mountain'.[9]

None the less, he ordered a forward movement. The main body of his
men would move round the Union right, around Cedar Mountain, while
others moved round the left, on the other side of the road that ran on one

side of the valley. Artillery on Cedar Mountain would keep the defences facing the main attack pinned down, and inhibit their reinforcement. The area beside the road was heavily wooded, save for a wheatfield of about 40 acres. The area between the road and the mountain consisted of fairly clear open meadows or meadows planted with American corn.

The flaw in this apparently excellent plan was that it assumed without any real proof that the main strength of the Union force was on the left side of the Culpeper Road, and that the Confederates attacking along the right would face little or no opposition and easily flank the main Union force.

The grey-clad soldiers set off. Soon vast clouds of dust from the marching feet and horses' hooves lay heavy in the hot, humid air. Breathing was difficult in the ranks. Men emptied their canteens quickly and found that the area lacked streams or wells with easily available water. 'The day was hot and the dust oppressive and the march was a slow one,' one staff officer recalled.[10] Many of the men had been on the road without a long break since 8.00 a.m. 'Many fell fainting by the wayside, and large numbers fell out to hunt a shady spot to cool their parching brain,' a 19th Georgia Infantry soldier remembered.[11] Few clouds blocked the burning sun's rays.

Actual fighting began when Confederate artillery opened up on Federal soldiers posted near where a small gate opened on to a lane that led to a farmhouse. This move, however, did not happen as quickly as Jackson anticipated; normally it took some hours to deploy long lines of marching infantry four abreast into two-deep battle lines, and this is what happened that day. It was an hour past noon when the infantry was in position to move out, but they had to wait. The artillery was not in position until closer to 2.00 p.m., when the cannon began firing

Finally, the chaplain of the 1st New Jersey Cavalry recalled, 'With one burst of thunder, twelve pieces of artillery opened upon our line, while the skirmishers of the enemy engaged warmly with our own. At the same time the Pennsylvanians on our right were attacked, and our own batteries rang out their defiant response to the enemy.'[12]

Then, at about 3.00 p.m., Jackson sent his infantry forward through the cornfield on the other side of the road of the wheatfield and gate against Union cavalry deployed dismounted, three men on the skirmish line while the fourth held the horses. Federal artillery drawn up behind Mitchell's Station Road supported the dismounted troopers. Just before the infantry began moving forward, Confederate artillery dashed along the road and unlimbered into position just beyond the gate.

In the meantime, Confederate infantry pressed the Union cavalry back.

Like the first drops of a thunderstorm, the shot pattered on the ground
around us, each striking up its little cloud of dust, while the air over
our heads was vocal with their whistles. "Steady there!" cried the
major, sternly, as there was a little confusion visible in the ranks of
Company A [1st New Jersey Cavalry]. Two men, Washington Raisner
and Albert Young, drew their horses out of the ranks and saluted, saying quietly, "We are hit, sir," as they moved to the rear. The ranks
closed up again like a wall, and in ten minutes these two men, instead
of nursing their hurts, had the balls extracted, the wounds bandaged
by the surgeon, and, before the blood had even fully clotted and dried
on the lint, were once more back in their places.[13]

Finally, however, the Union cavalry had to give way before the advancing Confederate infantry. Their advance was so smooth that some of the Confederates
were heard 'chatting about home and their sweethearts' while in the forward-
moving battle line.[14] The Federals halted briefly when they reached their
reserves, but were soon sent back again by several Confederate artillery shells.

More Confederate infantry was moving up on the left. They were led by
a native of Maryland, Charles S. Winder, who was well hated by his men for
his harsh discipline, but who had been given command of a division for this
battle. Their original commander had been wounded earlier during the
artillery exchange. Winder himself was unwell, but had left his bed because
of the coming fight. On taking the field he ordered a brigade led by Major
General Richard Garnett 'to move to the front under cover of the woods on
the left (west) side of the road until he arrived on the flank of the nearest battery, which he was then to charge,' one of Winder's staff officers recalled.[15]
He also held the brigade commanded by Brigadier General William Taliaferro [pronounced 'Tulliver'] near the gate to support his artillery.

Although Confederate artillery on top of Cedar Mountain, which had
begun firing as soon as each gun was unlimbered and in position, commanded the Federal left, preventing Banks from advancing in that direction, Banks' right was hidden by trees.

Shortly after arriving on the field Winder fell, terribly mangled by a
Union shell while trying to pass orders on to a nearby artilleryman. A cannoneer saw 'a tremendous hole ... torn in his side' as the general fell.[16] One
of Winder's aides reached his body, and:

... found General Winder lying dreadfully wounded by a piece of shell, which had passed between his left arm and side, tearing the flesh from the inside of the arm above and below the elbow and lacerating the left side as far back as the spine. He still had use of the arm, but it was evident that the wound was mortal. He had been placed on a stretcher, and was not suffering as much pain as he would have suffered if the shock had not been so great. I leaned over him and asked, "General, do you know me?". Turning his eyes to my face with a look of recognition, he answered, "Oh yes" and said some words of sorrow for his wife and children.[17]

Winder was taken off the field to a nearby building where, by 6.00 p.m., he slipped into unconsciousness and died.

Taliaferro, who later said he was 'ignorant of the plans of the general [Jackson], except so far as I could form an opinion from my observation,' assumed command of the left wing.[18] Unfortunately, Jackson and Taliaferro did not get along at all. Jackson, who rarely informed his subordinates of his plans, was doubly unlikely to let Taliaferro in on them.

Finally, and only after setting his troops in motion, Jackson received word of 'glistening bayonets of infantry ... moving stealthily to our left, through the woods'.[19] He then personally reconnoitred in that direction. Once he had seen the area he advised Garnett to watch his left flank carefully at all times. He also had Garnett call up reinforcements from Taliaferro towards the left. Then Jackson returned to the cabin in which he had set up his headquarters, just south of the gate. Meeting his staff officer of engineers there, he told the lieutenant to 'go off on the left and reconnoitre to find out whether it would be practicable to turn the enemy's right'.[20] His mind was obviously still set on one of his favourite flanking movements. Indeed, as the first of A. P. Hill's troops began to arrive he sent the lead brigade, Thomas' Brigade, around to the far Confederate right.

The reserve on the left was the famed Stonewall Brigade, Jackson's Bull Run brigade of Virginians, who felt, with some reason, they were the bravest fighting men in the Confederate army. This day they were led by one of the regimental colonels, Charles Ronald of the 4th Virginia. Ronald was not up to the job of brigade commander. He was ordered to support Garnett's Brigade, and placed them in a column of regiments, which meant that they would take longer to deploy into line when they reached their objective, and also that they would all be under artillery fire for a longer time than if they had advanced in line.

Moreover, after wandering confused through the woods for some time, Ronald finally brought the brigade out a good 450 yards south-east of Garnett's men. Then he halted and sent a courier to find out what to do next. Twenty minutes passed while the courier tried to find the overall commander in that part of the field. Taliaferro, meanwhile, rode over to the left-hand unit of Garnett's Brigade, the small 1st Virginia 'Irish' Battalion. He saw no Federals and returned to the centre of his line, across the road from the gate. Taliaferro also ordered Ronald to continue towards the front.

The Confederate line, from left to right, by now included Garnett's Brigade on the edge of the wheatfield and the Culpeper Road, Taliaferro's Brigade just on the other side of the gate, and Early's Brigade on Taliaferro's right. Artillery filled much of the gap between Early's infantry and the infantry on top of Cedar Mountain.

It was by now fairly late in the afternoon. The sun set at about 5.10 p.m., Philadelphia time, that day.[21] Yet Jackson himself did not get to the gate until around 5.15, about the time that A. P. Hill's division arrived. On the other side of the field, Banks was just getting his troops organised for an attack. He rode up and down his lines so quickly that his hat flew off, leading a regular US Army officer to quip that the general 'had also lost his head, but did not know it'.[22] Leaving a small brigade on his left and another brigade as a reserve in his rear, he placed the remainder of his men in line of battle. By 5.45, as shadows were growing deeper in the woods and in the shadow of Cedar Mountain, he ordered them all forward, one division on each side of the Culpeper Road.

On Banks' left, Major General Christopher Augur's Division started off confidently against the three Confederate brigades and artillery both on that side of the road and on Cedar Mountain. One of Jackson's couriers noted:

> The Yankees came on at a quick step and in what appeared to be a perfect line, without crook or curve, the skirmish line only a short distance in their front. They had almost passed from view beneath the bluff when the sound of the scattering volley of musketry fell on my ear, and a second later the most terrific roar of musketry that I had ever heard arose from the base of the hill on which we sat.[23]

Jackson, seeing the attack launched, scribbled an order on a blank book page and handed it to an orderly, telling him to 'carry this to General Hill', and adding 'be as expeditious as possible'. Hill received the orders quickly enough, and within minutes was forwarding reinforcements to the threatened spot. A captain in the 54th Georgia was among those reinforcements, and he later described what he had seen on the way up:

> The field we passed through was an extensive one, and presented to our sight, as we entered it, almost innumerable bodies of troops fighting, with nothing to protect them save the hand of God. Friend and foe were in open field, and such fighting is seldom witnessed. Troops of all descriptions – horses in every direction, with empty saddles – wounded and dead in all quarters.[24]

The Confederate defensive line was, however, based along a fence line that edged the cornfield which gave them, if not a great deal of protection, at least a line of battle that was easily visible.

The Confederate fire made an almost continuous roar, rather than the staggered volleys and single shots so often heard. Guns grew so hot that it was said that water had to be poured over the barrels to prevent them from firing prematurely when the next cartridge was rammed into the barrels. Artillery on Cedar Mountain itself added to the cacophony. Augur himself was hit shortly after his troops stepped off. Shot in the back as he turned in the saddle to call for his troops to move up, he was evacuated from the field. By the time the charge had turned back, three of the four general officers in the Union division had been wounded.

Unfortunately for the Confederates, however, the left-hand brigade in the line that faced Augur's Division was Taliaferro's Brigade. That brigade commander was, during the attack, understandably more concerned about his own brigade than the division strung out on the other side of the Culpeper Road. Moreover, the attack on the Confederate right hit well before there was any serious fighting on the left. Therefore, his natural inattention considerably helped the Union attack that came on their right, across the wheatfield. For it was on the right that the Union troops of Crawford's Division hit before the 10th Virginia had emerged from the woods to come to the support of the Irish Battalion. Some of the cannon sent to help defend the position had withdrawn before the Union troops appeared in the front. A cannoneer of the Rockbridge Artillery wrote:

By frequent firing during the campaign the vent of my gun had been burned to several times its proper size, so that at each discharge an excess of smoke gushed from it. After the captain's attention was called to it, it happened that a tree in front, but somewhat out of line, was cut off by a Federal shell just as our gun fired. Supposing the defect had caused a wild shot, we were ordered to take the gun to the rear, the other gun soon following.[25]

Not all the Confederate artillery had been so withdrawn, but every gun was shortly to count.

The first Union troops to arrive, just as Confederate guns were limbering up, were some companies of the 3rd Wisconsin. One of its members later wrote:

We hurried forward, pushed down the fence, and without stopping to re-form our line started on a run for that battery. I noticed as we went that Crawford's Brigade had not yet arrived, and that we were alone in the field. Suddenly, from the side of the slope and from the bushes and rocks on our front, arose the Confederate infantry, and poured into our ranks the most destructive musketry fire that I have ever experienced. Lieutenant Colonel Crane was killed, and fell from his horse at the first volley. Major Scott was wounded, being carried off by his horse. Captain Hawley, of the company on our right, was wounded, and a third of his men were killed or wounded at the same time. The right began to fall back, some of the men helping off wounded comrades, others loading and firing at the enemy as they slowly retreated to the woods.[26]

In fact, at about 6.00 p.m. Crawford's men were attacking at the same time as the Wisconsin troops, although hidden from sight by woods. They pushed forward with fixed bayonets, four regiments strong in line of battle. Hardly had Taliaferro arrived at the gate when word came that Federals were indeed in front of the Irish Battalion. The first Confederate volley shocked the Federals, causing many casualties, but they came on bravely, reaching the Confederate line that had been drawn up around a high rail fence, and dissolving it. Jackson's force had been flanked. Hurriedly, Taliaferro rushed the 10th Virginia Infantry to the aid of the hard-pressed Irishmen. The courier from the Stonewall Brigade arrived at about the same time, and Taliaferro told him to move that brigade to Garnett's aid as well.

The Stonewall Brigade was even further behind, and would be too late to save the right flank of Garnett's Brigade. Yet help was at hand. The 42nd and 48th Virginia Infantry Regiments, on the extreme right of the advancing Federals, poured volley after volley into the Federals. Still they came on. The Irish fire did not add much to the effect of the fire from the 42nd and 48th; indeed, an officer in the 28th New York recalled that their shots passed over the heads of the advancing Federals, causing not one casualty. 'By order the battalion fired as the enemy came within 150 yards of our position, with very little effect,' reported Major John Seddon, the battalion commander. 'We fired two more scattering volleys, all with little effect. By this time the enemy were close upon our front and had closed in upon our left flank. Seeing this, the battalion gave way, and retreated rapidly and in great confusion.'[27] The Battalion later reported losses of six killed and 37 wounded, actually one of the smallest losses of any unit in its brigade.

'The Yankees now made an advance with the line that had been concealed in front of the Irish Battalion and the 42nd Virginia,' wrote Private John Worsham of the 21st Virginia. 'Their line being longer than ours, the Yankees swung around the Irish Battalion into our rear and occupied the position from which we had advanced only a few minutes before.'[28] Indeed, the Irish Battalion, which later roster calls would reveal had lost one man killed here, broke and ran as soon as they saw the Federals come steadily on after receiving the ineffective Confederate volley. The Battalion had only ten wounded, with one man apparently killed by heat and exhaustion on the firing line. Other units from Garnett's Brigade, shaken by the flight, soon followed them. Then, starting with the left-hand unit of Taliaferro's Brigade, the 47th Alabama, that unit began to fall apart. The Federals were rolling up Jackson's line.

Worsham gathered the men around him and they started towards safety:

After a few steps I saw a Yankee sergeant step into the road about 50 or 75 yards ahead of us. At the same time I heard the firing of rapidly approaching enemy in our rear. A great dread filled me for Jackson, because I had seen him at this spot only a moment before. The Yankee sergeant, with his gun in his left hand and his sword in his right, turned up the road and approached us. A Yankee private stepped into the road just ahead of him. As this was the road on which we marched to get to our position, this showed that the enemy were not only in our front, flank, and rear, but actually had the Second Brigade surrounded! The Yankee sergeant did not stop his advance toward us until he actually took hold of one of the men of our regiment, pulled him out of ranks, and started toward the rear with his prisoner. One of our men, who was in the act of capping his gun, raised it to his shoulder and fired. The sergeant fell dead, not ten feet away.

By this time the road was full of Yankees, and there was such a fight as was not witnessed during the war. Guns, bayonets, swords, pistols, fence rails, rocks, etc. were used all along the line. I have heard of a "hell spot" in some battle; this surely was one. Our colour bearer knocked down a Yankee with his flag staff – and was shot to death at once. One of the colour guard took the flag, and he also was killed. Another, Roswell S. Lindsay of F Company, bayonetted a Yankee, then was immediately riddled with balls – three going through him. Four colour bearers were killed with the colours in their hands. The fifth man flung the riddled flag to the breeze, and went through the terrible battle unhurt.[29]

Jackson had not left the area, however, but was still on the scene. According to his topographer: 'The General and the three or four members of his staff who were still with him were exposed to the hottest of the fire and all were busy trying to rally the left wing after it fell back, the General appealing to the men to follow him, and he led a body of them to the fight'.[30] Jackson himself tried to draw his old cavalry sword to lead his troops back, but found it had rusted fast in the iron scabbard. Unsnapping it from the slings, he waved the sword, still in its scabbard, in one hand and a battle flag in the other as he rode, reins flapping at his sides, among the retreating troops. 'Rally, men,' he cried out. 'Remember Winder! Where's my Stonewall Brigade? Forward, men, forward.'[31]

Brigadier General Jubal Early, whose brigade was on the right of Taliaferro's, rode to where the Federals had broken through the line. He later wrote:

On getting to where I could see, I discovered that it had given way, and the men of several regiments were retiring rapidly to the rear, while a portion of the enemy had crossed the little stream in front of where my left had been. The only thing now standing, as far as I could see, was

Thomas' brigade on my right, the 12th Georgia, four companies of the 52nd Virginia, and part of the 58th Virginia.

It was a most critical state of things, and I saw that the day would probably be lost, unless I could hold the position I still occupied. I could not, therefore, go to rally my retreating men, but sent my Assistant Adjutant General, Major Samuel Hale, to rally them and bring them back, while I rode to the rest of my troops and directed their commanders to hold on to their positions at all hazards. On giving the directions to Captain Brown of the 12th Georgia, he replied: "General, my ammunition is nearly out, don't you think we had better charge them?" I could not admit the prudence of the proposition at that time, but I fully appreciated its gallantry. This brave old man was then 65 years old, and had a son, an officer, in his company.[32]

The 13th Virginia, in Jubal Early's Brigade, held on and fell back only slowly, firing into the Federals, whose advance slowed as they did so. The 12th Georgia poured in steady volley after volley. They acted 'as if we had been invited to a frolic,' one wrote later, adding, 'Talking and laughing continued as long as the battle lasted'.[33] Once the Union troops had visibly halted, the Georgians, aided by elements of the 52nd and 58th Virginia Regiments, counterattacked, and the Federal advance came to a dead halt.

The Stonewall Brigade, with the 10th Virginia, had also arrived. The 10th was quickly brushed aside, as well as the 27th Virginia regiment from the Stonewall Brigade. The route taken by the 27th was something of a shock to the rest of the army. Captain Charles Haynes, a temporary regimental commander, blamed his regiment's disgraceful retreat on the fact that a regiment on the right of the 27th fell back, while advancing enemy caught the regiment in a crossfire. Yet in his official report he admits, 'I lost three men killed and one wounded,' adding 'not having sufficient force to drive back the enemy and hold my position, the regiment was compelled to fall back. This, on account of thick brush and fallen timber that covered the ground, caused the regiment to scatter considerably.' Haynes tried to rally the regiment some 150 yards to the rear, but admitted that he 'only partially succeeded'.[34] The Stonewall Brigade would have to fight short of one regiment.

But the rest of the Brigade wheeled some 90° into line of battle, quite a difficult feat while under fire and keeping the companies dressed, and refused to be budged. Indeed, some of its units managed to pivot into the rear of the companies of the 3rd Wisconsin, which had been so battered in its initial attack, and send that unit packing. Private John Casler of the Brigade's 33rd Virginia recalled:

When we were about halfway across the field we met the enemy's line lying down behind a small slope. We commenced firing and advancing – the enemy returning the fire – but as our line on the left was about one regiment longer than theirs the brigade kept on advancing and coming around on a wheel. The first line of the enemy fell back on the second; and as our regiment reached the edge of the woods we came to a wheat field that was cut and shocked. There the firing was heavy.[35]

The left of the Confederate line was now apparently firm.

A Federal officer who had been captured earlier watched in awe as Jackson rode about the field waving his sword and flag. 'What officer is that, Captain?' he asked a Confederate.

'Stonewall Jackson,' came the reply.

The Federal turned back to the scene in front of him. 'Hurrah for General Jackson,' he yelled. 'Follow your general, boys!' Touched, the Confederate let the Federal slip away to safety in the confusion.[36]

Jackson, who had lost his hat in the woods, was busy directing Lawrence O'B. Branch's North Carolina brigade, on the west of the road, forward, supported by James Archer's Brigade. When he arrived at Branch's Brigade he found Branch, a former congressman, making a speech to his men to inspire them. One of Jackson's staff officers wrote:

It was a dangerous experiment, for I do not believe any general ever made a speech to his troops on the even of battle who did not do more harm than good. But no harm was done on this occasion for General Jackson hearing of this delay and the cause of it, started with an unfathomable smile and galloped to the spot. As he reached the right of the brigade he took off his hat, rode rapidly along the line looking the men steadily in their faces as he passed along. When he reached their commander, he said curtly, "Push forward, General, push forward!" and then moved to the front. The effect was instantaneous: this was an eloquence the men understood. Forward with quick step and then quicker went the whole line after their illustrious leader and then with an irresistible yell they charged over the field, their wild yell mingling with the rattle of their musketry. Several officers rushed up to Jackson and almost forced him to the rear, but the charging line swept past him with a shout and kept on.[37]

Branch's troops advanced, passing by the fleeing ranks of the 27th Virginia, which, the North Carolinians noted with some scorn, was a unit of the famed Stonewall Brigade. Jackson then sent Dorsey Pender's North Carolina Brigade to the left of the Stonewall Brigade to try to envelop the Federal right.

Banks, seeing his attack foiled as Crawford's men dribbled back out of harm's way, hurled a single regiment, the 10th Maine, at the Confederate left. It dissolved in a firestorm from Pender's Brigade and the Stonewall Brigade. So many of the 10th were hit in the forlorn effort that, one veteran recalled, 'It looked as if we had a crowd of howling dervishes dancing and kicking around in our ranks'.[38] Banks ordered the 1st Pennsylvania Cavalry, 164 men of all ranks, in a last desperate attempt across the wheatfield. All but 71 men were shot down in the valiant but foolish attempt. A Confederate later counted the corpses of some 29 dead horses in the field over which the Pennsylvanians had charged. As the survivors fled, a small, two-regiment-strong Federal brigade deployed into line at the edge of the woods. It was the last gasp of the Federals, and the brigade was quickly driven off.

It was now Jackson's turn. He ordered a general advance all along the line just as a sudden, brief, hard shower gave some relief to the exhausted men. The last intact Federal brigade near the wheatfield was caught by a flank attack. A third of the brigade's men were captured, killed or wounded before the survivors could escape. On the Confederate right, troops swept down off Cedar Mountain, past a millpond that slowed down their advance, and into the Federal line. The Federals turned and ran. 'The cannonade continued until long after dark and was a splendid sight,' Jackson's topographer noted in his diary.[39]

Banks himself was nearly captured by Confederate cavalry. One of his staff officers recalled how Confederate cavalry suddenly emerged from a wood near where the general and his staff were observing the action:

Turning suddenly, they yelled and poured in upon us a rapid and continuous volley from carbines and pistols. We mounted in hot haste, as the enemy were not more than fifty paces from us. In attempting to mount, General Banks was overthrown and his hip badly hurt by the horse of a dragoon, the rider of which was killed. By the time we had started across the field, the fire in our rear became more furious. The balls struck around us so rapidly that I thought it impossible for anyone to escape. Colonel Ruggles, the adjutant general, and Captain Rowley of the Signal Corps lost their horses by shot. Major Meline streaked it afoot, his horse having escaped from his groom. General Pope stuck his head down and, striking spur, led off at full speed. I gave my mare the reins and, as we crossed a hollow, a regiment of our own infantry seeing a dark mass of cavalry advancing opened fire. Thus we had it front and rear and only our being in a hollow saved us.[40]

'We kept up the pursuit until 9 or 10 o'clock that night,' Private Worsham of the 21st recalled, 'when we were halted and allowed to rest for the night.'[41] The brief shower had not cooled off the field much; the mercury stood at 86° at 8.00 p.m., even though the sun had set by that time. Many Confederates spent much of the night finding wounded companions and Federals hidden in the woods and bringing them to help. Unhurt Federals, also hidden in the woods, escaped danger and surrendered to the first southern soldier they saw.

Rickett's division had drawn up a mile behind Banks' troops, and there the survivors finally halted as it became too dark to fight any longer. Jackson, too, halted his men. As night fighting was very difficult, at best, Jackson decided that his men had done enough. They had completely routed Banks and stopped Pope's advance guard. Jackson himself dismounted on a grassy spot of ground, not wanting to deprive the wounded of the shelter of any nearby buildings, and said he would sleep there. When asked if he wanted anything to eat first, he replied, 'No, I want *rest*, nothing but *rest!*'[42]

Banks had lost 314 men killed, 1,445 wounded and 594 missing, some 400 of whom were prisoners. In addition, according to Jackson's topographer, the Confederates captured a cannon, 3,000 strand of arms, and twelve wagon loads of much-needed ammunition. Jackson had lost but 231 men killed and 1,107 wounded, nearly half of whom were in Garnett's and Taliaferro's Brigades. Jackson's gamble so unnerved Hallack in Washington that he refused to allow Pope to advance further across the Rapidan until he had been heavily reinforced. Pope had halted, and Jackson was free to go on the offensive.

Notes

1 Alexander, Bevin, *Lost Victories, the Military Genius of Stonewall Jackson*, New York, 1992, p.142.
2 McDonald, Archie P., *Make me a Map of the Valley, the Civil War Journal of Stonewall*

Jackson's Topographer, Dallas, Texas, 1973, p.65.

3   *ORs,* Series I, Vol. XII, Part II, p.182.

4   Ropes, John C., *The Army Under Pope,* New York, no date, p.21.

5   Douglas, Henry Kyd, *I Rode with Stonewall,* Chapel Hill, North Carolina, 1940, p.123.

6   Krick, Robert K., *Stonewall Jackson at Cedar Mountain,* Chapel Hill, North Carolina, 1990, p.45.

7   McDonald, Archie P., *op. cit.,* p.66.

8   Towsend, George A., *Rustics in Rebellion,* Chapel Hill, North Carolina, 1950, p.225.

9   Freeman, Douglas Southall, *Lee's Lieutenants,* New York, 1944, Vol. 2, p.16.

10 Krick, Robert K., *op. cit.,* p.63.

11 Krick, Robert K., *ibid.,* p.65.

12 Pyne, Henry R., *Ride to War,* New Brunswick, New Jersey, 1961, pp.60-61.

13 Pyne, Henry R., *ibid.,* p.63.

14 Krick, Robert K., *op. cit.,* p.58.

15 Howard, McHenry, *Recollections of a Maryland Confederate Soldier and Staff Officer,* Dayton, Ohio, 1975, p.169.

16 Krick, Robert K., *ibid.,* p.96.

17 Howard, McHenry, *op. cit.,* p.170.

18 Vandiver, Frank E., *Mighty Stonewall,* New York, 1957, p.341.

19 Early, Jubal A., *op. cit.,* p.97.

20 Krick, Robert K., *op. cit.,* p.108.

21 Sturges and Pritchard, *Farmer's Almanac for the Year 1862,* Mansfield, Ohio, p.18.

22 Krick, Robert K., *op. cit.,* p.120.

23 Oates, Dan, ed., *Hanging Rock Rebel,* Shippensburg, Pennsylvania, 1994, p.120.

24 Krick, Robert K., *ibid.,* pp.130-136.

25 Moore, Edward A., *The Story of a Cannoneer under Stonewall Jackson,* New York, 1907, p.96.

26 Hinkley, Julian W., *A Narrative of Service with the Third Wisconsin Infantry,* Madison, Wisconsin, 1912, p.34.

27 *ORs,* Series I, Vol. XII, Part II, p.205.

28 Worsham, John H., *One of Jackson's Foot Cavalry,* Jackson, Tennessee, 1964, p.64.

29 Worsham, John H., *ibid.,* p.65.

30 McDonald, Archie P., *op. cit.,* p.66.

31 Vandiver, Frank E., *op. cit.,* p.342.

32 Early, Jubal A., *Narrative of the War Between the States,* New York, 1989, p.99.

33 Krick, Robert K., *op. cit.,* p.199.

34 *ORs,* Series I, Vol. XII, Part II, p.197.

35 Casler, John O., *Four Years in the Stonewall Brigade,* Dayton, Ohio, 1994, p.103.

36 Vandiver, Frank E., *op. cit.,* p.342.

37 Douglas, Henry Kyd, *op. cit.,* pp.124-125.

38 Krick, Robert K., *op. cit.,* p.223.

39 McDonald, Archie P., *op. cit.,* p.66.

40 Strother, David Hunter, *A Virginia Yankee in the Civil War,* Chapel Hill, North Carolina, 1961, p.77.

41 Worsham, John H., *op. cit.,* p.66.

42 Vandiver, Frank E., *op. cit.,* p.343.

Benham Attacks Secessionville

THE GAMBLE: *that a Federal Corps-sized force can successfully cross terrible terrain to capture a fort being built by Confederate forces near Charleston before the fort is too complete to take.*

If there was one place other than Richmond that Federal forces desired to take, it was Charleston, South Carolina. There, in that lovely city by one of the best bays in America, southerners declared the Federal constitution null and void, and the government dissolved. They had done it before, decades earlier, but a show of Federal governmental strength, directed by southern President Andrew Jackson, put an end to it – for the time being. But South Carolina leader John C. Calhoun kept alive the idea of secession, of the supremacy of each state government over the Federal government, in the decades that followed.

Then, when the will of the majority, as judged under the Federal Constitution, indicated that Republican and slavery foe Abraham Lincoln was to be the next President of the United States, it was in Charleston that South Carolinians met and declared that they were no longer a part of the old United States of America. Having done that, it was at Fort Sumter in Charleston that the first shots against the United States flag were fired, to start the war. So Charleston was not an objective simply because of its port, its quartermaster depot and its size. It was an objective for revenge.

But Charleston would be a hard nut to crack. It was set well away from the ocean, on the western side of a well protected bay. Along the ocean the land was dissected up by marshes, swamps and rivers, and dozens of small islands dotted the inlets. The land was fairly easy to fortify and difficult to capture.

In November 1861, however, almost at the war's beginning, the northern forces scored well by making a rather easy capture of the Port Royal region, some 70 miles south of Charleston, along the coast. The sea islands featured

two decent sized towns, Beauford and Hilton Head, that the Federals fortified. That capture enabled Federal Navy ships to be resupplied relatively
close to Charleston itself, instead of having to make the long trip back to
Virginia's coast. In addition, the area made an ideal staging ground for further attacks on other seaside Confederate posts. Major General David
Hunter, commander in the area, made his headquarters at Hilton Head.

Hunter, an 1822 US Military Academy graduate, had been a major in the
paymaster department before the war. Writing to Lincoln after the presi-
dential election earned him a seat on Lincoln's train to Washington, and the
confidence of the man himself. Although his campaigns were invariably
defeats, he had the ear of the president in his new command, and was
known to be a man of some influence in the government. More influence,
in fact, than most major generals are capable of. His influence would be
greatly enhanced were he to capture Charleston.

Port Royal's capture concerned another general as well, Major General
John C. Pemberton, Pennsylvania-born commander of the Confederate
Army's Department of South Carolina and Georgia. He pulled a number
of his troops back from the small islands around Charleston to the largest
island in the area, James Island. There he set up a line of defence that ran
between Fort Johnson on the north-east corner and Fort Pemberton on
the north-west corner. On the island there was one town of real notice,
Grimball's, which lay considerably south of Fort Pemberton on the road
to Charleston. One road from that town led to Fort Johnson, whose guns
also covered the south channel of Charleston's harbour. No roads ran
between the two forts; indeed, James Island Creek, and marshy land on
either side of the creek, made direct travel between the two forts almost
impossible.

Besides Grimball's, there was a small town almost in the very centre of
the island. It was called Secessionville, not because of any Civil War political connection, but because it was made up of summer homes that were so
isolated from the inhabitants and activities of the rest of the island that their
inhabitants joked that they lived in Secessionville. The town, almost
directly east of Grimball's, lay on the very edge of useful land. To its other
three sides lay swamp, and it was close to a large body of water almost
directly in the centre of the island. The Confederates took advantage of its
position to build an observation tower, protected by an earthworks fortification. Pemberton began improving this fortification shortly after Port
Royal fell.

Grimball's was built on the Island side of the Stono River, and fairly soon after Port Royal's capture Federal warships began to probe the river. They found little resistance, and landed a corps of two divisions there, some 11,000 men, under Brigadier General Henry W. Benham, on the night of 2 June 1862. Now an entire Federal corps was only a day's march from Charleston.

If Hunter was out of his league with such a command, Benham was even more so. An unhappy childhood apparently left him unable to deal with others save in a manner of cold contempt. Even so, he was an extremely intelligent, if egotistical, individual who had graduated first in his class at the US Military Academy in 1837. As traditionally happened with those who came first in their classes, Benham had been posted to the Corps of Engineers. He continued in the Corps, having turned down a majority in the infantry after the Mexican War, through the 1861 campaign in West Virginia. There his service as chief engineer earned him a commission of brigadier general of volunteers, with a command in the line to match. Unfortunately he lacked a veteran infantryman's instinct for ground; for when to attack and when not to do so. His actions in West Virginia showed this, and were criticised by some of his fellow soldiers. None the less, he was reassigned to South Carolina, where Hunter considered him 'industrious, energetic, and wholly devoted to his duties'.[1]

Benham learned that the fortifications at Secessionville, which were within range of his artillery, consisted of only 'a common earthwork', which would soon be strengthened. On 9 June he met with Hunter to discuss the situation. He urged that it was important to 'have and hold those points for the security of our camps and even for the occupation of the Stono'. Deserters had told his troops that the fort there lacked a stockade and its front was only covered with the interwoven brambles called *abatis*. There were between four and six cannon mounted on it, he was told, but another six or seven were ready to be mounted. He may or may not have known that one of the guns mounted there was an 8in Columbiad, a huge shore-defence gun that could clear an entire deck with one shot. Finally, the post was garrisoned by only two battalions of infantry. Benham felt that a quick assault before the Confederates could finish their works was a gamble well worth taking, for the capture of Secessionville would place the Federals square in the centre of the island, not only aiming them directly at Charleston, but protecting their camp on the Stono River.

Benham produced a map with a line drawn through the point where the Confederate works and signal tower at Secessionville were located, showing his superior how they threatened his position. Later he would report, 'I considered it indispensable that we should have and hold those points for the security of our camps and even for the occupation of the Stono ...' Moreover, he added, he feared that the Confederate works 'would be a good foundation for driving us from the Stono entirely'.[2]

Hunter agreed that the works presented a threat, but was concerned that the Federals did not have enough reliable information on the enemy's strength. He later claimed that he 'gave positive orders to General Benham that no advance should be made until further explicit orders had been received from these headquarters'.[3] Indeed, Hunter returned to his headquarters at Hilton Head on 10 June, leaving a note to Benham saying, in part:

> ... in any arrangements that you may make for the disposition of your forces now in this vicinity, you will make no attempt to advance on Charleston or to attack Fort Johnson until largely reinforced or until you receive specific instructions from these headquarters to that effect. You will however provide for a secure intrenched [*sic*] encampment, where your front can be covered by the fire of our gunboats from the Stono on your left and the creek from Folly River on the right.[4]

The imprecise statements in these orders were enough for Benham. He understood that he could not attack Fort Johnson or Charleston, but he felt he had received sufficient authorization to clear the enemy at Secessionville so as to have a 'secure intrenched encampment'. 'I understood him distinctly as assenting to and approving of my representation,' he later claimed.[5] As far as Benham was concerned, he had been allowed to gamble with an attack on the Secessionville works.

Benham was ready to move straight away. However, he was convinced by his subordinates that the troops needed rest after landing and building their camps and works despite several days of steady rain. Many of them had also been involved in a skirmish on the 10th. Benham postponed the attack until 15 June, a Sunday. In the meantime he had a battery of three rifled guns placed where it could fire on the works at Secessionville. The cannoneers began firing immediately and continued a steady, but apparently ineffective, fire.

On the evening of the 15th Benham gathered his top officers, Brigadier General Horatio Wright, commander of his 1st Division, Brigadier General Isaac I. Stevens, commander of the 2nd Division, and Colonel Robert Williams, commander of the 3rd Brigade. Captain Percival Drayton, the US Navy's senior naval officer in the area, was also present. Benham announced his plans to take the Confederate works by force, and, according to later testimony, the three were aghast. Stevens said that the Federal artillery fire had been useless, and that as soon as the firing ceased the enemy came out to man their guns again as strong as ever. Stevens also said that he felt that volunteer troops had never stormed works as strong as those at Secessionville, and they would not this time.

Benham did not hear anything the three said. According to him this was to be a reconnaissance 'made in force, with the object, if it were successful and the fort not too strong, of capturing and holding the same'.[6] Wright objected, telling Benham that his orders were not for a reconnaissance, they were orders to fight a battle. Drayton, whose ships would provide artillery support for the assault, was concerned by the lack of enthusiasm for such an assault exhibited by the Army officers present.

Despite this, Benham would not be dissuaded from his gamble. Overruling the others, he outlined his plans. According to Wright:

> The division of General Stevens was to form the assaulting column against the enemy's works at Secessionville, and, being formed in the utmost silence at is outer pickets, was to move forward at the first break of day upon the enemy's batteries, while the remainder of the troops, comprising Williams' brigade and a part of my division, moving together from the camp at Grimball's, were to act as a support to General Stevens, protecting his left and rear from an attack of the enemy's forces from that direction.[7]

The important part of these orders was that the attack could come at daybreak, which was around 4.53 on 16 June.[8] Therefore, Benham wanted Stevens' men charging at the fort, bayonets levelled, by three in the morning, 'before good aiming light, and with guns loaded'.[9]

'General, may I ask what is the plan of battle?' asked one of Stevens' officers on his return from the meeting.

'Damn it, sir,' an angry Stevens burst out, 'there isn't any plan. You will fire when you get a chance, and be careful not to hit any of our own men.'[10]

Stevens, who had earlier urged with his usual lack of success that a day-light attack would be a better plan, because the targets would be distinct, understood Benham to mean that he should begin his attack at 4.00, still 50 minutes before clear daylight. He therefore had his division roused at about 1.00 a.m. and in formation by 2.00. Then he started off, reaching their outer picket line by 3.30.

It was neither a good night nor good terrain for marching. Clouds hid the stars, and the moon had set almost four hours earlier. 'It was so dark that one man could not follow another except at very short intervals,' Stevens reported.[11] The troops had to march along narrow, sandy lanes bordered by dense woods. When they reached the Confederate picket line the Union troops would have to cross a deep ditch, climb a six foot-high embankment topped by a thick myrtle bush hedge, cross another ditch and break through another myrtle hedge. They would then be on relatively clear ground, in an old cotton field left to weeds which had grown some three feet high. Years of previous cultivation had left deep ruts between the rows on which cotton had been planted, making it slow to cross. Once across this field, they still had to charge some 400 yards across a narrow causeway. Impassable marshes on either side of the causeway prevented at attack over those areas.

At that point, too, they would come under Confederate fire from the fort, and the Confederates were ready for them. Brigadier General Nathan G. 'Shanks' Evans, a member of the US Military Academy class of 1848, com-manded the overall area including the fort, which was commanded by Colonel Thomas G. Lamar, 1st South Carolina Artillery. Lamar's garrison comprised two companies of his own regiment, numbering some 150 troops.

Lamar first noticed unusual activity in the Federal camp on the afternoon of the 15th, while the Federal commanders were meeting. He notified Evans that he was convinced that the Federals would attack that night or the next morning. Then, later, he saw flickering lights in the Federal camps through the darkness, indicating unusual activity, the movement of a great many men. He became convinced that the Federals were already on the move to attack his position, and at 2.00 a.m. so notified Evans. At the same time he had his own troops roused and in position, weapons loaded and at the ready. They were joined by a company of the 22nd South Carolina Infantry that had been ordered to the fort for fatigue duties.

Evans immediately gathered all the troops he could and sent them to Lamar's post. Then he hurried to the scene himself. It was now getting close to daybreak, and the first Federal troops attacked the Confederate picket line. They were men of Companies C and H of the 8th Michigan, who had been detailed to serve as advanced skirmishers and the attacking party; a group that would have earlier been called the 'forlorn hope'. Behind them came Company E, 1st New York Volunteer Engineers, with axes, saws and shovels slung in black leather holsters on their backs, to remove the *abatis* and brush in the attackers' path.

In the darkness the advance group captured four Confederate pickets, possibly dozing, and sent them to the rear. Their movement attracted several shots, which undoubtedly raised the fever pitch of Colonel Lamar even further, but they had been ordered to keep complete silence and did not return the southern fire. Finally they broke through the rough terrain into the open field and deployed into open skirmish order. They then halted, kneeling silently, as the rest of the regiment emerged from the hedge line and went into full line of battle behind them. As his companies were turning to the left and coming on to line, brigade commander Colonel William Fenton, a middle-aged volunteer officer who had risen from a sick bed for the fight, examined the Confederate position through his glasses. By now the false dawn had brought sufficient light to the scene to enable him do so, but the dark blue coats were fairly well hidden against a dark green hedge background.

Stevens later described what Fenton saw:

The front on which the attack was made was narrow, not over 200 yards in extent, stretching from the marsh on the one side to the marsh on the other. It was at the saddle of the peninsula, the ground narrowing very suddenly at this point from our advance. On either hand were bushes on the edge of the marsh for some little distance. The whole space at the saddle was occupied by the enemy's work, impracticable abatis on either hand, with carefully prepared *trous de loup* on our left and in front a ditch 7 feet deep, with a parapet of hard-packed earth, having a relief of some 9 feet above the general surface of the ground. On the fort were mounted six guns, covering the field of our approach. The whole interior of the work was swept by fire from the rifle pits and defences in the rear, and the flanks of the work itself and the bushes lining the marsh on either hand were under the fire of riflemen and sharpshooters stationed in the woods and defences lying between the work and the village of Secessionville.[12]

Fenton decided the position directly in front of him was too hard to attack. Instead, he saw that higher ground to his right would enable his men to fire into the Confederate position. At the same time, the following regiments could follow his lead to get into the best position. He therefore ordered his men to march forward at an oblique angle to the Confederates. At the same time he sent couriers back to let the following regiments know what he was doing.

Fenton had been told not to stop to fire, but dash on and take the works with the bayonet. However, the alerted Confederates spotted the 8th as it started to move, and opened fire. The Columbiad, in the centre of the works, had been loaded with all sorts of scrap, including broken glass, horseshoes and spikes, and tore great gaps in the Federal line. Lamar himself acted as gun commander for this weapon, sighting it before each discharge. 'My reason for pointing the Columbiad myself,' Lamar said, 'was to fire at the centre of the line and thereby break it, in order to cause confusion and delay, so that I might get my infantry into position previous to their reaching my lines.'[13] His plan worked.

Fenton wrote:

> During this advance, the enemy opened upon our lines an exceedingly destructive fire of grape, canister, and musketry, and yet the regiment pushed on as veterans, divided only to the right and left by a sweeping torrent from the enemy's main gun in front. This brought a portion of the regiment to the left near the tower or lookout, and a brisk fire of musketry was soon opened on both sides. The enemy's fire proved so galling and destructive that our troops on the parapet were compelled to retire under its cover, and that of the ditch and slope on our right at the marsh, slope and trees on our left.[14]

A 23-year-old second lieutenant from Stevens' staff, Benjamin Lyons, who had previously scouted the area, led the attack. 'Come on, boys,' he yelled as he dashed down into the ditch and up the other side.[15] There, at the bottom of the earthworks, he fell, badly wounded. Others dashed by him as he turned and limped back to a field hospital in the rear. Although he reached help, he later died from his wounds. The New York Engineers dropped their tools, unslung their muskets and fixed bayonets and dashed forward with the first attacking wave. Heavy artillery fire tore through their ranks, and several paused. Corporal George Hughes twice grabbed stunned engineers and shoved them forward, keeping up the momentum of the attack.

The 8th Michigan, which led the assault, actually managed to cross the ditch in front of the fort's walls, dash up the slope and reach the top of the fortifications. But, because the troops behind them halted, they were without support, and had to fall back. A large number of their officers fell, both in the attack and on the parapets, and the leaderless regiment lost cohesion. Finally, the survivors gathered around the colours, which had been brought off the field, but effectively they were out of the rest of the fight. They had lost 182 killed, wounded and missing out of 509 they had brought into the fight. The engineers also lost many of the tools they had dropped before making the attack.

Lamar took advantage of the pause caused by the stalled attack to rush additional reinforcements from his reserves, some 250 men from the 1st and 9th South Carolina Battalions, into positions behind the works. The 1st, which arrived first, was posted on his left where the Michigan attack fell, while the 9th lined the works along the right and centre. By now Lamar had 500 men to defend against a total attacking force of 6,600. The advantage of numbers was largely nullified, however, by the narrow causeway which limited the attackers' front.

The 8th had been told to wait for the 7th Connecticut so that the two could advance on line together. In fact they had not done so, and the 7th Connecticut formed into line as the Michigan troops were scrambling up the earthworks. Despite the orders not to return fire, many of the men of the 7th now stopped some 130 yards from the fort and opened fire at the Confederates. Their fire was joined by howitzers of the 1st Connecticut Light Battery, which opened up on the fort from a range of about 500 yards. As their canister and spherical case exploded over the works they were joined by a James rifle from the battery's right section that also came on to line. The 28th Massachusetts, a largely Irish regiment, came up behind the men from Connecticut, but their organisation fell apart when their ranks were parted by the *abatis*. The second attack collapsed. The 7th halted behind the hedge, many of the men going on the battle side to add their musket fire to that of the artillery. Finally, however, Stevens ordered the 8th, 7th and 28th to return to camp.

Stevens had the rest of his men fall back some 1,200 yards from the fort and re-formed his so far untried troops for a second attempt. In answer to an urgent plea from Fenton, the 2nd Brigade came up on line as support, led by the 79th New York, with the 100th Pennsylvania following. Then Stevens ordered the line forward on the double quick.

As they came up to where the 1st Connecticut Light Battery was firing away, he called to its commander, 'Connecticut boys, go in and the day is ours'. Immediately they limbered up and headed after the infantry. Cannoneer Edward Griswold recalled:

> We had to cross a cotton field, some 800 yards, and the enemy was raking that field with cannonades, and the seacoast howitzer that had been taken from the Government. The cannoneers were not mounted ... Corporal Scannton mounted one of the limbers and sitting astride, managed to hold on. I grasped the muzzle of the gun, with my thumb over the sight pin. How those horses went.

Reaching a point not far from the fort's walls, the battery halted and ran their guns on to line, under heavy fire from Confederate cannon. 'We worked the guns lively, and most of the time in a stooping position,' Griswold wrote. Astonishingly, not a single cannoneer was hit by enemy fire.[16]

But Confederate artillery fire took its toll of the next attacking wave. According to 2nd Brigade commander Colonel David Leasure:

> We entered the range of a perfect storm of grape, canister, nails, broken glass, and pieces of chains fired from three very large pieces on the fort, which completely swept every foot of ground within the range, and either cut the men down or drove them to the shelter of the ravine on the left. I now turned to look after and lead up the One-hundredth Pennsylvania Regiment, and found its centre just entering the fatal line of fire, which completely cut it in two, and the right, under Major Leakey, obliqued to the right, and advanced to support the right of the Seventy-ninth New York, and many of the men reached the foot of the embankment, and some succeeded in mounting it, with a few brave men of the Seventy-ninth, who were there with a portion of the Eighth Michigan.[17]

Not all the Michiganers had managed to retire. Some had laid between the cotton rows, and jumped up to join this second charge.

Private John P. Wilson, Company C, 100th Pennsylvania, wrote:

We ran up close to the fort, and the rebels were raining showers of grape, canister, chains, and musketballs, but I did not care for them a bit more than if it had been a shower of rain. Henry Guy has three holes through his blouse, but he is not hurt. There was one ball struck my bayonet. I was the only one standing for several rods around for a while. The rest laid down to avoid the grape, but I wanted to see where it was coming from. Several that laid down never got up again, but there was not one of the balls touched me. We could not get in the fort when we got to it. We stayed for over an hour and then we got the order to retreat.[18]

Still other Union infantry reached the fort's walls and began scrambling up to the top. Lieutenant Colonel David Morrison of the 79th New York actually reached the top and stared in, impressed by the strength of a fortification that he had been told was only in its early stages. Then he fell with a wound to his head. He was just one of many Federal officers wounded on top of the works. Captain Richard N. Doyle of the 8th Michigan paused to fire his revolver into the Confederates below until he fell, shot. Captain Benjamin B. Church of the 8th had been cheering his men on, waving his sword, when a Confederate bullet found him and he fell dead into the works.

Neither were the Confederates having an easy a time of it. Lieutenant James Campbell of the 9th South Carolina found himself without a weapon and grabbed a handspike, the baseball-bat-like wood spike used to move gun tails, and began clubbing Federals left and right. Finally he found a dropped musket to use.

Determined fighting like that of Lieutenant Campbell stalled the Federal attack. Largely leaderless with so many of their officers down, many of the Federals now ducked behind the outside of the earthen walls and fired at Confederates on the other side. This stalemate continued for some 20 minutes, when the survivors of the assault began to give up hope and fled back the way they had come. For 'God's sake', Leasure pleaded to an officer of the 1st Division, which was drawn up silently watching the scene, 'come up to the front and support me in a charge ...'[19] The officer, who possibly recalled previous orders not to reinforce a failed attack, declined, saying that the troops could not be ordered into battle by anybody from the 2nd Division.

Giving up, Leasure ordered his brigade to retire. The 79th New York left some 40 dead or badly wounded behind them, bringing back another six of their dead and 60 wounded. Benham, however, was yet to yield. He ordered the 1st Brigade to fall back and re-form, to prepare for yet another attack. At the same time he ordered Williams to bring his 3rd Brigade, some 1,500 strong, to move out in open order and provide covering fire for the retiring 1st Brigade.

Once again the pause allowed Lamar to stiffen his defences with reinforcements. The 4th Louisiana Infantry Battalion, some 250 strong, arrived and was placed along the right just as Benham's next assault was launched. 'Remember Butler', they yelled at the attacking Federals, recalling the harsh treatment of residents of New Orleans by Major General Benjamin Butler.[20]

Williams sent forward his two dismounted units, the 3rd New Hampshire and the 97th Pennsylvania Infantry. At first they dashed straight ahead to the front, halting in a deep ditch some 200 yards from the Confederate works. There they ducked under heavy fire. Williams then ordered the 97th to a point on the left. A swamp lay between the two positions, and Colonel Henry Guss had to dismount and fight with his horse, which tore at its reins to escape, while leading it through the morass. Finally they found a ditch and dropped into it, while the colonel sent a reconnaissance party to find a way to attack the Confederates. Then they all moved a bit further forward and again lay down. The excitement and exhaustion of a long night march had so wearied the men that many of them fell asleep there, despite cannonballs from both sides bursting overhead.

Even so, men of the 97th took casualties. Private James Starr of Company F looked on in horror as one of his close friends, George Wright, suddenly rose from his knee, exclaiming, 'Oh, my God, I'm shot,' and dropped dead.[21]

A heavy artillery unit, the 3rd Rhode Island Regiment, was ordered out to support the 3rd and 97th. When they reached their position, Major Edwin Metcalf spotted a Confederate battery, partly hidden in a thicket alongside the works, that was firing into the 3rd New Hampshire. He had the men act as infantry, taking advantage of the heavy woods to work their way to the enemy guns. Some of his lead men actually reached a point where they could see the enemy's three guns and count the couple of infantry companies supporting them. Metcalf, under fire for the first time, as was his regiment, was unsure of himself. There were no experienced infantrymen around him, and he decided to call off the attack and return to his starting position.

Wright also ordered the 47th New York to the left of the line to silence fire coming from a low row of bushes behind a very marshy ravine. The regiment took a position 400 paces from the fort, with enemy canister bursting among them. They would spend some 15 minutes there, firing volleys at an unseen enemy.

But all this Federal fire took its toll of the defenders, too. Lamar was hit on the head by a bullet during the second charge and, exhausted from the loss of blood, turned over his command to Lieutenant Colonel P. C. Gaillard, commander of the 9th South Carolina. Gaillard had not been in command long when he, too, was wounded, and he turned over command to Lieutenant Colonel Thomas M. Wagner, 1st South Carolina Artillery. Captain Samuel J. Reed, commander of the 1st's Company B, fell while overseeing the operation of one of the fort's guns.

Finally, Benham got his troops in line and ordered them forward for another try. Again the Confederate guns poured out their odd mixture of scrap, while southern muskets covered the killing grounds in front of the fort. This attack was stopped dead about 500 yards from the fort, the survivors streaming for the rear and the relative safety of the hedge line.

The sun was high in the sky by now, about 8.00 a.m. Stevens gathered his survivors around their colours to prepare for yet another attack. As he formed his ranks he sent word back to Benham that they were going to make yet another attempt. But as he was waiting for subalterns to get their companies formed he saw Williams' brigade pulling back, under Benham's orders, he learned from a staff officer. A messenger brought him word that Wright's division was also withdrawing. He decided to wait where he was pending further orders.

The Confederates kept up a steady fire on the retiring Federals. Captain DeWitt Clinton Lewis of Company F, 97th Pennsylvania, saw one of his men fall in the swamp, pulled down under the stagnant water by his heavy wet woollen uniform and full cartridge box and canteen. Almost without thinking, Lewis ran back through the fire, splashed through the swamp and reached the drowning man. He pulled him up and half-dragged, half-carried him back to where the rest of the company was waiting. For this action he was awarded the Congressional Medal of Honor.

By 9.00 a.m. Stevens received orders from Benham to join the general withdrawal. He waited until all of Wright's regiments but the 97th were past, then began his own division's retreat. His division had lost 133 killed, 365 wounded and 31 missing. Most of these men fell between 5.00 and 5.30

a.m. The 8th Michigan bore most of the casualties, losing 13 of the 22 officers who led it into the fight. Fenton wandered among his survivors, crying, 'My poor boys! My brave boys! Where are my boys?'[22] In many regiments men wrote letters home like the one written by Lieutenant Philo S. Morton to the father of one of his soldiers: 'Whilst near the Fort a Shower of Grape came in our ranks, one of which struck your Son, James, and we think tore off one of his legs, near the body. He fell! This is the last we saw of him.'[23]

The Confederates, on the other hand, had very few losses. Only five officers and 47 enlisted men had been killed, with another dozen officers and 132 enlisted men wounded. Eight men were missing, most of them pickets grabbed by advancing Federals before the fight began. Benham's gamble had been a disaster.

But Benham still had a fight to fight. Those who made the attack were united in condemning the general's gamble. 'Let there be no mercy shown to one who shows no mercy. He must be crushed at once or we are all lost,' wrote Captain William T. Lusk of the 79th New York to his uncle. 'I will not enumerate half the examples of imbecility he has shown, or the wickedness of which he has been guilty. The last act is too real.'[24] Benham was detested even among the ranks for the attack. 'I think general H. W. Benham was the highest in rank and was responsible for the proceedings,' wrote Sergeant John B. Porter of Company B, 76th Pennsylvania Infantry. 'I believe there never was a court martial on the case, although there was loud talk of bringing him to [at the] time.'[25]

A shocked Hunter had Benham arrested, reporting back to Washington that his orders had been disobeyed. Benham defended himself in his report by calling the attack a 'reconnaissance' with the idea of 'ascertaining the nature of the fort and the position in front on our rear, as also the character of the ground in advance of our left as far as may be necessary to secure our camps here ...'[26] This reconnaissance he said was accomplished. He also tried to blame Stevens for not attacking earlier, something that brought a strongly protesting Stevens into the paper battle. Stevens accused Benham of attacking against the advice of all of his subordinates.

Hunter had Benham sent back north. There Major General Henry C. Halleck, the army's general-in-chief, had Benham's brigadier general's commission revoked that August. Benham was out of the army, but he fought this battle better than he did Secessionville, persuading five New England governors to apply to Lincoln for his reinstatement. Lincoln asked the US

Judge Advocate General, Joseph Holt, a man with no military experience, to look into the case. Holt's finding was that Benham did not technically disobey Hunter's orders. Indeed, the orders were so vague that they could have been reasonably interpreted as calling for just such an attack as Benham ordered. Holt went further than that. A lawyer and attorney who had worked as Commissioner of Patents, Postmaster-General and, for a few weeks in 1861, Secretary of War, he wrote that the failure of the attack was due to Stevens' lateness in launching the attack, and his failure to direct 'personally and in proper order the march of troops in their advance ...'[27]

Vindicated by a non-soldier in uniform, Benham had his commission restored in February 1863 and was returned to brigade command. But he would never again be able to waste soldiers' lives in combat. He was given command of the Army of the Potomac's Volunteer Engineer Brigade, a two-regiment unit that spent much of its time in workshops in Washington, with details being sent out to line units to perform such duties as bridge building.

Notes

1 Gragg, Rod, 'A Bloody Half-Hour', *Civil War Times Illustrated*, January/February 1994, p.48.
2 *ORs*, Series I, Vol. XIV, p.45.
3 *ORs, ibid.*, p.42.
4 *ORs, ibid.*, p.46.
5 *ORs, ibid.*, p.45.
6 *ORs, ibid.*, p.52.
7 *ORs, ibid.*, p.54.
8 Clarke, H. C., *The Confederate States Almanac, and Repository of Useful Knowledge for 1862*, Vicksburg, Mississippi.
9 Gragg, Rod, *op. cit.*, p.51.
10 Gragg, Rod, *ibid.*, p.50.
11 *ORs, op. cit.*, p.49.
12 *ORs, op. cit.*, p.59.
13 *ORs, op. cit.*, p.94.
14 *ORs, op. cit.*, p.65.
15 *ORs, ibid.*, p.71.
16 Niven, John, *Connecticut for the Union*, New Haven, Connecticut, 1965, p.148.
17 *ORs, op. cit.*, pp.72-73.
18 Schriber, Carolyn P., 'A Scratch with the Rebels', *Civil War Times Illustrated*, January/February 1994, p.49.
19 Gragg, Rod, *op. cit.*, p.55.
20 Gragg, Rod, *ibid.*, p.55.
21 Starr, James, *A Song of the 97th P.V.*, collection, Chester County Historical Society, West Chester, Pennsylvania.

22 Gragg, Rod, *op. cit.*, p.56.
23 Schriber, Carolyn P., *op. cit.*, p.49.
24 Niven, John, *op. cit.*, p.149.
25 Chisman, James A., ed., *76th Regiment Pennsylvania Volunteer Infantry*, Wilmington, North Carolina, 1988, p.21.
26 *ORs, op. cit.*, pp.52-53.
27 Gragg, Rod, *op. cit.*, pp.56-57.

Magruder Bluffs at Yorktown

THE GAMBLE: *that a small army can bluff a vastly superior army into think-ing that an equally large force confronts it in an invulnerable position, thereby buying time to allow a defence to be organised.*

The grand Army of the Potomac under George B. McClellan had stolen a march on the Confederates, leaving the ground route from the north to sweep around and land on the tip of a small peninsula separating the York and James Rivers. Richmond was within a day's march at best, were McClellan to move swiftly and decisively.

Jefferson Davis later wrote:

> As soon as we ascertained that the enemy was concentrating his forces at Fortress Monroe, to advance upon our capital by that line of approach, all our disposable force was ordered to the Peninsula, between the James and York Rivers, to the support of General John B. Magruder, who, with a force of seven to eight thousand men, had, by availing himself of the Warwick River, a small stream which runs through a low, marshy country, from near Yorktown to the James River, constructed an entrenched line across the Peninsula.[1]

Magruder's force was rather grandly named 'The Army of the Peninsula'.

Yorktown was then a small farming town. Much of its land was cut up by small artificial hills and valleys, reminders of a much earlier siege when an American/French army under George Washington had besieged a small British/German army under Earl Cornwallis. Cornwallis' eventual surrender marked the beginning of the end of the American Revolution. The area was not only rich in history, but it was one that was naturally suited for defence.

The commanding general was known to his fellow soldiers as 'Prince John' Magruder because of his lavish parties, courtly manner, fashionable dress, elaborate full dress parades and his pomposity. Born in Virginia in 1807, he was an 1830 graduate of the US Military Academy, and had been brevetted three times for gallant and meritorious conduct in the Mexican War. He subsequently served at posts where he could indulge his passion for high society, especially at Fort Adams, near Newport, Rhode Island, at Fort Leavenworth, Kansas, and finally in Washington. Tall, with a soldierly bearing, he even affected a fashionable, 'Horse Guards' lisp. Friends recalled the occasion when he had especially impressed visiting British officers with his dinner and wines, and one asked exactly how much an American Army officer earned. Feigning surprise, Magruder said he had no idea, and that he would have to ask his servant. In fact he had no independent income at all, and much of his lifestyle was little more than a grand bluff.

At Yorktown, Magruder was in the right place at the right time, for keeping McClellan at bay, even given the Union general's psychology, called for a gambler who knew how to bluff. When Magruder, who had been commissioned a Virginia Volunteer colonel at the war's outbreak and given command of artillery around Richmond, arrived at Yorktown in late May, he found little even with which to bluff. He had a handful of infantry and no cavalry. None the less, he set to work erecting fortifications, while at the same time bombarding the new War Department in Richmond with requests for 8,000 to 10,000 men. Without them, he indicated, he would be forced to retreat in the face of any enemy.

Even without these reinforcements, however, Magruder inflicted one of the first land victories of the Confederacy on advancing Federal troops on 10 June 1861. In a relatively small action that in later days would not even rate the name of a battle, Magruder's infantry, supported by an artillery battery, met an advancing enemy at Big Bethel. Federal attacks were poorly conducted. Indeed, some of their units, clad as volunteers in grey uniforms, mistook others in their own force for Confederates, and further broke up the Union advance by firing among themselves. Although Magruder had some 1,400 men in his command, no more than 300 Confederates were in action at any one point in the skirmish. Confederate losses were only 11 men, compared with Federal losses of 75 out of a force of 4,400 men.

This early war action, small as it was, brought instant fame to the Virginian, even though the Confederate fighting forces on the field had actually been commanded by a professional soldier from North Carolina, D. H. Hill. Even so, the Richmond *Dispatch* of 15 June 1861 described Magruder as all that 'fancy had pictured of the Virginia gentleman, the frank and manly representative of the chivalry of the dear Old Dominion' (Virginia is nicknamed the 'Old Dominion State'). Magruder was promoted to the rank of brigadier general.

Magruder redoubled his efforts in building up his defences. Davis wrote:

Having a force entirely inadequate to occupy and defend the whole line, over thirteen miles long, he built dams in the Warwick River, so as to form pools, across which the enemy, without bridges, could not pass, and posted detachments at each dam to prevent the use of them by attacking columns of the enemy. To defend the left of his line, where the stream became too small to present a serious obstacle to the passage of troops, redoubts were constructed, with curtains connecting them.

Between Yorktown and Gloucester Point, on the opposite shore, the York River is contracted to less than a mile in width, and General Magruder had constructed batteries at both places, which, by their crossfire, presented a formidable obstacle to the ascent of ordinary vessels. The fortifications at Norfolk and the navy-yard, together with batteries at Sewell's Point and Craney Island, in conjunction with the navy, offered means of defence against any attempt to land troops on the south side of the James River.

As a second line of defence, a system of detached works had been constructed by General Magruder near to Williamsburg, where the width of the Peninsula, available for the passage of troops, was only three or four miles.[2]

These fortifications were fine, but Magruder could not obtain nearly as many cannon as he needed to defend them. Indeed, all that Magruder, the professional artilleryman, had been able to obtain and mount were some fifteen guns, including a number of light field guns. Moreover, he had only 30 to 60 rounds of ammunition for each one, depending on the calibre. So the showman decided to gamble on a bluff. He had logs shaped to resemble cannon barrels, with slightly flaring mouths, and painted black. These 'Quaker guns', as they were called at the time, were mixed with real cannon all along the fortification. Although Magruder planned to replace the wooden dummies with real cannon, given time and supplies, in the meantime he was willing to gamble that his dummy guns would slow up an advancing enemy just enough.

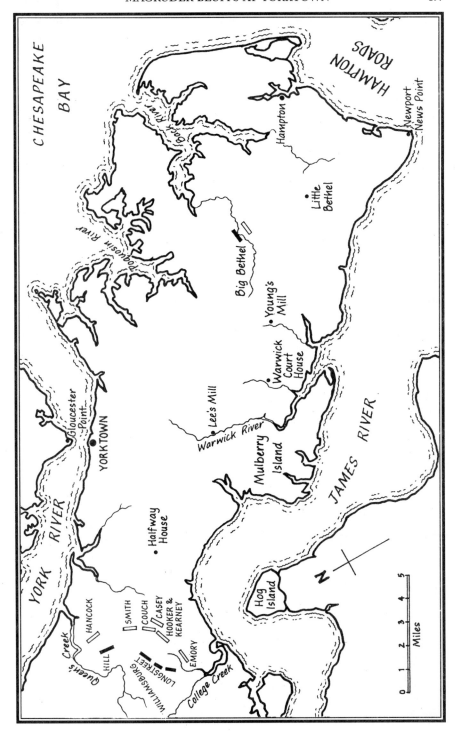

A Federal surgeon was among a group of troops who came across one of these dummy cannon which had been abandoned by its Confederate crew as the Union troops advanced on them.

> As we passed this place on our outward march, we saw at a distance what appeared to be a heavy gun, but as we approached it proved to be a large cart, on which was mounted a great wooden mortar, which had, perhaps, been used by negroes for cracking corn. When we returned a hog's head was fixed in the mouth of the mortar. "There," remarked an officer, "is the first Quaker we have seen on the Peninsula".[3]

Magruder and his men were not to be allowed enough time to replace all of the dummy guns. On 2 April McClellan his men anchored off Fort Monroe, and 36 hours later they were slogging ashore. Their landing was unopposed, only a handful of Confederate scouts watching as they brought some nineteen batteries of field artillery, 66,700 men and endless trails of wagons ashore. Quickly the Federals formed up and marched off, one column heading directly towards Yorktown and another along the Lee's Mill Road, with the intention of outflanking Yorktown. Deserters from the Yorktown garrison who had earlier come into Federal positions reported that there were no more than 8,000 men available, and McClellan was filled with optimism.

Unfortunately he did not use that optimism to push his troops forward with any speed. 'The march was slow and tedious,' a Federal infantry officer noted in his diary under 4 April. 'Halts were frequent on acct [account] of difficulty with baggage and artillery.'[4] When they halted after the first day's march they were only halfway to Yorktown.

'Everything has worked well today,' McClellan wrote his wife. 'I have gained some strong positions without fighting and shall try some more manoeuvring tomorrow.'[5] But events were already starting to burn the edges of McClellan's optimism. Next day the advancing Federal troops found the roads to be worse than they had expected. Told before setting foot on the Peninsula that the roads were largely sandy with natural drainage, they found in pouring rain on the morning of 5 April that the roads were really sticky clay under a light layer of loam and shell marl, and turned into thick mud fairly quickly.

'The roads, which at first were dry and firm, were as we advanced badly cut up, and great difficulty was experienced in getting the trains up,' wrote a Union surgeon. 'Infantry could get along well enough, but artillery and army wagons had a hard time of it. Each piece of artillery made the road worse, until the axles dragged in a river of mud.'[6]

On top of the problems with the roads, McClellan discovered that his flank move around Yorktown was not to go unopposed. Indeed, Confederate fortifications had been placed where he had not expected any, and troops manning these fortifications offered what McClellan regarded as stiff opposition.

Still, Magruder had fewer than 10,000 men to cover his entire line of fortifications. Against him, McClellan had a force that could have forced its way easily. Some years after the war, McClellan whined:

Then, on the 5th of April, I found myself with 53,000 men in hand, giving less than 42,000 for battle, after deducting extra-duty men and other non-combatants. In our front was an intrenched [*sic*] line, apparently too strong for assault, and which I had now no means of turning, either by land or water. I now learned that 85,000 would be the maximum force at my disposal, giving only some 67,000 for battle.[7]

Still, Magruder had no way of knowing that McClellan was beginning to feel unease about the roads and his numbers, so he pulled yet another, even more astonishing bluff. He had units moved about, in and out of cover, to make it seem that yet more units were arriving in his fortifications. 'The way Magruder fooled them was to divide each body of his troops into two parts and keep them travelling all the time for twenty-four hours, till reinforcements came,' recalled a lieutenant in the 14th Louisiana, which marched from Yorktown to the James River six times that day. Another Alabama private wearily noted in his diary: 'This morning we were called out by the "Long roll" and have been travelling most of the day, seeming with no other view than to show ourselves to the enemy at as many different points of the line as possible'.

When Federals appeared in front of the 11th Alabama Infantry, Captain H. McMath recalled, the unit jumped out of the entrenchments and ran through enemy fire 'until we got out of sight just around the point of a hill. We were halted there some 1/2 hour, when we were counter-marched over to a place we started from.'[8]

Magruder had trains roll into places behind his lines, blowing whistles, then quickly turn round and back up several hundred yards before going through the same exercise again. When a train screeched to a halt, drummers and buglers sounded assembly, while men, greatly enjoying the theatrics, shouted orders to non-existent regiments. All the time, Magruder had his men maintain a running fire all along the front.

Jubal Early, whose Confederate infantry brigade had been rushed to Magruder's aid on 9 April, later wrote:

> The assuming and maintaining the line by Magruder, with his small force in the face of such overwhelming odds, was one of the boldest exploits ever performed by a military commander, and he had so manoeuvred his troops, by displaying them rapidly at different points, as to produce the impression on his opponent that he had a large army.[9]

Magruder's gamble paid off. McClellan halted his infantry and called up his artillery to probe the Confederate defences. It was slow work, pulling up cannon on rutted, muddy roads and getting them into position, their limbers drawn up behind them. A Louisiana chaplain wrote home:

> As soon as we were aware of their presence we hastened to salute them with a salvo from our cannon. They returned the greeting in kind. Then during the course of the day they fired on us some twenty times, but no one was injured or even really frightened, though many of their shells exploded in the midst of our troops. During a period of one hour, four of these shells passed right over my quarters. The Yankees' aim was always too high. Our own artillery reciprocated with more effect: one shot blew up one of their caissons (I saw this myself from the height of one of our ramparts where I happened to be), and another managed to knock an officer clean off his horse. On the next day, Sunday, we were still exchanging occasional volleys, but to no one's advantage; and ever since that time the cannon have remained silent. But the skirmishes which began Saturday night along the creek have continued up till now.[10]

With the artillery, McClellan brought up an observation balloon in its first use on an American battlefield. Directed by a civilian, Thaddeus Lowe, who had been a professional balloonist before the war, the small staff of military volunteers attached to Lowe's 'Aeronautic Department' filled the balloon with gas generated by portable coal-gas generators dragged along with the army. Slowly the tethered balloon, manned by Lowe, who was being paid a colonel's salary as head of the Aeronautic Department, rose above the tree line behind McClellan's lines. Magruder, instantly aware of what was happening, having heard rumours of an the earlier use of Federal balloons at the First Bull Run, continued running his troops in and out of clumps of trees as if they were newly arriving formations. Lowe dutifully reported all of these movements to McClellan's headquarters using the telegraph key installed in his balloon basket.

On the right, Brigadier General Charles S. Hamilton, whose division faced the Confederate line between Yorktown's main fortifications and where the Warwick River began, saw through Magruder's bluff. He reported to his corps commander, Brigadier General Samuel P. Heintzelman, that the Confederate defences were quite thin on his front. He said that one push should go right through them, and that he wanted to make a reconnaissance in force there. The two generals went to McClellan's headquarters with the request, but McClellan, armed with notes from the military amateur Lowe and backed up by Chief Engineer John Barnard and one of his favourite officers, Fitz John Porter, flatly rejected the idea. A siege was the only way to conduct this operation, the three from the rear echelon agreed.

On the left, however, which was a naturally stronger position, behind the Warwick River which had been deepened in parts by dams built by Magruder, an unordered reconnaissance in force almost destroyed Magruder's careful deception. There, Brigadier General William F. 'Baldy' Smith sent two regiments under a hard-fighting soldier, Brigadier General Winfield Scott Hancock, to scout out the river line and find holes in it. Shortly after Hancock left, orders came from McClellan's headquarters calling for that part of the line to dig in for a siege. Smith left his corps commander, Major General Erasmus Keyes, and went off to find Hancock to tell him the reconnaissance was off.

When Smith found him, Hancock was enraged by the orders to disengage and fall back. He had already found a weak spot and was ready to tear through it and roll up the Confederate army. No matter, Smith said, orders were orders and Hancock was to fall back. Hancock, the good soldier, did so. For the rest of his life Smith believed that, had McClellan's orders been two hours later in arriving at his commander's headquarters, the attack would have succeeded and Richmond would have fallen.

What Hancock did bring back actually encouraged McClellan in his belief that no attack could succeed. With Hancock's troops came four prisoners from the 14th Alabama, full of the news that there were some 40,000 Confederate troops along the Warwick and that soon they would have 100,000 in position there. The South's leading soldier, Joseph Johnston, was due with another 8,000 men on that day alone.

It was a very different McClellan than the one who had been so confident on the day of the landing on the Peninsula who telegraphed Washington on 7 April: 'All the prisoners state that General J. E. Johnston arrived in Yorktown yesterday with strong reinforcements. It seems clear that I shall have the whole force of the enemy on my hands, probably not less than 100,000 men and possibly more.' The result, he believed, was that 'my force is possibly less than that of the enemy'. No attack could succeed. 'Were I in possession of their entrenchments and assailed by double my numbers I should have no fears as to the result.'[11]

Magruder had bluffed, and McClellan, the professional military engineer who had been in the Crimea during that war, had bought the bluff. He halted his troops, paralysed by the knowledge that his well-thought-out plan was now worthless. The roads were worse than expected; his forces were smaller than he had wanted; the Navy could not land troops up either river easily; and now a huge Confederate force had dug in along a creek that he thought was merely a dry line on a map. Indeed, while intelligence told him that Magruder had no more than 15,000 men at the most, he figured that nobody, let alone a professional soldier, would attempt to hold 15 miles of entrenchments with such a small force.

McClellan did the only thing a professional soldier could have done – or so he convinced himself. He ordered his troops to halt and dig in for a full siege. McClellan later wrote:

Whatever may have been said afterward, no one at the time – so far as my knowledge extended – thought an assault practicable without certain preliminary siege operations. At all events, my personal experience in this kind of work was greater than that of any officer under my command; and after personal reconnaissances more appropriate to a lieutenant of engineers than to the commanding general, I could neither discover nor hear of any point where an assault promised any chance of success. We were thus obliged to resort to siege operations in order to silence the enemy's artillery fire, and open the way to an assault.[12]

Rarely did McClellan learn from past events. Even after it became general knowledge that his forces outnumbered the Confederates in the Peninsula, he went on to believe equally falsely that he was outnumbered in Maryland in 1862. However, he did apparently learn from his studies of Sevastopol in the Crimean War that a siege had to be conducted when the enemy fortified his lines. McClellan ordered just such a siege.

Federal engineers came forward and laid out a line of entrenchments, including batteries for mortars and large siege cannon. Pioneers cut down trees and began digging parapets. Once Magruder saw that he had won the first part of his bluff and McClellan was stalled dead in his tracks, he realised that the second part of the gamble would be even harder. He would have to convince the enemy well dug-in in front of him that they were unable to push through the smaller Confederate force with a direct assault. This would require even more acting than simply dancing regiments back and forth through the woods in front of Federal scouts.

Magruder did his best to win the rest of his gamble. He knew, however, that the odds were against him. He telegraphed his capital, Richmond, on 6 April that all of his lines were under observation, from the air as well as by land, and that the Federals had been active along it all during the day. He noted that the Federals had already probed one weak point in the defences and that he had reinforced that place, but that eventually the superior numbers of the Union army would prevail. Reinforcements were on the way, he was told. A brigade arrived on 5 April, and another two regiments on the 6th.

In the meantime, Magruder did his best to keep up appearances. He made a point of riding all along his lines in enemy view in full uniform, accompanied by a large and brilliantly attired staff. Two more brigades of infantry arrived 7 April, followed by a third on the 8th. Another brigade climbed off its railway cars on the 10th, followed by three more brigades on the 11th, bringing Magruder's defences at Yorktown to 34,400 – a significantly smaller number than the 100,000 McClellan had estimated the Confederates to have along his front.

Once he had enough troops to man the basic posts, Magruder sent out small groups of troops to keep Federal work parties off their balance. 'On the 11th of April General Magruder ordered sorties to be made by small parties from all the main parts of the line for the purpose of fooling the enemy,' General Early recalled.[13]

It worked. Federals working on their entrenchments had to take twice as much time as they should have, because they always had to be wary of Confederate sharpshooters and scouts. Colonel Francis Vinton of the 43rd New York Infantry reported sending out all of his brigade pioneers to work in his front. 'The sharpshooters of the enemy at this point fired at the regiment, which I am afraid they saw too plainly. They killed a man. He was shot in the forehead with a small bullet. I did not return the fire. At their next discharge they wounded two men. I then allowed the regiment to break into groups and take cover on its line of battle.' Vinton then ordered general firing at the elusive enemy, but was unable to clear them from their entrenchments. 'He fired with some persistence, and finally wounded another man and a lieutenant. I aimed low. The water splashed as far as I could see.

'At about 11 o'clock I was ordered to retire my line within the picket line. The pioneers had already finished what they had to do along the ravine.'[14] Work on the lines was tough and, especially for relatively green troops that made up both armies in the spring of 1862, fearful.

On the 11th, too, the much-feared CSS *Virginia* steamed towards the Federals in Hampton Roads, scattering small Union vessels in its wake. The plan was to draw the Federal ironclad USS *Monitor* into the upper bay and close with, board and capture the smaller boat. Specially trained boarding parties would throw wet sailcloth over the pilot house, blinding her commander, while others would drive wedges between the turret and deck to prevent it revolving, and still others would toss turpentine-soaked lit cotton waste down the ventilators to drive her crew on deck. In fact, the southern ship was not able to decoy the *Monitor* away from guarding the rest of the squadron, so the entire plan went for nothing. None the less, the very appearance of the *Virginia* effectively sealed off the James River, neutralised the Union fleet and added to McClellan's discomfort.

Luckily Magruder was sitting across the battlefield poker table from only one other player, McClellan. The rest of the Union forces, many of whom could see that one stiff assault could take the Confederate lines, did not have a voice in how the cards were to be played. First Lieutenant Charles B. Haydon of the 2nd Michigan Infantry noted in his diary on 13 April:

I have great faith in General McClellan, still there are matters ab[ou]t which I have my own thoughts and speculations. I do not believe Napoleon would have spent so much time in preparation. Indeed everyone knows he would not and knows equally well he would have succeeded. We all know that as a rule delay means defeat to the invader and victory to the invaded. Knowing this, seeing our delay without knowing the cause, it is but natural, in view of the vast expense, the dangers of foreign interference and the unexpected misfortunes to which every nation is liable, that many should feel anxious and some should have serious misgivings. I wait with confidence but not without emotion the perfect vindication of our much honoured General's plan of operations.

So far as we are personally concerned we are very impatient of delay.[15]

On 12 April Joseph Johnston arrived in Richmond and assumed command of both Magruder's besieged Army of the Peninsula and the Confederate troops at Norfolk in a new formation that would gain fame as the Army of Northern Virginia. A trained engineer, he was more in McClellan's mould, a cautious soldier, afraid to commit to battle unless assured of victory. Very little ever pleased him. Indeed, when he inspected the defences at Yorktown he reported that they were all wrong; no avenues for attack had been left, the lines were badly drawn and incomplete, and they were quite vulnerable to flank attacks by the superior Federal force. Johnston returned to Richmond with this report on 14 April, when he told Jefferson Davis that he wanted to give up the Yorktown positions altogether. It would be much better, he said, to fall back and prepare for a single decisive battle with the advancing Federals.

Davis, very loath to give up any southern soil, was unhappy with this report. He convened a council including Robert E. Lee, Secretary of War Randolph, Major General James Longstreet and General Gustavus W. Smith to discuss their options. 'It was the first time that I had been called to such august presence, to deliberate on momentous matters, so I had nothing to say till called on,' Longstreet recalled. When asked his opinion, Longstreet started to say that McClellan was a cautious engineer and would not move before 1 May, but, before he could get to his proposal, Davis interrupted him to say that he would not hear a word disparaging McClellan. 'McClellan had been a special favourite with Mr Davis when he was Secretary of War in the Pierce administration, and he seemed to take such reflections upon his favourites as somewhat personal. From the hasty interruption I concluded that my opinion had only been asked through polite recognition of my presence, not that it was wanted, and said no more.'[16]

But Johnston did speak up, offering two alternative plans. One would be to abandon Yorktown and concentrate all the troops, including garrison troops from Georgia and the Carolinas, near Richmond to force a show-down battle. The second plan called for Magruder to hold Yorktown as long as possible, while the main army under Johnston moved towards Washington. He was sure that the US government would recall McClellan when its own capital was threatened. Smith agreed, going further by suggesting that the Confederate army should not stop at Washington but go on through Baltimore and Philadelphia to New York. He does not appear to have offered a suggestion as to how Johnston's army could escape from New York once there.

Lee favoured holding Yorktown and falling back if necessary only slowly. He pointed out that the enlistments for one year that most Southern soldiers had made were ending even as they were speaking. Congress earlier approved conscription, so that effectively every soldier who took his discharge at the end of the year was instantly drafted into his regiment again. To sweeten this, however, they allowed men to elect new officers and even change units if possible. As a result, veteran, hard-disciplining officers were suddenly booted out and new officers with minimum experience replaced the retired ones. Entire units were being broken up. It would take time, Lee said, to build these units into an effective army again, and therefore they should fight on the lower Peninsula. And they should do so without troops from Georgia and the Carolinas, whose removal could mean the loss of Charleston, South Carolina, and Savannah, Georgia.

The Secretary of War added that giving up Yorktown would mean giving up the Norfolk Navy Yard, where the *Virginia* was based and where a number of other Confederate Navy vessels were currently under construction.

After a discussion lasting many hours, Davis, who had not given an opinion, announced his decision. Johnston would take command at Yorktown, a post which he was to hold as long as possible. All the troops under his command would join him there. Johnston, however, believed from the beginning that Yorktown could not be held and mentally, at least, began his plans for withdrawing from the line.

So Johnston began pouring his men into the basic line roughed out by Magruder's brilliant acting force. They went to work adding to trench lines, some of which were originally dug by British troops in 1781, and strengthening weak points. In the meantime, McClellan's thorough preparations for a full siege continued, with 111 heavy siege guns being brought forward and emplaced to turn the Confederate lines into a copy of the craters of the moon. Much of his work here was based on the siege of Sevastopol, his wife sending him books on the subject as his entrenching work continued. Balloon observations continued, and there was a thrilling episode when Fitz John Porter, observing alone, noticed that the balloon in which he was riding had broken free of its moorings and had drifted over Confederate lines. Luckily a shift in the wind direction brought him back across Union lines, and he managed to release gas from the balloon and descend safely.

The Confederates, too, assembled their own balloon, but it had to be filled with gas in Richmond, because the south had no portable coal-gas generators, and brought up to the front tied to a flatboat – the world's first aircraft carrier. It, too, broke loose one day, only to be brought back to safety by a lucky wind gust.

For the most part, however, the siege took on a long, boring life of its own. There was constant danger from enemy sharpshooters and constant boredom from a lack of anything to do but dig. Sergeant W. H. Andrews, 1st Georgia Regulars, recalled:

> The works were occupied by lines of battle relieving each other every 34 hours, and just after night as no movement of troops could be accomplished during the day, only under a heavy fire from the enemy. Under the fallen treetops above and below the dam, the enemy's sharpshooters would conceal themselves before day every morning, and it was worth a man's life to show his head above the works, five of the Regulars being killed by trying the experiment. Many nights while below the dam, we would sit with water up to our knees and sleep under the inspiring music of the frogs. Whoever thought there was music in the hollering and croaking of the frogs? Under certain circumstances there is. It is a well-known fact that frogs will not holler when the water is disturbed, and in that fact lay the music. As long as they kept up their music, we knew that the yankees were not crossing the swamp.[17]

On 16 April McClellan authorised a raid on a post on the Warwick River near Dam No. 1 – the very spot Hancock had earlier wanted to attack in strength. In a small action later known as the Battle of Lee's Mills, Union artillery plastered the Confederate works, while infantry from the Vermont Brigade kept the Confederate infantry under cover with small-arms fire. After three hours, return fire had all but ceased, and skirmishers splashed their way across the pond to see what was up. They reported that the enemy post was empty.

Two companies of the 3rd Vermont Infantry were ordered forward. They were told that the water there was but waist high. They were misinformed. The Vermonters dashed through the creek, firing at the scattered enemy in their front as they came. In minutes they were behind cover in the enemy trenches and had cleared the enemy from their front. However, in crossing the creek many of the paper cartridges in their leather cartridge boxes had become soaked, making them useless. The Vermonters scrounged ammunition from cartridge boxes of the wounded and dead Confederates or their own comrades.

But no reinforcements came to help them. McClellan himself was on the scene, observing. He said nothing about the blue coats fighting on the other side, only turned his horse away to ride back to his headquarters. The division commander, Baldy Smith, was twice thrown from an unruly horse and was too stunned to see what a handhold in the enemy line could mean. The Vermont Brigade commander started to send reinforcements, but they were stopped by the sheer volume of fire from the Georgia and Louisiana brigade that had deployed to save the position. The Federal reinforcements fell back behind the tree line, where they could not see either the Confederates or their friends across the stream. Finally, the survivors from the 3rd Vermont simply turned and bolted down the creek bank and across the creek to safety on the Union side. 'Why, sir, it was just like sap-boiling, in that stream, the bullets fell so thick,' a 16-year-old Vermont private recalled.[18]

One Vermonter waiting on the other side wrote home, describing how his comrades made their way back: 'In a few minutes squads of men were seen emerging from the woods with their wounded comrades, carrying some of them on their backs, some on stretchers, and others were assisted hobbling along the best way they could; and many, alas! were left that could not be recovered.'[19]

McClellan's only attack on the Confederate lines at Yorktown was over. The long hours of tedious work for Federal infantry and artillerymen pressed into duty as pioneers, and Confederates waiting for the attack that was sure to come, continued.

The main job for the Federal troops was placing the siege guns, a giant assortment of two 200lb Parrott rifles and a dozen 100lb Parrotts, rifled guns that outgunned any number of cannon the Confederates had in their lines. Smaller, 20lb and 30lb Parrotts and 4.5in Rodman guns added their weight to the force. For vertical fire McClellan bought up 41 mortars that could fire their balls high into the air so that they would drop nearly vertically into trenches and gun emplacements. Some of these included 13in seacoast mortars which fired shells weighing 220lb. In all, the guns would be able to fire 7,000lb of iron directly into the Confederate line at Yorktown.

Johnston and his men could hear all this preparation, the ringing of woodsmen's axes on trees indicating where roads were being cut and emplacements made. Jubal Early recalled:

> The enemy continued to work very busily on his approaches, and each day some new work was developed. He occasionally fired with artillery on our works, and the working parties engaged in strengthening them and making traverses and epaulments in the rear, but we very rarely replied to him, as our supply of ammunition was very limited. During the month of April there was much cold, rainy weather, and our troops suffered greatly, as they were without tents or other shelter. Their duties were very severe and exhausting, as when they were not on the front line in the trenches they were employed in constructing heavy traverses and epaulments in the rear of the main line, so as to conceal and protect the approaches to it. In addition to all this, their rations were very limited and consisted of the plainest and roughest food. Coffee was out of the question, as were vegetables and fresh meat. All this told terribly on the health of the men, and there were little or no hospital accommodations in the rear.[20]

Johnston knew that he would have to withdraw before the Federal metal began to fall among his men and make withdrawal difficult, if not impossible. His first notification to Richmond came on 27 April, when he alerted the government to the fact that the Federal parallels were almost completed. Then, on 29 April, he wrote: 'The fight for Yorktown, as I said in Richmond, must be one of artillery, in which we cannot win. The result is certain; the time only doubtful ... I shall therefore move as soon as it can be done conveniently.'[21]

By now Johnston had some 56,600 men and 36 batteries of field artillery under his command at Yorktown. This large a force could not just tiptoe away, even from someone as slow as McClellan. And an army in retreat is vulnerable to attack. None the less, it was a job that had to be done. He ordered all tentage and the like not visible to the enemy to be packed and withdrawn immediately. The complete withdrawal was to be made on the night of 3 May, and anything not packed up and carried off by then would be left behind.

It was not a totally secret move. An escaped slave from Yorktown reported to a northern newspaper correspondent several days before the retreat that he had seen military wagons loaded up and heading back towards Richmond. When the correspondent reported this to McClellan's chief of staff he was told that the army knew for a fact that the Confederates were totally committed to a last-ditch defence of Yorktown, and no withdrawal was being considered by them. Indeed, McClellan could see no reason why a Confederate force of some 100,000 to 120,000, as his intelligence chief reported it, would ever consider retreating.

On 3 May, as dusk came, the Confederates opened fire on the Union lines with every gun they could muster. They fired for some time and finally, one by one, ceased fire. For the first time in a month the entire line was quiet. Early wrote:

> The object of this was to dispose of as much of the fixed ammunition as possible and produce the impression that we were preparing for an attack on the enemy's trenches. The cannonading was continued during the next day, and, on one part of the line, we were ready to have commenced the evacuation at the time designated, but a little before night on that day (Friday the 2nd) the order was countermanded until the next night, because some of Longstreet's troops were not ready to move. We therefore continued to cannonade on Friday night and during Saturday. Fortunately, after dark on the latter day the evacuation began and was conducted successfully – Stuart's cavalry having been dismounted to occupy our picket line in front, and then men attached to the heavy artillery remaining behind to continue the cannonade until near daylight next morning, so as to keep the enemy in ignorance of our movements.[22]

The next morning, a Sunday, Lowe of the Aeronautic Department could not see a single man in the Confederate line from his vantage point high in the air. Slowly, Union pickets crossed what had been a deadly no-man's land. The enemy was gone. The Confederates had folded their hand.

After the siege had ended, civilian Mary Chestnut, whose husband was an important South Carolina political figure in the government in Richmond and who was, therefore, fairly knowledgeable about current affairs, noted in her diary: 'Magruder did splendidly at Big Bethel – out there. It was a wonderful thing, how he played his ten thousand before McClellan like fireflies and utterly deluded him – keeping down there ever so long.

'It was partly the Manassas scare we gave them. They will never be fool-hardy again.'[23]

Notes

1 Davis, Jefferson, *The Rise and Fall of the Confederate Government*, New York, 1881, Vol. II, p.83.
2 Davis, Jefferson, *ibid.*, pp.83-84.
3 Stevens, George T., *Three Years in the Sixth Corps*, Albany, New York, 1866, p.31.
4 Sears, Stephen W., *For Country Cause and Leader*, New York, 1993, p.215.
5 Sears, Stephen W., *To the Gates of Richmond*, New York, 1992, p.36.
6 Stevens, George T., *op. cit.*, p.34.
7 *B&L*, Vol. II, p.171.
8 Stephen V. Sears, *To the Gates of Richmond*, *op. cit.*, pp.37-38.
9 Early, Jubal A., *Narrative of the War Between the States*, New York, 1989, p.59.
10 Buckley, Cornelius, M., SJ, trans, *A Frenchman, a Chaplain, a Rebel; the War Letters of Pere Louis-Hippolyte Gache, SJ*, Chicago, 1981, p.106.
11 Sears, Stephen W., *To the Gates of Richmond*, *op. cit.*, p.43.
12 *B&L*, *op. cit.*, p.171.
13 Early, Jubal A., *op. cit.*, p.61.
14 *ORs*, Series I, Vol. XI, Part I, p.395.
15 Sears, Stephen W., *For Country Cause and Leader*, *op. cit.*, pp.220-221.
16 Longstreet, James P., *From Manassas to Appomattox*, New York, 1991, p.66.
17 Andrews, W. H., *Footprints of a Regiment*, Atlanta, Georgia, 1992, p.33.
18 Waite, Otis, F. R., *Vermont in the Great Rebellion*, Claremont, New Hampshire, 1869, p.125.
19 Rosenblatt, Emit and Ruth, eds, *Hard Marching Every Day*, Wichita, Kansas, 1992, pp.20-21.
20 Early, Jubal A., *op. cit.*, pp.62-63.
21 Sears, Stephen, *To the Gates of Richmond*, *op. cit.*, p.59.
22 Early, Jubal A., *op. cit.*, p.66.
23 Woodward, C. Vann, ed, *Mary Chestnut's Civil War*, New Haven, Connecticut, 1981, p.401.

A GAMBLE AT ARMY LEVEL

Sherman Marches Through Georgia

THE GAMBLE: *that an entire army can cut itself from its line of communications and supply and head overland deep into enemy territory without being destroyed, as was Napoleon's in Russia.*

'Atlanta is ours', wired Major General William T. Sherman to the War Department in Washington on 3 September 1984, 'and fairly won.'[1] That single event revitalised the lagging spirits of the north; it swung votes towards Abraham Lincoln, then running for a second term as president against a peace platform presented by the Democratic Party. The war that had seemed to be deadlocked after earlier victories that opened the Mississippi River now appeared to be going against the south. As newly-minted Lieutenant General Ulysses S. Grant wrote: 'The news of Sherman's success reached the North instantaneously, and set the country all aglow'.[2]

Until then, Sherman had not been considered one of the north's leading generals. He still needed to build his reputation. Early in the war he had been forced to resign from his command because of what appears to have been a nervous breakdown, but his good friend U. S. Grant, who had had faith in Sherman's abilities, put him in ever higher command positions. Sherman later wrote that, while he was a US Military Academy cadet, he 'was not considered a good soldier, for at no time was I selected for any office, but remained a private throughout the whole four years. Then, as now, neatness in dress and form, with a strict conformity to the rules, were the qualifications required for office, and I suppose I was found not to excel in any of these.'[3] Indeed, in terms of appearance, the years had not improved the professional soldier. One of Grant's staff officers, Colonel Horace Porter, met him in Atlanta shortly after its fall. He was seated on a porch, 'sitting tilted back in a large armchair, reading a newspaper. His coat was unbuttoned, his black felt hat slouched over his brow, and on his feet were a pair of slippers very much down at the heels.'[4]

Sherman then rested his army after its long campaign that had ended in the taking of Atlanta, and turned Atlanta itself into an armed fortress by expelling whatever civilians had remained after its long siege. In the meantime, the Confederate Army that had been defending Atlanta withdrew slightly to the west. Its commander, Lieutenant General John Bell Hood, a fiercely aggressive, if not over-brilliant fighter, was sure to strike again.

But it would not be that easy. Hood reported back to his headquarters in Richmond that his troops, gathered to the west of Atlanta, had been badly demoralised by the retreat. President Jefferson Davis, gravely concerned, took the long trip to Hood's headquarters by a rail system that could no longer pass through the direct route via Atlanta, but wound round much further south.

When he got there, Hood produced a plan that called for the Confederate capture of the railroad that connected Atlanta with the main supply area of Chattanooga, Tennessee. Hood's army would then capture Federal supply depots, to annoy Sherman into attacking him on ground of his choosing. If good ground would not be available, he would retreat to Gadsden, followed by Sherman, where, joined by local militia, he would offer 'a final stand' for 'a decisive battle,' Davis recalled.

If victorious, as under the circumstances it was hoped we should be, the enemy could not retreat through the wasted country behind him, and must surrender or disperse. If Sherman should not pursue our retiring army to Gadsden, but return to Atlanta to march toward the seacoast, he was to be pursued, and, by our superiority in cavalry, to be prevented from foraging on the country, which, according to our information as to his supplies on hand at Atlanta, and as to his inadequate means of transportation, would be indispensable for the support of his troops. Should Sherman, contrary to that information, have supplies and transportation sufficient to enable him to march across the country, and should he start toward the seacoast, the militia, the local troops, and others who could be employed, should obstruct the roads and fords in his front by felling trees, and, by burning bridges and other available means, delay his progress until his provisions should be consumed and absolute want should deplete if not disintegrate his army.[5]

To boost the sagging morale of the Confederate Army of Tennessee, Davis and his Secretary of State, Robert Toombs, went round making speeches to different units, praising their heroism and telling them of the great things that would happen in the future. A number of their talks found their way into southern newspapers which eventually were read in the north. Sherman noted one saying that Confederate cavalry, led by noted cavalry leader Major General Nathan B. Forrest, was already cutting roads in middle Tennessee and that Hood's army would soon join him there. Confederate troops from Kentucky and Tennessee would soon be home, the newspapers quoted Davis as saying. Back east, Grant read some of them and remarked, 'Mr Davis has not made it quite plain who is to furnish the snow for this Moscow retreat through Georgia and Tennessee. However, he has rendered us one good service at least in notifying us of Hood's intended plan of campaign.'[6]

Sherman had suggested just such a move from Atlanta east to the beaches of the Atlantic Ocean to his superiors even before taking Atlanta. He had been in contact with that famed gambler, Grant, who was now in command of all the US armies in the field, with the suggestion that Sherman's troops be allowed to cut loose from Atlanta and head to the sea, possibly to the Alabama River, or St Mark's, Florida, or even Savannah. What Sherman actually wanted to do was take perhaps the largest gamble of the war. He wanted to take the bulk of his army, some 63,000 men with 64 cannon, south to destroy Confederate manufacturing and agricultural facilities and make the southern civilian population decide to renounce their independence and give up fighting the war. 'I want to make a raid that will make the South feel the terrible character of our people,' he told one of his subordinates.[7]

While awaiting Grant's response to this plan, Sherman started gathering intelligence about Georgia, possible targets in the state, its defences, the potential for living off the land in the state, and eventual goals. On 14 September he sent a letter to a woman in New Orleans asking her to 'go to Augusta, Georgia, and keep me advised of things along the Savannah River and as far out as Milledgeville. I will pay you and your messengers well.'[8]

While Grant approved of the idea in principle even before Atlanta fell, he thought that Sherman's leaving Hood in his rear was dangerous, and left the most important job Sherman faced essentially undone. Sherman's plan was common knowledge among the officers of Grant's staff, who spent much time gathered around maps studying the potential for such a move.

On 12 September Grant called one of those staff officers, Horace Porter, into his office. After lighting a cigar he said:

Sherman and I have exchanged ideas regarding his next movement about as far as we can by correspondence, and I have been thinking that it would be well for you to start for Atlanta tomorrow, and talk over with him the whole subject of his next campaign. We have debated it so much here that you know my views thoroughly, and can answer any of Sherman's questions as to what I think in reference to the contemplated movement, and the action which should be taken in the various contingencies which may arise ... I can comply with his views in regard to meeting him with ample supplies at any point on the sea-coast which it may be decided to have him strike for. You can tell him that I am going to send an expedition against Wilmington, North Carolina, landing the troops on the coast north of Fort Fisher; and with the efficient co-operation of the navy we shall no doubt get control of Wilmington harbour by the time he reaches and captures other points on the sea-coast.[9]

Porter, armed with Grant's ideas, started immediately to Sherman's head-quarters.

Porter arrived at Atlanta on 20 September and promptly produced a letter from Grant asking for ideas on what the next move should be now that Atlanta was in Federal hands. 'After reading General Grant's letter, he [Sherman] entered at once upon an animated discussion of the military situation East and West, and as he waxed for intense in his manner the nervous energy of his nature soon began to manifest itself,' Porter wrote.[10]

After lunch, Sherman confided in Porter, 'I want to strike out for the sea'. After pointing out how important it was for the Union to capture ports at Mobile, Alabama; Wilmington, North Carolina; and Savannah, Georgia, he said that if the Savannah River were in Federal hands:

I would feel pretty safe in picking up the bulk of this army and moving east, subsisting off the country. I could move to Milledgeville, and threaten both Macon and Augusta, and by making feints I could manoeuvre the enemy out of Augusta. I can subsist my army upon the country as long as I can keep moving; but if I should have to stop and fight battles the difficulty would be greatly increased. There is no telling what Hood will do, whether he will follow me and contest my march eastward, or whether he will start north with his whole army, thinking there will not be any adequate force to oppose him, and that

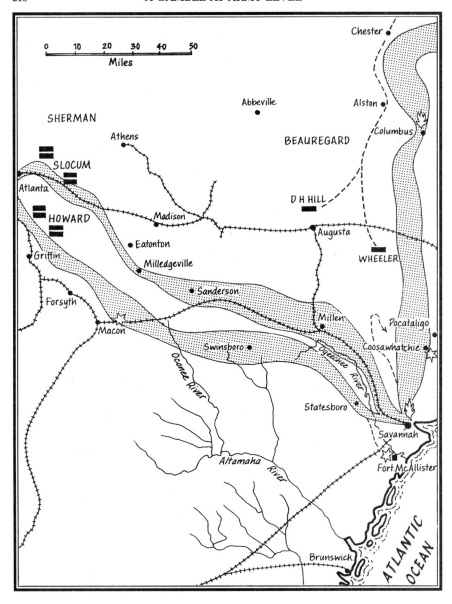

he can carry the war as far north as Kentucky. I don't care much which he does. I would rather have him start north, though; and I would be willing to give him a free ticket and pay his expenses if he would decide to take that horn of the dilemma. I could send enough of this army to delay his progress until our troops scattered through the West could be concentrated in sufficient force to destroy him; and then with the bulk of my army I could cut a swath through to the sea, divide the Confederacy in two, and be able to move up in the rear or Lee, or do almost anything else that Grant might require of me.[11]

Of course, the question remained about Hood's announced plans to move north against the railroad lines and perhaps even major Federal positions in Tennessee. Sherman had an answer to that, too. He would send two infantry corps and most of his cavalry, commanded by Major General George H. Thomas, straight up to Nashville before Hood could get there. Thomas could defend Nashville easily enough.

Sherman outlined these ideas in a long letter to Grant on 20 September, which Porter took with him when he started back to the eastern headquarters. Porter claimed later that Grant immediately decided to let Sherman have his way, with a remarkable little concern about allowing Hood's army to remain in existence. In fact, Porter, with the benefit of knowledge of how successful Sherman's march would be, probably made Grant appear more supportive of Sherman's plan than he actually was.

And Grant appreciated the possibilities of Sherman's plan even more than Lincoln or his Secretary of War, Edwin Stanton. 'The President feels much solicitude in respect to General Sherman's proposed movement and hopes that it will be maturely considered,' Stanton telegraphed Grant, adding that a 'misstep by General Sherman might be fatal to his army.'[12] On November 7 one of President Lincoln's secretaries noted in his diary that, 'Talking with the President a day or two ago about Sherman, he told me that Sherman was inclined to let Hood run his gait for a while, while he overran the Gulf States in Hood's rear. Grant seems rather inclined to have Sherman strike and destroy Hood now, before going South, but gives no orders in the case.'[13] Stanton even paid a special trip to visit Grant, quite probably on behalf of the President, to be sure that Grant felt that Sherman would not lose his army by such a march.

Staff officer Porter wrote:

There were some who thought Grant manifested unnecessary anxiety on this subject, but it must be remembered that just one year before, Lee had sent Longstreet's whole corps to northern Georgia; that it was not discovered until it was well on its way to join Bragg's forces against Rosecrans's army at Chickamauga; and that it accomplished the reverse which occurred to our arms on the field.[14]

Heated debate continued among Grant's staff as to the possible failure or success of Sherman's plan. Grant's chief staff officer, Brigadier General John Rawlins, was convinced that, if Hood fell back slowly before the western Union army, Sherman would not be able to supply his force once cut loose from Atlanta and would be destroyed. On the other hand, if Hood were to strike north, Sherman could not stop him and the Federal forces available would not keep the Confederates from reaching the Ohio River. Others expressed concerns about the coming winter which, in that part of the country, could bring rains or even snows that could stall an army with muddy roads, much as Burnside's Army of the Potomac had been stalled in January 1863 along the Rappahannock. Indeed, most military men looked to Napoleonic examples, and had only to note the 1812 Russian campaign to see what mud could do to an advancing army. Grant kept his own counsel, however, and simply listened to the raging debate within his military family.

Before a decision could be made on Sherman's plan, on 21 September, Federal scouts discovered that Hood had pulled his army to Palmetto Station, sending his cavalry to the west side of the Chattahoochee River. Sherman looked at his maps and decided that, in opening the way for the Federals to advance into Central Georgia, Hood intended to do pretty much what Sherman had actually wanted him to.

On 25 September Sherman telegraphed Washington that Hood's army was on the move. 'If I were sure that Savannah would soon be in our possession, I should be tempted to march for Milledgeville and Augusta; but I must first secure what I have.'[15] So Sherman dispatched one division to Chattanooga and another one to Rome, Georgia.

Grant was not wholly satisfied with these defensive moves. 'It will be better to drive Forrest out of Middle Tennessee as a first step, and do any thing else you may feel your force is sufficient for,' he telegraphed Sherman on 26 September. The last thing that aggressive-minded gambler Sherman wanted to do was split up his army in penny packets, defending every little post and chasing grey ghosts throughout Tennessee. 'It would have a bad effect,' he telegraphed Lincoln directly in Washington, 'if I were forced to send back any considerable part of my army to guard roads, so as to weaken me to an extent that I could not act offensively if the occasion calls for it.'[16]

None the less, Sherman detached yet another division from his force to the Chattanooga garrison. And he telegraphed Washington on 29 September that he took it 'for granted that Forrest will cut our road, but think we can prevent him from making a serious lodgment'. As to chasing Forrest, 'his cavalry will travel a hundred miles where ours will ten'. Instead, he harped on his old, but as yet neither approved nor rejected plan. 'I prefer for the future to make the movement on Milledgeville, Millen, and Savannah,' he concluded.[17]

On 1 October, however, leaving the XX Corps to hold Atlanta, Sherman led his troops out, north, after Hood, towards Marietta, Georgia. By 3 October his lead troops reached and crossed the Chattahoochee River, and by 4 October signals received from a small Union garrison at Allatoona indicated that Hood had that position surrounded. Sherman ordered his army to move quickly to their relief.

By 5 October Sherman himself had reached heights near Allatoona. His signal corps officer was able to make out a flag message through the smoke of gunfire, 'Corse [the garrison's commander] is here'. As Sherman brought his army up, Corse's men stood off an attack. 'I am short a cheek-bone and an ear, but am able to whip all hell yet!' Corse notified Sherman the next morning.[18] The railroad lines that Hood's men had torn up were quickly repaired by Sherman's engineers, most of whom were volunteers in the 1st Michigan Engineers and Mechanics. The end effect of all their cavalry raids on Federal transportation lines was little more than the effect of a ship making a wake through the ocean.

Sherman brought the rest of his troops into Allatoona only to find that the enemy had disappeared. In a desperate plea to Grant to let him turn around and carry out his original scheme, he telegraphed:

> It will be a physical impossibility to protect the roads, now that Hood, Forrest, Wheeler, and the whole batch of devils, are turned loose without home or habitation. I propose that we break up the railroad from Chattanooga forward, and that we strike out with our wagons for Milledgeville, Millen, and Savannah. Until we can repopulate Georgia, it is useless for us to occupy it; but the utter destruction of its roads, houses, and people, will cripple their military resources. By attempting to hold the roads, we will lose a thousand men each month, and will gain no result. I can make this march, and make Georgia howl![19]

Still, he continued on a march after Hood; a march he considered worthless. On October 11 he again telegraphed Grant, pointing out that, 'We cannot now remain on the defensive'. While admitting that Hood with his numbers and speed could break the lines of communications pretty much at will, Sherman said that he preferred simply to destroy his own lines of communications with the north and turn towards the sea. Hood, he argued, may turn towards Tennessee and Kentucky, but would probably follow Sherman's men. 'Instead of my guessing at what he means to do, he will have to guess at my plans,' he telegraphed. 'The difference in war would be fully twenty-five per cent.'[20]

Sherman's men, weary from their long marches, would have agreed with their commanding general had they known his views. 'General Hood's army being less in numbers and more lightly equipped can move faster than we, through these mountains,' an artillery staff officer wrote home.[21]

Still Grant kept silent, leaving Sherman to continue his pursuit and gnash his teeth at the gamble not taken. Hood made an attempt at taking the post at Resaca, Georgia, but was beaten off after some skirmishing. In the meantime he tore up more rail lines, capturing the 24th US Colored Troops in the process. Sherman's men came after him, passing through one of the many gaps in the lines of mountain ranges on 14 October, but found nothing. Again, he tried to pin Hood down near Lafayette, but by the time he could concentrate his forces Hood's men were gone and Sherman's men were in a foul mood. On 17 October one of Sherman's disgusted staff officers wrote home, 'We have been following General Hood since the 4 inst. and have marched about 100 miles. General Sherman has failed to overtake Hood and bring on a general battle as he had hoped to do.'[22]

Thomas, who had been told of Sherman's plans, was not thrilled at being left behind with a hostile force somewhere nearby. 'I hope you will adopt Grant's idea of turning [Major General James] Wilson [the Federal cavalry commander] loose, rather than undertake the plan of a march with the whole force through Georgia to the sea, inasmuch as General Grant cannot co-operate with you as first arranged.' When he received this telegraph, Sherman realised that, despite his pleas and eventual approval, 'neither General Grant nor General Thomas heartily favoured my proposed plan of campaign'.[23]

It was certain that Grant was not in favour, heartily or otherwise, of Sherman's plan as long as there was a Confederate Army in being that threatened territory already captured. He telegraphed on 1 November:

Do you not think it advisable, now that Hood has gone so far north, to entirely ruin him before starting on your proposed campaign? With

Hood's army destroyed, you can go where you please with impunity. I believed and still believe, if you had started south while Hood was in the neighbourhood of you, he would have been forced to go after you. Now that he is far away, he might look upon the chase as useless, and he will go in one direction while you are pushing in the other. If you can see a chance of destroying Hood's army, attend to that first, and make your other move secondary.[24]

Sherman, who by now was spending more time fighting his military superiors over telegraph lines than Hood's men over battlegrounds, replied the next day that he felt pursuing Hood would be useless; that Thomas could defeat him were he to move north; and that Hood would be successful if, by manoeuvre, he would force Sherman's army to retire north, out of Georgia. 'If I turn back, the whole effect of my campaign will be lost,' he wired. 'I am clearly of opinion that the best results will follow my contemplated movement through Georgia.'[25]

Finally, Grant resolved to trust in Sherman's instincts and let him make the gamble. Reluctantly, on 2 November, he authorised the march which was to end below Savannah. 'I do not see that you can withdraw from where you are to follow Hood, without giving up all we have gained in territory,' Grant telegraphed. 'I say, then, go on as you propose.'[26]

Grant's approval reached Sherman while he was still on the march after Hood. He immediately halted his troops and telegraphed Thomas in Nashville to return the two divisions earlier sent as reinforcements to that city. Then he ordered his quartermaster to gather sufficient provisions to last the army for 30 days, and send everything else in stores back. By 1 November, Sherman ordered, nothing was to be in Atlanta but what would be necessary and could be carried with the army on a march through enemy territory, a march that would end on the Atlantic coastline.

Word that the army was going to start out on another long campaign, one that promised to be as long, if not longer, than the one that ended in Atlanta, spread quickly through Sherman's army. 'Have been on a long [trip] for the last month chasing up Mr Hood,' wrote Sergeant Andrew McCornack of Company I, 127th Illinois Infantry Regiment. 'Thomas has got an army up there now that will take care of him and we came back to Atlanta. Expect will have to trikie [sic] out for Savannah or some other sea port far in the South.'[27] Sherman had kept his men, as well as the enemy, mystified as to their eventual goal. 'We be came convinced that we were going somewhere, no one knew where,' Private Robert H. Strong, 105th Illinois Infantry Regiment, wrote after the war. 'Some guessed one place, some another. The most general guess was Baton Rouge, Louisiana, where there was reported to be a large Rebel Army. Others thought we were going to Andersonville to release the prisoners held there.'[28] 'I hoped that it would be Charleston,' wrote the adjutant of the 3rd Wisconsin Infantry, 'for I wanted the people of South Carolina who started the war to feel its effects and to reap their share of the horrors.'[29]

Indeed, Sherman was so secretive about his goal that even one of his wing commanders, Major General O. O. Howard, had no idea what it was. 'From present appearances we shall be cut off from communication for some little time,' he wrote home on 11 November. 'I don't know myself where we shall go, but we have stripped for a trip in the enemy's country.'[30]

The Confederate high command, too, wondered where Sherman would head. 'It was supposed that Augusta, on account of our principal powder-manufactory and some important workshops being located there, would be the first objective point of Sherman, should he march toward the east,' President Davis wrote.[31] But all they could learn was what Sherman published in one of his general orders that, 'It is sufficient for you to know that it [the coming march] involves a departure from our present base, and a long and difficult march to a new one'.[32]

At any rate, Sherman's men packed their haversacks and knapsacks with all their valuables and all the food they could, while commissaries and quartermasters boxed spare equipment and foodstuffs and sent it back to Thomas. Many men took the chance to write home to let anxious loved ones know that they would be gone for some time, probably out of touch, but not to worry. One officer wrote home:

> Wherever we have been on this campaign we have, so far as the country afforded supplies, levied off of the country and have pretty effectively cleaned it of all that man or beast could eat. The people who were so unfortunate as to live on the line of march of either of the armies will be sufficiently hungry this winter to regret that Hood ever made this raid. But this is one of the misfortunes of war, and war, at the best, is scientific cruelty.[33]

On 11 November the same officer jotted a quick note at ten in the morning noting that the last train was to leave Atlanta at noon, whereafter Fed-